Taming the Lizard Brain

In this practical guide, Shannon Hodges draws on his 40 years of experience as counselor, clinical supervisor, consultant, author, and trainer in sharing information to help clinicians and clients in the healing journey of treating PTSD, anxiety, phobias, and stress.

This book provides a comprehensive treatment approach to treating trauma as well as managing anxiety and stress and provides simple, effective techniques for overcoming trauma symptoms. It offers an efficacious, self-reflective, mindfulness-based approach to treatment. Written in workbook style, the text offers practical exercises that provide step-by-step guidance for using a mindfulness-based cognitive and narrative exercise approach within therapy. The text is supported by a strengths-based philosophy of "What has happened to you?" rather than a "What's wrong with you?" approach to healing. It guides readers from fundamentals to provide a foundation for understanding trauma through various connected topics to enable readers or their patients to address their trauma, self-soothe, manage trauma, and more. Each chapter offers practical, self-guided exercises designed to assist the reader in addressing trauma healing, anxiety, and stress reduction in a personal manner. The text is most suitable for ages ranging from 12 years onward, with a wide range of activities involving scaling questions, fill-in-the-blanks, short writing exercises, and creative activities like the empty chair conversation, letters to your younger self and future self, forgiveness exercises, and many more.

This book serves as a valuable resource for mental health professionals, clients in therapy, and former clients continuing their healing journey. It's also beneficial for students in counseling, psychology, and social work programs. The guided, hands-on approach helps build resilience across various contexts, making it widely applicable for both clinical practice and personal development.

Shannon Hodges, PhD, LMHC, has been a longtime professor of Clinical Mental Health Counseling (CMHC), co-founder, and assistant coordinator of the Center for Mindful Practice and served as department chair and coordinator of the CMHC program at Niagara University. He has taught at the University of the Sunshine Coast in Australia for the past few years. Shannon has 25 years of experience providing counseling and training in community agencies, university counseling services, residential living communities, South African orphanages, and remote Australian schools. He is a former director of a university counseling center, former director of a community mental health clinic, and specializes in trauma treatment utilizing mindfulness-based cognitive therapy (MCBT). He has authored numerous professional publications, including books, book chapters, journal articles, and essays. His videos, *Trauma Informed Mindfulness-Based Care* and *Self-Care for Professionals: Preventing Burnout and Creating a Healthier Life*, are popular training videos.

During a 40-year career, Shannon has been awarded for his research and teaching, served on and chaired national committees and task forces, and sat on editorial boards of professional journals, including the *Journal of Counseling & Development*, *Journal of Mental Health Counseling*, and *Journal of College Counseling*, among others. He is a longtime member of the American Counseling Association and holds membership in the Australian Counselling Association. Shannon has taught internationally (in Australia) and delivered professional trainings and keynotes on six continents.

Taming the Lizard Brain

A Mind, Body, Breath, and Spirit Approach to Healing Trauma, Anxiety, and Managing Everyday Stress

Shannon Hodges

Routledge
Taylor & Francis Group
LONDON AND NEW YORK

Designed cover image: stellalevi

First published 2027
by Routledge
4 Park Square, Milton Park, Abingdon, Oxon OX14 4RN

and by Routledge
605 Third Avenue, New York, NY 10158

Routledge is an imprint of the Taylor & Francis Group, an informa business

British Library Cataloguing-in-Publication Data
A catalogue record for this book is available from the British Library

ISBN: 9781041173458 (hbk)
ISBN: 9781041173441 (pbk)
ISBN: 9781003689232 (ebk)

DOI: 10.4324/9781003689232

Typeset in Galliard
by codeMantra

This text is dedicated to Dr. Tim Osberg, Professor of Psychology at Niagara University for 43 years, my former colleague, close friend, and brother from another mother. Tim, you have long been the educator I have strived to become.

Contents

Author's Note *xv*
Foreword *xvi*
Preface *xviii*

1 Understanding and Managing Trauma 1
Trauma: What's the Story You Are Telling Yourself? 2
Here Are a Few Additional Considerations 3
Examples of Trauma 5
Trauma Defined 5
Trauma's Impact on Survivors 6
Post-Event Factors 8
My Ability to Address Trauma 9
Self-compassion 10
Post-Traumatic Stress Disorder (PTSD) and Acute Stress Disorder (ASD) 10
ASD and PTSD Criteria on Exposure Include 11
Post-traumatic Stress Disorder 11
PTSD Symptoms 12
Type I and Type II PTSD 14
The PTSD Checklist, 5th Edition. (PCL-5) 16
PCL-5 16
Trauma Memory and Reframing: The Story You Are Telling Yourself 19
Promises Made and Kept 20
Your Power of Belief 21
Remembrance for Healing 21
Phase I: Safety and Stabilization 23
Phase II: Remembrance and Mourning 23
Phase III: Reconnection and Integration 23

The Arms of Love Exercise 24
My Healing Journal 24
Lessons Learned 25

2 **Establishing Safety and Security** 26
Establishing Safety and Security 27
Feeling Grounding: The What and the How 28
Reflective Exercises on Safety 29
Exercise: Establishing Safety in Your Life 30
My Safe Place Visualization 31
Visualizing Your Safe Place 31
Safety Checklist 32
Relaxation: It All Starts with Breathwork 32
Tips for Practicing Meditation 33
Mindfulness: What Is It Exactly? 34
Checking in with Yourself: Taking a Recess from This Workbook 36
Lessons Learned 38

3 **Addressing Your Trauma** 39
The SUDS Scale 39
Dissociation 40
Treating Trauma-Related Dissociation 41
Body-Oriented Interventions 42
Vagus Nerve Voo Exhale 42
Light Stream Technique 42
Flashbacks and How to Manage Them 42
Addressing and Managing Flashbacks 43
Replay and Review Flashback Technique 44
Addressing Flashbacks in the Mind, Body, Breath, and Spirit 45
Detailed EFT/Meridian Tapping Points 46
Addressing Nightmares 50
Suggestions for Facing Your Nightmare: 51
Exercise: Revising your Trauma Nightmare 52
Your Trauma History 53
My Resilience Record 53
Writing Your Trauma Timeline 54
When You Are Ready, Here's a Three-Part Question to Address in Your Healing Journal 54
Writing My Healing from Trauma Story 54

Here Are a Few Suggested Steps for Writing Your Trauma Recovery Journal 55
Lessons Learned 56

4 Self-soothing Interventions When You Are Triggered 57
Managing and Soothing Triggers 57
Managing My Triggers 59
Narrative Exercise for Managing Trauma Triggers 60
Steps in the Narrative Trauma Management Exercise 60
Narrative Trauma Healing Exercise 61
Final Draft: The Worst Moments 63
The Concluding Paragraph 63
Suggestion: How I Have Showed Courage 63
Ways I Have Demonstrated Courage 64
Lessons Learned 65

5 Managing Trauma When It Arises 66
Procrastination 66
The Miracle Question 67
Separating a Traumatic Memory into Smaller Sections 68
The Purpose of a Traumatic Memory 69
Self-talk Regarding a Traumatic Memory 70
Rescripting and Revising the Dominant Narrative 70
The Problem with Dissociation 71
When I Dissociate 71
How We Can Manage Dissociation 71
Behaviors Resulting from Untreated Dissociation 72
Ways I Avoid Potential Trauma 73
Addressing Trauma-Related Dissociation 74
Facing Your Most Common Triggers 75
Addressing the Triggers That Lead to Avoidance 76
What I Have Learned about Dissociation 77
Self-injurious Behaviors (SIBs) and Ways to Reduce and Stop Them 77
Symptoms of SIBs Can Include 77
Forms of Self-injury 78
Treatment for SIBs 78
My Self-injurious Behaviors 79
Prolonged Exposure Therapy (PET) 80
Types of Exposure 80
Steps in Imaginal Exposure 80

In Vivo Exposure 81
Case Example: Imaginal Exposure 81
Case Example: In Vivo Exposure 82
Prolonged Exposure Caution 83
Practice: Prolonged Exposure Therapy 83
Imaginal Exposure 83
Real-Life Exposure 84
The Empty Chair Exercise 85
Empty Chair Example 85
The Empty-Chair Technique: Practice 86
Lessons Learned 87

6 Regaining Trust and Developing Self-compassion 88
Negative Beliefs and Self-talk 88
Beliefs Regarding My Trauma 88
The Three Cs to Healing Negative Beliefs 89
The Case of Scott 89
Cognitive Revision Example (3 Cs) 90
3Cs Practice 91
Commitment: The Hard Part Exercise 91
What Is Forgiveness? 92
The Effects of Holding onto Anger 92
How Can I Begin to Achieve a State of Forgiveness? 93
Setting Healthy Boundaries with Others 93
Basic Steps to Setting Healthy Boundaries 93
Setting Healthy Boundaries Practice 94
What If I Am Having Difficulty Forgiving? 95
The Miracle Question Applied to Forgiveness 95
The Empty-Chair Forgiveness 95
Practicing Self-compassion 95
Daily Gratitude Practice 96
Self-forgiveness 97
Self-forgiveness Practice 98
Trust 99
What Does Trust Mean? 99
Reflections on the Previous Trust Exercise 100
Challenging My Beliefs about Power and Control 100
My Beliefs about the Power of Choice (and Relinquishing Control) 101
Self-affirmations: Reminding Ourselves of Our Talents and Capabilities 101

Steps to Take 102
Lessons Learned 103

7 **Addressing Trauma Symptomology: Negative Self-talk, Social Isolation, and Incongruent Emotional Expression** 104
Persistent Negative Emotions 104
Start Where the Dysregulation Starts: Fear 105
Questions Regarding Fear 106
The Top Ten Negative Thoughts that Cause Me Anxiety and the Strategies I Use to Manage That Anxiety 108
Top Ten Negative Thoughts That I Will Challenge by Practicing the 3 Cs 109
Expressing My Anger 109
How My Anger Has Wounded Me 110
Ways I Can Express My Anger in a Healthy, Appropriate Manner 111
Depression and Subsequent Guilt 111
A Suicide Intervention Plan 112
Guilt and Shame: The Terrible Twins 113
Unpacking Feelings of Guilt and Shame 113
Self-compassion Intervention on Guilt and Shame 113
Ask the Guilt and Shame Twins: 113
Healing My Shame Beliefs 114
Remember Your Healing Companions: Mind, Body, Breath, and Spirit 115
Healthy Communication: Asking for Our Needs to Be Met 117
Active Listening 119
Tip 1: Don't Hijack a Conversation 119
Tip 2: Be Present in the Relationship 120
Tip 3: Set Healthy Limits 121
My Responsibility to Heal 121
My Short Essay on How I Began to Heal My Trauma (or Manage My Anxiety or Stress) 123
Lessons Learned from This Chapter 124

8 **Calming the Lizard Brain for Home Life, Improved Work Relations, and Quality Sleep** 125
Creating More Restful Sleep 125
Trauma Survivors 126
For Trauma Survivors, Consider the Following to Prepare for Sleep 126

Other Pre-bedtime Wind Down Activities for Sleep 128
My Relaxation before Bedtime Routine 129
What about Those Nights When I Cannot Sleep? 129
Strategies to Relax on Those Nights When I Have Insomnia 130
Cognitive Reframing of Upsetting, Unpleasant, and Traumatic Thoughts: Healing the Second Arrow of Pain 130
Recognizing My Anger Signals: Keeping the Second Arrow Unloaded 132
My Approach to Anger Management 133
Situations That Cause Me to Become Angry 135
My Forgiveness Routine 136
The Verbal Approach to Forgiveness 136
The Narrative Approach to Forgiveness 137
The Creative Approach to Forgiveness 137
The Forgiveness Meditation 137
The Forgiveness Activity 138
Note to Readers 138
Personal Boundaries: Setting Limits with Others 138
Saying No: Practicing One of the Hardest, But Most Necessary Expressions 139
Practical Boundary Practice: Finding and Maintaining Your Safe Space 141
Respect My Boundaries Assertiveness Worksheet 142
My Healthy Boundaries Checklist 143
Writing Your Personal Short Story on Healing 144
Drawing Your Healing 145
Lessons Learned 145
One Percent Better 146
Tough Decisions 146
Courage 146

9 Managing Stress: EFT Tapping, Breathwork, Meditation, and Movement 147
Basic Facts Regarding Chronic Stress 148
Breathwork 148
Box Breathing 148
Mindful Meditation 149
Walking Meditation 149
Vagus Nerve Breathwork 149
Voo Exhale (Also Called the Voo Breath) 150
Meridian Tapping Points 150

Additional Information on Tapping 151
Healing Movements 151
Trauma Release Exercises 152
Therapeutic Massage 154
Common Somatic Concerns in Trauma Recovery 154
Benefits of Therapeutic Massage 155
Acupuncture for Trauma Reduction and Healing 155
Chair Yoga 155
To Start Chair Yoga 156
Tai Chi 156
Qigong 157
Movement Meditation 157
Getting Started 158
Some Tips for Getting Started 158
Self-Reflection Questions Regarding Your Activity/Fitness Plan 160
Lessons Learned 161

10 Helping First Responders 163
Asking for Help: It Takes Strength and Courage 164
Tips for Being a Good Listening Friend or Colleague 165
Self-Reflection on Seeking Help 166
Developing Presence to Help Others 169
Narrative Responses for Adjusting to Past Trauma 170
First Responder Re-entry Questions for Exploration 171
Addressing Survivor Guilt 172
Becoming Aware of Survivor Guilt Signs 173
Writing and PTSD: A Cathartic Approach 175
The Narrative: Telling My Story 175
Telling My Story 176
Reflections on Telling My Story 177
My Trauma Recovery Journal 178
Lessons Learned 180

11 Creating a Meaningful Life: Practical Exercises 181
Meaning in Life 182
Some Questions Regarding Meaning in Life 183
Writing a Meaning in Life Journal 184
Drawing: Another Creative Outlet 187
Reflective Questions on Your Drawing (or Collage) Journal 189

Lessons Learned 189

12 Lessons Learned through Healing: Post-traumatic Growth's Rewards 190
Significant Reflections on Your Healing 191
Charting Your Healing Journey 192
Start at the Beginning 193
Charting Your Healing from Trauma 195
Healing Meditations 198
Some Tips to Remember If You Are New to Meditation 198
Self-Guided Healing Meditation 199
Vagus Nerve Guided Meditation 201
Reflecting on the Vagus Nerve Meditation 202
What Disappointment Is Trying to Teach Me 203
Some Potential Lessons from Disappointment 203
Life Lessons, Trauma Healing, and Post-traumatic Growth Have Taught Me 205
Conversations with Myself 209
Lessons Learned from This Chapter and Beyond 210
Postscript 210
Afterword 211

References *213*
Index *219*

Author's Note

This workbook is designed to be utilized by mental health clinicians treating patients with acute stress disorder (ASD), PTSD (especially complex trauma), anxiety, and stress. The workbook is also appropriate for individuals who have completed trauma treatment or who are far enough along in treatment to apply the exercises as an aftercare type of support. The text is also designed to assist people in managing anxiety and everyday stress, but it is not intended as a substitute for professional counseling and psychotherapy with a qualified mental health professional.

Foreword

Dr. Katrina Andrews, *Senior Lecturer in Counseling, University of the Sunshine Coast, Australia, December 2025*

As I sit down to write this, the air in Australia feels heavy. On Sunday, December 14, 2025, the serenity of Bondi Beach, Sydney, was shattered by a targeted attack on the Jewish community. It is a stark, heartbreaking reminder that trauma is not merely a clinical concept discussed in university lecture halls; it is a visceral, lived reality that can arrive unannounced on a sunny afternoon.

In the immediate aftermath of the news, my first instinct was to reach out to the author of this book, Shannon, and his wife, who is a proud member of the Jewish community. I needed to know they were safe. When we spoke, despite the shock and the encroaching shadow of grief, I witnessed something profound. They were deeply upset, yes, but they were already in motion—reaching out to family, checking on friends, and turning toward one another for support. In the midst of acute stress, they were instinctively practicing the very resilience and connection that this workbook champions.

That moment crystallized why *Taming the Lizard Brain: A Mind, Body, Breath, and Spirit Approach to Healing Trauma, Anxiety, and Managing Everyday Stress* is not just timely; it is urgent.

We are living in an era where global conflicts are escalating, and the ripple effects of terror and instability are felt across oceans. Whether you are a clinician in Sydney, a first responder in New York, or a community member in London, the nervous system speaks a universal language. When safety is threatened, the "Lizard Brain"—our primal survival mechanism—takes the wheel. While this mechanism is designed to keep us alive, it can, if left unmanaged, trap us in a cycle of reactivity, anxiety, and disconnection.

This book serves as a vital bridge between clinical evidence and human experience. As a senior lecturer in counseling, I value resources that are rigorously informed yet accessible. Shannon has achieved this balance by refusing to adhere to a single, rigid dogma. Instead, he has curated a holistic "toolkit" that borrows from the most effective evidence-based treatments available today—integrating narrative therapy, CBT, somatic practices, and mindfulness.

The structure of this workbook mirrors the journey of healing itself. It begins, as all trauma work must, with *safety and stabilization* (Chapters 1 and 2).

Shannon guides the reader through the physiological realities of Type I and Type II trauma, offering immediate, tangible tools like box breathing and safe-space visualization to bring the nervous system back online.

As the text progresses, it courageously moves into the heart of **processing** (Chapters 3–5). The exercises provided here regarding triggers, flashbacks, and dissociation are treated with immense care. I was particularly moved by the "Empty Chair" exercises, which allow for a compassionate dialogue with one's own trauma and triggers—shifting the narrative from "What is wrong with me?" to "What is this trying to teach me?"

Crucially, this book addresses the **wounds of connection** (Chapters 6 and 7). Trauma often steals our ability to trust and isolates us in shame. Through exercises on boundaries, forgiveness, and the healthy expression of anger, this workbook offers a roadmap back to community and self-compassion.

Finally, the text transcends mere symptom management and aims for **meaning and growth** (Chapters 10–12). Whether addressing the specific burdens of first responders or guiding a survivor toward post-traumatic growth, the ultimate goal of this work is not just to survive but also to build a life rich with purpose.

This book is intended for an international audience, and rightly so. Trauma knows no borders. However, writing from Australia, in the wake of recent tragedy, I see this text as a beacon. It is a resource for the mental health clinician seeking practical interventions for clients with ASD and PTSD. It is a companion for the community member who has completed a program and is asking, "What now?"

Taming the Lizard Brain is an invitation to reclaim your story. It is a testament to the fact that while we cannot always control the events that happen to us—or the state of the world around us—we possess profound capacity within our mind, body, breath, and spirit to heal.

I commend this work to you with hope and resilience.

Preface

Within this workbook, you will encounter numerous self-reflective exercises and interventions designed to help you heal your trauma in your mind, body, breath, and spirit (meaning and purpose). You will notice there will be some repetition of exercises in this workbook, and that is by design, as repeating exercises reinforces both the concept and one's belief in that concept. While I have written this workbook in a particular manner, with Chapters 1–12, feel free to skip around if you desire (another reason for my repetition of exercises). Please feel free also to take a break from the chapters if you are feeling triggered. If your triggers seem unmanageable, please contact your therapist ASAP.

One more thing I wish to express before you begin this workbook. For readers who have experienced trauma (likely, that's most readers), your healing process involves a transformation process from wounded and emotionally dysregulated to post-traumatic growth and healed. In some ways, you might consider the lifecycle of a caterpillar in the process of becoming a butterfly. That is, you are undergoing your own personal metamorphosis. The caterpillar forms a cocoon, in which it sheds its old self with the aid of imaginal cells. Imaginal cells are those that remain dormant within the caterpillar's body and contain the blueprint for the butterfly. Human imaginal cells, however, are metaphoric. The therapeutic process represents the chrysalis of post-traumatic growth, as your new self emerges, ready for flight.

1 Understanding and Managing Trauma

First, some reflections and suggestions:

I have spent decades treating people with post-traumatic stress disorder (PTSD), as well as those grappling with general anxiety, stress, suicidality, grief, etc. PTSD will be the primary focus of this workbook, but many interventions herein can easily be adapted to address anxiety and stress. I would also like to offer congratulations to readers who are challenging their fears (e.g., anxieties, PTSD, and stress) by using this workbook. I expect many, if not most, readers have previously worked with a therapist. While I am a long-time counselor/therapist with four decades of experience, I also have spent several years addressing my own anxiety, depression, and PTSD. I have spent considerable time as a counseling client working on these challenging issues (or perhaps more appropriately, growth opportunities), and I have learned from sitting in the client's chair. I do believe that having much experience as a client has made me a better therapist. I hope that I pass on the lessons I have learned as a clinician treating trauma, anxiety, stress, addiction, etc., and those learned while being treated for the sundry issues that accompany trauma.

I would further encourage readers to remember that healing from trauma, managing stress, and anxiety is as individual and personal as it is a scientific process. In my long history of counseling trauma survivors, for example, I have noticed that progress is seldom linear. Many clients (Note: I will use the term "clients" rather than "patients" as that was what I was taught; however, I have no issue with the term "patient") have come to my various offices, having previously received treatment from other clinicians. Often, they would work with me for several sessions and then request a break from therapy. Later, many returned to my office, while others likely continued their therapeutic journey with someone else. Healing, especially from complex trauma (i.e., long-term trauma), is often completed in increments punctuated by breaks from sessions.

Regarding the previous paragraph, work your way through this book at a rate congruent with your own healing. Take your time and tell yourself that incremental healing is still healing, something I regularly remind my clients. In this workbook, you will encounter numerous cognitive, somatic, reflective, and breathwork exercises. Some of these exercises will seem a better fit for you and your recovery than others, and this is natural because people vary in what

DOI: 10.4324/9781003689232-1

works for them. So, work on the exercises, giving a sincere effort, especially with those interventions that seem to be the best fit for you. I also encourage readers to commence writing what I term a "Trauma Recovery Journal." For readers using this text to manage regular anxiety and stress, call it a "Personal Growth Journal" or anything you like. You may become weary of my suggesting you complete every exercise in this journal. I encourage writing out the exercises, as that implies greater commitment and suggests you are more likely to commit to what you have written (Pennebaker, 2004). Therefore, throughout this workbook, you will read me constantly encouraging you to answer the exercises in your Trauma Recovery Journal.

In addition, self-monitor how often you use this workbook. Healing can be stressful work, so permit yourself to go slowly, take breaks when needed, and always revise your self-talk to be self-compassionate. While there are many factors in healing trauma, managing anxiety and stress (e.g., working the exercises, counseling, refraining from self-medication), the most salient of all is what one tells themself about their ability to heal. The old self-fulfilling prophecy is very true. As my crusty high school counselor was fond of expressing, "If you believe you can succeed, you will do so, at least to some extent. Conversely, if you believe you can't succeed, you are completely right." So, dear readers, your mantra for healing is, "I will take whatever time is necessary and heal my trauma/anxiety/and manage my stress." If you habituate these words and believe them, you will heal. Some of the most damaged people I have treated for complex PTSD were survivors of long-term sexual, physical, and verbal abuse who self-medicated their pain for years; some were homeless and with lots of defeat and personal loss, yet they worked their steps and healed because they believed they could heal. So, cultivate that positive, self-fulfilling attitude that you will heal. If you believe you can heal and then put in the work, you are going to heal, at least to some extent.

One consideration I strongly encourage all readers to adopt, especially those healing from trauma (likely most readers), is the Japanese philosophy of kintsugi. Kintsugi is the Japanese philosophy characterized by embracing imperfection and treating healing as an essential part of human experience, or, as some might express, celebrating beauty in brokenness. The word is composed of two Japanese words, "kin," meaning "gold" and "tsugi," meaning "to mend." Thus, kintsugi highlights filling cracks rather than hiding them, and second, kintsugi is the idea that repair, or healing, makes the creation more interesting than before it was broken. So, regularly remind yourself that healing your pain or brokenness creates a stronger, more beautiful, more interesting you (Navarro, 2019).

Trauma: What's the Story You Are Telling Yourself?

Brene Brown is a popular author, educator, and mental health professional. One of her most popular books and favorite sayings is *What's the Story You Are Telling Yourself?* (2017). The reason this statement is so critical is that trauma healing is as much about the story as it is about the trauma itself. All trauma clients I have treated have been more focused on their trauma story, what they were telling themselves, than their actual trauma. One reason for this is that dissociation is one of the most common methods of surviving trauma (van der Kolk, 2014). During ongoing trauma (e.g., sexual abuse, torture, psychological abuse), victims dissociate, that is, go offline, as a means of survival. Dissociation is a primary reason trauma survivors have memory gaps. Survivors fill those gaps with their own version of the story (e.g., "I am a victim and will always be broken," or "I am a survivor and when healed will be a thriver!"). The stories we tell ourselves are very important because we believe those narratives. Basically, if we believe we can heal, we will, as we are likely to put in the required work, and because belief plus the work becomes self-fulfilling. Conversely, if we do not believe healing is possible, we won't, because if healing is impossible, why put forth any effort? So dear reader, the story you need to tell and re-tell yourself is, "I am going to heal by putting in the required work, and one day I will move from trauma survivor to that of posttraumatic growth."

I would also be remiss if I did not address the reality that many readers likely will skip around the different chapters in this workbook as opposed to working sequentially from Chapters 1 to 12. Once again, find what works for you, so long as you put in the work.

Here Are a Few Additional Considerations

1 What is your personal mission statement? If you are like most people, you likely have never considered the matter. Yet companies, schools, colleges, and non-profit organizations have mission statements. A mission statement defines an organization's core reason for existence and communicates its purpose, values, and goals to employees, stakeholders, clients, and customers. A mission statement serves as a guide for operations and strategic decision-making, ensuring that the organization remains focused on and consistent with its long-term mission.

   Again, I'd suggest you begin keeping a Trauma Recovery Journal (or one for managing anxiety or stress) and begin by writing a personal mission statement. You will need to reflect on your purpose, values, and goals, and how you ensure congruence with these goals and values.

2 I suggest you address the following question: In what ways have I demonstrated courage in my healing journey? Addressing trauma takes courage, as healing requires facing traumatic memories that no one would want to face. So, write about your courage and give yourself credit for keeping up that courage, as I know very well, it is not easy.

3 Keep constant positive visual reminders up regarding healing and positive change. One friend was fond of posting encouraging and inspirational messages on her refrigerator. This way, several times a day, she would be reminded of why she was a psychologist serving a challenging population of traumatized children.

4 What would you hope to gain from this workbook? There are lots of helpful resources out there, and yet you have selected this as one to use. I would suggest you write your reason for selecting this as a resource and then record how well it helped in your Trauma Recovery Journal. In my work, I make much use of scaling questions to assess improvement and decline. When completed, answer the question: "On a scale of 1 to 10, with 10 being high, how helpful has this workbook been to you?"
5 Finally, this workbook can serve as a healing resource alongside readers who are currently in therapy or have completed therapy. Many interventions in this text, such as breathwork like meditation and box breathing, would not require previous therapeutic work. Others, like addressing specifics related to the abuse, would certainly work with a qualified therapist. Furthermore, should you begin to feel triggered while using this workbook, please contact a mental health therapist ASAP. For U.S. readers, you can also call the National Crisis Lifeline at 988.

Trauma, unfortunately, is an all-too-common human experience. Virtually everyone experiences trauma in some form during their lifespan. Trauma can be short-term and remit naturally within a short period (say, under 30 days), making it an acute stress disorder (American Psychological Association, 2022), or last for decades, and what mental health professionals' term post-traumatic stress disorder or PTSD (APA, 2022). Trauma may be caused by a single episode, such as an auto accident, or be ongoing, as when suffering long-term sexual or domestic abuse, which many of us call complex trauma.

Fortunately, help is more readily available for most people, given that more professional therapists are trained to provide effective treatments for trauma (e.g., EMDR, mindfulness-based CBT, cognitive processing therapy, prolonged exposure) and through the advent of online therapy via secure mediums or in traditional in-person counseling. What is important is doing what all 12-step programs emphasize in their approach, namely, admitting that one has a problem and needs help to address the issue. My own experience is that far too many trauma sufferers carry their trauma in secret, suffering anxiety, sleep difficulty, heart palpitations, and snapping in anger at loved ones and colleagues when triggered, while self-medicating their symptoms with alcohol and various other substances and careening from one broken relationship to another.

So, the first step in addressing trauma is to admit that it is a reality and is causing distress in one's life. Trauma can impact thoughts, emotions, relationships, dreams, attitudes, and somatic difficulties. However, recognizing trauma is present in one's life (the crisis) also provides the opportunity to address and heal that trauma and become liberated from a variety of personal maladies (the opportunity). I would further add that in my long experience as a clinician treating trauma, the simple, holistic approach (e.g., mind, body, breath, and spirit) is what works best. Throughout this text, numerous examples of simple narrative self-reflective exercises (cognitive reframing), body work (e.g., EFT/Meridian tapping, massage, exercise), breathwork (e.g., meditation, box breathing), and even spirit (meaning and purpose) will provide the reader the opportunity to address and challenge fears and ultimately live a healthier, more fulfilling life. The tougher part, however, is that like sobriety and physical fitness, there is no point whereby a person can say, "Okay, I'm healed, and my work is done, and I can just relax." No, you will need to continue the discipline of reframing self-defeating thoughts, using meditation and other breathwork, maintaining physical activity and meaningful relationships, and setting firm, although healthy, flexible boundaries with others.

Examples of Trauma

Perhaps you have experienced something traumatic. Maybe you have a history of childhood sexual abuse, or as an adult, have been trapped in a violent relationship, or are a refugee and are forced to flee your native country. Maybe you were in an automobile accident or observed a terrible industrial accident where a colleague was seriously injured or killed. Maybe none of this unfortunate list is what has impacted you. Perhaps your occupation involves daily interactions with trauma, such as paramedics, firefighters, police, military personnel, emergency room staff, and other hazardous occupations. In many instances, there simply is no way to escape or avoid trauma.

Fortunately, help is available, and this text focuses on providing information and self-reflective exercises that may be completed at a rate congruent with the readers' pace.

Trauma Defined

The term *trauma* has become a very familiar word in all societies. You have likely heard of it via social media, the internet, TV, film, podcasts, etc. Wars throughout the globe have brought trauma up close and personal to loved ones on all continents, as family members have been killed, seriously maimed, and experienced the destruction of their homes. Post-traumatic stress disorder (hereafter PTSD) is a label applied to a series of symptoms published in the *Diagnostic and Statistical Manual of Mental Disorders* (*DSM-5-TR*; American Psychiatric Association, 2022). The short definition, DSM-5-TR defines trauma as Criterion A and specifies exposure to actual or threatened death, serious injury, or sexual violence (APA, 2022). The exposure may be experienced directly, witnessed, or learned about, particularly if it involves a close family member or friend.

Trauma may involve the aftermath of a hurricane that kills thousands, a tornado, a flood, a plane crash, or a homicide in the neighborhood. Trauma may involve physical, sexual, or emotional harm or both, not to mention the loss of a sense of personal security. In essence, for the traumatized person, it usually means a paradigm shift from a worldview of safety and security to one of an unpredictable, callous, and hostile world. My experience in treating trauma survivors is that the changing mindset from general safety to that of constant hypervigilance is as much the challenge as the trauma itself. Most particularly, the stories that survivors continue to tell themselves about their trauma, in my experience, can be more problematic than the actual trauma. What we tell ourselves is powerful and self-efficacious, meaning that we believe the stories we tell ourselves, even when they are erroneous (Ellis, 2011). So, people recovering from trauma must tell themselves they will heal. I have worked with some very traumatized people who healed because they believed they would. While I would say that my work with these clients was helpful, their belief and their work were just as important as my help in their recovery. If you believe you can heal, likely you will. Conversely, if you believe you cannot heal, you will also be correct, as why put out any effort if you do not believe healing is possible? So, remember to be judicious in what you tell yourself, as that will become your belief, and your belief will hold strong predictive validity in your healing process.

Trauma survivors may be those who directly experienced the trauma (via sexual, physical, or emotional violence), those who witnessed the violence, or those exposed to survivors of trauma. We call this latter type of trauma vicarious or secondary trauma. While providing trauma and suicide intervention trainings and even counseling in South African orphanages and remote First Nation schools in Australia's Northern Territory, where there was a high rate of trauma among the children, many of the orphanage staff and remote schoolteachers suffered from vicarious trauma, as they worked with a very traumatized population. First responders (e.g., paramedics, police, military personnel) and many other professionals are very likely to be impacted by vicarious trauma and need good self-care programs (Figley, 1995; Stamm, 2009).

Trauma's Impact on Survivors

Trauma can have a significant impact on survivors' thoughts and behaviors. Survivors may initially experience shock, panic attacks, disorientation, dissociation (as if being out of one's body), memory gaps, and somatic problems, to cite just a few potential symptoms. Many survivors report a sense of constantly being on edge (hypervigilance) as they are always asking themselves this question: "Will I be safe or will I be hurt?" Every trauma survivor I have treated in a very long career has articulated some variation of this question. In his seminal book, *The Body Keeps the Score: Brain, Mind, and Body in the Healing of Trauma*, Bessel van der Kolk (2014) recounts numerous tales of patients lashing out at others in otherwise normal, non-threatening human interactions. The survivor lashes out due to overreacting to otherwise typical human interactions. The survivor overreacts to stimuli reminders of trauma, be that reminder sight (witnessing the unpleasant), smell (the abuser's cologne), the feel of the train passenger's hand on their back (tactile), a coach's whistle reminding them of their incarceration (hearing), or tasting food their abuser forced them to eat.

Numerous predisposing factors can influence how one responds to a traumatic event. The reaction to a traumatic event can vary due to age (younger people usually react more distressfully), whether one had time to prepare (for example, time to get to the basement before a tornado hit); previous traumatic history (i.e., survivor of long-term sexual abuse), the extent of injury to the survivor (physical, emotional, or spiritual) or to one's home, and the level of death and destruction witnessed. These are just a few of the factors that determine the level of trauma reactions for survivors. A survivor's willingness to actively seek help may also impact the level of trauma suffered. Consider a trauma survivor of a terrible flood that kills scores of people and destroys their neighborhood. If that person seeks shelter, food, medical attention, counseling, and even spiritual assistance from a place of worship or their 12-step program, their trauma, while significant, will very likely be less than the survivor who isolates themselves from human support.

It is also worth mentioning that some people are naturally more resilient to trauma than others. This likely explains why some military veterans who experienced combat develop PTSD while others do not. PTSD statistics vary among studies, with some suggesting PTSD rates of 13% to over 30% of combat veterans (Reisman, 2016). Other factors may include family and social support, degree of physical wounds and disability, aftercare during post-discharge, and what a person tells themselves about the trauma. Regardless, while most combat veterans do not develop PTSD, a significant percentage do.

A perusal of the trauma literature will mention the three major types of factors influencing the development of PTSD: pre-event factors, event factors, and post-event factors. While PTSD is the most serious and best-known trauma type, acute stress disorder is far more common and shorter in duration (under 30 days) (APA, 2022). Roughly 15% of people exposed to a traumatic event will develop PTSD. However, the rate can be significantly higher depending on the type of trauma. Survivors of long-term childhood sexual abuse and combat veterans with multiple deployments will very likely have higher rates of PTSD (van der Kolk, 2014). Regardless of the type of trauma or how long it lasted, a survivor's goal is to heal their trauma and emerge into what is termed post-traumatic growth. (We'll explore this in more detail later in the text.)

Pre-event Factors for Trauma

Examples of pre-event factors for trauma may include:

- Previous exposure to traumatic events such as child sexual abuse, domestic violence, persistent neglect, or witnessing neglect and abuse. Sometimes, these are termed adverse childhood experiences or ACEs.
- Early life anxiety or depression, or bullying.
- Family instability, separated from family of origin, and removed from family home due to neglect or abuse.
- Family history of criminal behavior.

- Absence of social or peer support.
- Ineffective coping skills.
- Gender, as females are twice as likely to develop PTSD as males. LGBTQ+ have significantly greater rates of PTSD.
- Early substance abuse.
- Genetics, with close biological relatives diagnosed with PTSD.
- Again, what the trauma survivor tells themselves about the trauma. (i.e., "I can heal with help" vs. "It's hopeless").

Event Factors

Some examples of trauma event factors may include the following:

- Geographic nearness to the event
- Level of exposure to the event, as greater exposure, leading to a greater likelihood of PTSD
- What the survivor tells themselves about the trauma. Or "What's the story you are telling yourself about the trauma?" (Brown, 2015)
- Less protective adults in one's life during childhood trauma
- Witnessing death, especially if violent
- Being a combat veteran, especially of multiple deployments
- Being in an occupation that regularly exposes you to traumatic events
- Being a survivor of sexual assault
- Duration of the trauma
- Poor coping skills

Post-Event Factors

The final category of PTSD risk factors includes those that exist after the traumatic event. These can be either positive or negative factors. These post-event factors may include:

- Poor social and family support
- Being female as opposed to male
- Having poor self-esteem
- Self-medicating with alcohol and drugs
- Inability to find meaning in suffering. Conversely, finding meaning through suffering (Frankl, 2006)
- Willingness to seek therapy for their trauma
- A belief that they can heal from their trauma
- Experiencing a strong reaction (startle) during the traumatic event or after the event that includes high blood pressure and avoidant or numbing symptoms (Friedman, 2000)

An additional important factor in managing trauma and stress is having an internal locus of control. That is, understanding that your power lies in how you manage and adapt to stressors around you, while realizing that you cannot control others' behavior; maintaining optimism and a sense of meaning that while traumatic events may lie outside your control, you maintain the ability to heal from trauma and lead a full life; confidence in your ability to cope with stressful situations; and finally, being strong enough to seek help when your coping strategies have reached their limit.

My Ability to Address Trauma

Check any of the following statements that you believe are true for you.

1 ___ I maintain a belief in my ability to effectively cope with and manage stress.
2 ___ I believe that I am a resilient person capable of managing personal difficulties.
3 ___ I am an optimistic person who believes difficult times will pass.
4 ___ I find that I am usually able to complete the tasks I have begun.
5 ___ I find meaning even during difficult periods in life.
6 ___ I have a supportive group of family and friends who help me manage difficulties.
7 ___ I maintain a strong sense of hope.
8 ___ I am a very spiritual person or have a strong sense of purpose in life.
9 ___ I realize that difficult times will eventually pass and that life will become more enjoyable again.
10 ___ I have a regular workout routine (e.g., walking, jogging, cycling, 4 or more days a week).
11 ___ I am willing to seek professional help should trauma, anxiety, stress, etc. become more that I can manage alone.
12 ___ I believe in my ability to manage the stressors in my life.
13 ___ I am willing to make important changes to improve my life.
14 ___ I enjoy a good challenge, as it motivates me to improve in some way.
15 ___ I believe in my ability to persevere during difficult times.
16 ___ I rely on my support network and well-being/self-care plan to manage difficulty and refrain from self-medication with alcohol or drugs to alleviate stress.
17 ___ I have a healthy, appropriate sense of humor that helps me cope with stressors.
18 ___ I am a generally friendly person.
19 ___ I believe the source of my power lies within me.
20 ___ I make plans and take action to improve my personal and occupational situation.

For the following two questions, I suggest you make use of your Trauma Recovery Journal.

1 Review your answers to the previous statements. What do you learn from your results?
2 What do you learn from the items you did not check?

Self-compassion

There has been considerable discussion and agreement regarding the importance of self-compassion in recent years (Neff, 2011). The best way to think about self-compassion perhaps lies in the question, "If you were to advise a friend being overly harsh on themself/themselves, what might you say?" Likewise, if you are being self-critical over what you did not check in the checklist, consider speaking to yourself as your own best friend (as opposed to your worst critic). My experience from 40+ years in the mental health field is that harsh self-criticism only compounds trauma, anxiety, and depression. On that note, fill in the blank below:

One way I can practice self-compassion is ______________________________.

Post-Traumatic Stress Disorder (PTSD) and Acute Stress Disorder (ASD)

In the DSM-5-TR edition, post-traumatic stress disorder (PTSD) requires exposure to a traumatic event and symptoms from four clusters: intrusion, avoidance, negative alterations in cognition and mood, and arousal/reactivity that persist for at least one month. Acute stress disorder (ASD) criteria are similar to PTSD but include symptoms for at least three days but no more than one month after the trauma. The primary distinction between ASD and PTSD is the duration of symptoms and the specified time frame following the traumatic event.

To summarize *DSM-5-TR*:

PTSD and ASD Criteria

- **Criterion A**: **Stressor**. Exposure to actual or threatened death, serious injury, or sexual violence (directly, witnessing, or learning about it happening to a close loved one).
- **Criterion B**: **Intrusion Symptoms**. At least one re-experiencing symptom (e.g., intrusive memories, nightmares, flashbacks).
- **Criterion C**: **Avoidance.** At least one avoidance symptom (e.g., avoiding thoughts/feelings or external reminders of the event).
- **Criterion D**: **Negative Alterations in Cognitions and Mood**. At least two negative alterations (e.g., inability to remember parts of the trauma,

persistent negative beliefs, distorted blame, diminished interest in activities, feelings of detachment, or inability to experience positive emotions).

- **Criterion E: Alterations in Arousal and Reactivity**. At least two hyperarousal symptoms (e.g., irritability, angry outbursts, reckless behavior, hypervigilance, exaggerated startle response, or problems with concentration/sleep).
- **Criterion F: Duration**. Symptoms in criteria B, C, D, and E last for at least one month.
- **Criterion G: Functional Significance**. Symptoms can cause clinically significant distress or impairment in social, occupational, or other important areas of functioning.
- **Criterion H: Exclusion**. Symptoms are not attributable to substance use, another medical condition, or better explained by another mental disorder.
- **Specifications**: PTSD can be specified as "With Delayed Expression" if the full criteria are not met at least six months after the event or "With Dissociative Symptoms" if there are significant depersonalization or derealization symptoms.

ASD and PTSD Criteria on Exposure Include

The criteria for exposure do not include internet news, photos, or TV, unless the exposure is work-related. At least 9 of the following fourteen symptoms must be present while symptoms continue from 3 days to 1 month after the trauma exposure; they cause clinically significant distress or impairment in social, occupational, or other areas of functioning; and the reaction is not due to physiological effects of a substance or other medical conditions (American Psychiatric Association, 2022).

Post-traumatic Stress Disorder

Javier is a combat veteran of the Gulf War, having been discharged and subsequently returned home to his previous job as a construction worker. While in Afghanistan, the armored vehicle he was riding in the Green Zone hit an IED. Javier was seriously wounded, and two of his fellow soldiers were killed. Loud sounds such as motor vehicles backfiring, fireworks, gunshots, and the like trigger him, and he lives in a constant state of hyperarousal, constantly on guard. Once, while having a cookout with his family, something in the fire made a loud popping sound, and Javier dove to the ground, taking his 5-year-old daughter underneath him to shield her from perceived danger.

Harriet is a nurse in an inner-city school located in an area of the city rife with gang violence. She is dedicated to the children in her school, knowing many of them are constantly on the periphery of violent injury or death. She has also attended the funerals of many former students who have died in gang wars or the crossfire of gang violence. One afternoon, a rival gang enters the school playground and opens fire on several students, killing two and seriously wounding several others. Harriet rushes out to provide first aid and try to save lives until the ambulances arrive. While providing CPR to a child, the student dies despite her best efforts. When the paramedics arrive, Harriet's clothes are soaked with the children's blood. Over the next two months, she experienced flashbacks, nightmares, and intrusive thoughts related to the carnage she witnessed on the school playground.

Javier and Harriet both suffer from PTSD, which has become all too prevalent in many societies. General prevalence rates for U.S. men and women run 4% and 8%, respectively (National Center for PTSD, 2020). Military veterans and first responders like Javier and those working in geographically violent areas like Harriet, have significantly higher rates of PTSD than the general population (Briere & Scott, 2015; van der Kolk, 2014).

PTSD Symptoms

As previously stated, trauma symptoms that persist for over 30 days, or if symptoms occur at least 6 months after the event occurred, are generally diagnosed as PTSD. Regarding PTSD, the traumatic event must be catastrophic or severe, involving death or threatened death, serious injury, or sexual violence, and not a nonaccidental or extended medical condition or media exposure, apart from in the line of duty (see categories A and H below). To be diagnosed with PTSD, you must experience at least 1 of the 5 symptoms listed in Category B; included in those symptoms, flashbacks are now considered to be dissociative reactions occurring on a continuum. You must experience 1 of 2 avoidance symptoms in Category C. Category D includes alterations in cognition and mood, and risk-taking and self-destructive behaviors are part of Category E, of which 2 or more are required for a diagnosis. Finally, to be diagnosed with PTSD, as opposed to ASD, symptoms must continue beyond a 1-month diagnostic term (Category F).

Complex trauma (PTSD) is a common term used to describe multiple episodes or ongoing trauma, such as in childhood sexual abuse or combat. Although complex trauma is not an official diagnostic category, many clinicians like me commonly refer to it. Thus, complex trauma is very real, especially to anyone who has survived long-term abuse (van der Kolk, 2014). The following list offers DSM diagnostic criteria for PTSD for children (over 6 years of age), adolescents, and adults.

A **You have been exposed to actual death, threatened death, serious injury, or sexual violence through one of the following:**

- Direct experience or exposure
- Witnessing the events in person
- Indirect exposure, learning about events happening to a close relative or friend (if exposure involves death, it must be violent or accidental)
- Repeated or extreme exposure to aversive details of traumatic events as part of your line of work (paramedics, police, military, etc.), not through electronic media, TV, or films unless it's work-related

B **Your intrusive symptoms include one or more of the following:**

- Recurrent, involuntary, intrusive, and distressing memories; in children, possibly expressed through play
- Recurrent and distressing dreams related to the traumatic event; in children, dream content may not be directly related to the event.
- Dissociative reactions (for example, flashbacks) as if events were recurring; in children, possibly reenacted through play.
- Intense or prolonged psychological distress when exposed to internal or external cues symbolizing or resembling some part of the event.
- Marked physiological reactions to internal or external cues symbolizing or resembling some part of the event.

C **You persistently avoid stimuli associated with the event(s) afterwards, and this avoidance takes the form of one or both of the following:**

- Avoiding distressing memories, thoughts, or feelings about the event
- Avoiding or trying to avoid external reminders that lead to distressing memories, thoughts, or feelings

D **The following category addresses repetitive alterations in cognitions (thoughts) and moods (emotions) associated with the event(s) that begin or get worse after the events occurred. You experience two or more of the following symptoms:**

- Inability to remember an important aspect of the event(s), typically due to dissociative amnesia, which may occur only once or multiple times. Dissociative amnesia is not common forgetting but is directly related to the traumatic event or events, leading to some degree of functional impairment, and is not a result of physiological conditions.
- Persistent, often distorted, exaggerated negative beliefs or expectations about yourself, others, and the world.
- Persistent negative cognitions (thoughts) about causes or consequences of the event(s), including persistent distorted blame of yourself, others, and the world.
- Persistent negative trauma-related emotional states (fear, horror, anger, guilt, shame).
- Markedly lowered interest or participation in important pre-trauma activities.
- Feelings of detachment, alienation, or estrangement from others.
- Persistent inability to experience positive emotions (happiness, satisfaction, love) and less outward display or expression.

E **Your arousal and reactivity symptoms that are associated with the event(s) include two or more of the following:**

- Irritable behavior and angry outbursts (with little provocation) expressed as verbal or physical aggression to people or objects

- Reckless or self-destructive behaviors
- Hypervigilance
- Exaggerated startle response
- Problems with concentration
- Difficulty falling asleep, staying asleep, or having restless sleep

F **The duration of your symptoms is more than 1 month.**
G **The PTSD disturbance causes clinically significant distress or impairment in social, occupational, or other important areas of functioning.**
H **This disturbance is not due to the physiological effects of a substance or to any medical condition.**

The clinician providing treatment to you may inquire if you have responded to the trigger (stressful) events by depersonalization. Depersonalization describes a sense of being detached from outside yourself, observing actions happening to you (like watching a film), and feeling that what you are experiencing is not reality.

A related issue involved persistent or recurrent experiences of unreality of surroundings, also known as derealization. These experiences have a feeling of unreality or a lack of familiarity. You may feel as if you are in a dream state or fog, or having some barrier between yourself and the external world around you (American Psychiatric Association, 2022). The world itself may appear unreal, and derealization often includes visual distortions (blurriness, greater acuity, altered distances, wider or narrower visual fields), which can impact both interpersonal and occupational areas of life. You may also experience decreased emotionality, difficulties with focusing, and problems related to retaining information.

Type I and Type II PTSD

There has been considerable discussion and research regarding types or subtypes of PTSD (Birkeland et al., 2022). Type I PTSD refers to people experiencing or witnessing traumatic events that are single, catastrophic, and unanticipated experiences. Type I PTSD examples include a one-time sexual assault, an automobile accident, and a natural disaster like a tornado, hurricane, or flood. The Type I traumas are sometimes referred to as critical incidents. If you have experienced a Type I trauma, you may have a detailed, clear memory of what occurred. These traumatic memories often remain active, causing distress when you are triggered by similar experiences, hearing about them, or seeing them in the media.

Type II PTSD refers to multiple traumatic experiences, like long-term sexual abuse, ongoing domestic violence, having been a prisoner of war (POW), or those who lived or are living in a war zone and represents what professionals like me refer to as "complex trauma."

Type I and Type II trauma often involve the same type of symptomology. Type I, the single-episode type, is often more amenable to therapy (van der

Kolk, 2014). However, a catastrophic Type I trauma experience (i.e., losing your entire family to a flood) can be as traumatic as Type II trauma.

Type I and II trauma may be experienced in the following manner:

1. Based on previous trauma, you sense danger and begin to feel anxious (weak stomach sensations, increased blood pressure, racing, disturbing thoughts, etc.)
2. You feel overwhelmed and out of control when triggered.
3. Feeling threatened, you lash out against the perceived threat through an angry verbal outburst, perhaps involving obscenities, threatening language, becoming physically assaultive by shoving, punching, kicking, etc., or by fleeing the situation (e.g., walking or running away), or simply by "freezing up" to the perceived threat. (or fight, flight, or freeze).
4. After the threat passes or after the fight, flight, or freeze ends, the aftermath begins. There is some relief about decreased blood pressure, reduction of disturbing thoughts, and a sense of equilibrium returning.
5. Sometime later, you may realize that you have overreacted and that unpleasant consequences are likely. (e.g., verbal reprimand, fired from a job, legal problems)

Now, regarding Type I trauma, consider the following situation regarding Sylvia.

Sylvia was relaxing at her favorite coffee shop, reading the online news, when someone ran into the shop screaming, "Run, he's got a gun!" At that moment, a man entered the coffee shop and began shooting at the woman. Sylvia, momentarily stunned, then motivated by her surging blood pressure and thoughts of death, jumped to the floor, rolled quickly, and then scampered around the counter, finding refuge behind a tall set of plants. She watched in horror as the assailant shot several patrons before rushing from the shop. As sirens began wailing, Sylvia felt frozen to the floor before rushing behind the counter and grabbing several towels, whereupon she approached a survivor and held the towels against an adolescent female's wounds. The girl looked at Sylvia in shock, asking, "Am I dying?" Suddenly, paramedics arrived and roughly pushed Sylvia out of the way and began administering immediate care. Sylvia stood and watched as if viewing a scene from an upsetting movie, unable to hear the background sounds of multiple police and ambulance sirens.

Over the next two months, Sylvia reexperienced the event in her dreams, was regularly triggered by sirens, loud pops of boxes and plastic bags, and high blood pressure, and began to have trouble remembering workplace meetings and appointments. Sylvia then began self-medicating with alcohol, increasingly withdrawn from peers, and feared leaving her apartment might result in bodily harm or even death.

Now, Sylvia has experienced severe single-episode Type I trauma resulting in PTSD, as her symptoms have continued for the past 1 month and even worsened in severity. Remember, single-episode trauma can be as upsetting and unremitting as Type II trauma depending on the extent of trauma itself.

The following is an example of Type II trauma:

Ben had enjoyed a happy childhood until he was 8 years old. His mother was a single parent, with neither she nor Ben having contact with the father. When Ben was 8, his mother married a man named Steve. Steve initially seemed friendly and even kind, purchasing both Ben and his mother things they previously could not afford. However, 6 months into the marriage, Steve began sexually abusing Ben weekly. Ben was confused about what was happening, and soon he began to feel depressed and angry. With no outlet for his anger, he began self-mutilating on his arms and legs, hiding his cuts with jeans and long sleeves. However, one day during PE, the teacher noticed Ben was bleeding and took him to see the school nurse. The nurse examined Ben, noticing the cuts, and after some questioning, Ben explained why he was cutting himself. The nurse alerted the school counselor and principal, and Child Protection Services were notified. After an investigation, Steve was arrested and taken to jail awaiting trial. Ben's mother, shocked to lose Steve's affection and his significant salary, accused Ben of lying about the abuse. Ben then felt even worse, and thus his trauma was multiplied, believing he had been the one to blame.

Now, regarding the Type I trauma case of Sylvia and the Type II case of Ben, these are two case study examples based on actual clients I counseled in different clinical settings. Both Type I (single-episode trauma) and Type II (multiple or ongoing trauma) had long-term devastating effects on Sylvia and Ben. I treated both Sylvia and Ben (both pseudonyms) many years after their initial exposure to their traumas. Both Sylvia and Ben healed from their trauma, mainly due to their belief in their ability to heal, their commitment to working the treatment plan, and with strong social support in their lives.

The PTSD Checklist, 5th Edition. (PCL-5)

The Post-traumatic Stress Disorder Checklist (PCL-5) is a free, helpful, self-screening assessment in the public domain, meaning anyone can use it free of charge. (There is also a military version of the PCL-5).

Instructions: There is one question about the stressful experience or event, followed by 20 multiple-choice questions. These questions have been designed for adults. You may take the assessment here or download it from the website (https://novopsych.com/assessments/diagnosis/ptsd-checklist-5-pcl-5/). Disclaimer: This self-assessment is not a substitute for clinical diagnosis or professional therapeutic advice. By using the PCL-5, you accept any responsibility, as the website and not this text are responsible for outcomes. As always, I recommend you address your trauma with a qualified mental health professional.

PCL-5

Instructions

Below is a list of problems that people sometimes have in response to a very stressful experience. Keeping your worst event in mind, please read each problem carefully and then select one of the numbers to the right to indicate how much you have been bothered by that problem in the past month.

In the past month, how much were you bothered by:	*Not at all*	*A little bit*	*Moderately*	*Quite a bit*	*Extremely*
1 Repeated, disturbing, and unwanted memories of the stressful experience?	0	1	2	3	4
2 Repeated, disturbing dreams of the stressful experience?	0	1	2	3	4
3 Suddenly feeling or acting as if the stressful experience were actually happening again (as if actually back there reliving it)?	0	1	2	3	4
4 Feeling very upset when something reminded you of the stressful experience?	0	1	2	3	4
5 Having strong physical reactions when something reminded you of the stressful experience (e.g., heart pounding, trouble breathing, sweating)?	0	1	2	3	4
6 Avoiding memories, thoughts, or feelings related to the stressful experience?	0	1	2	3	4
7 Avoiding external reminders of the stressful experience (e.g., people, places, conversations, activities, objects, or situations)?	0	1	2	3	4
8 Trouble remembering important parts of the stressful experience?	0	1	2	3	4
9 Having strong negative beliefs about yourself, other people, or the world (e.g., having thoughts such as: I am bad, there is something seriously wrong with me, no one can be trusted, the world is completely dangerous)?	0	1	2	3	4
10 Blaming yourself or someone else for the stressful experience or what happened after it?	0	1	2	3	4

(*Continued*)

In the past month, how much were you bothered by:	*Not at all*	*A little bit*	*Moderately*	*Quite a bit*	*Extremely*
11 Having strong negative feelings such as fear, horror, anger, guilt, or shame?	0	1	2	3	4
12 Loss of interest in activities that you used to enjoy?	0	1	2	3	4
13 Feeling distant or cut off from other people?	0	1	2	3	4
14 Trouble experiencing positive feelings (e.g., being unable to feel happiness or have loving feelings for people close to you)?	0	1	2	3	4
15 Irritable behavior, angry outbursts, or acting aggressively?	0	1	2	3	4
16 Taking too many risks or doing things that could cause you harm?	0	1	2	3	4
17 Being "superalert" or watchful or on guard?	0	1	2	3	4
18 Feeling jumpy or easily startled?	0	1	2	3	4
19 Having difficulty concentrating?	0	1	2	3	4
20 Trouble falling or staying asleep?	0	1	2	3	4

A PCL-5 score of 38 or higher is indicative of PTSD. It is recommended that clinicians using this scale initially administer it to develop a baseline and at different points to measure treatment progress. For readers not in treatment, it is strongly recommended that you contact a mental health professional if your score is around or above the 38-cut-off score. (In fact, I recommend you contact a therapist if you score 30 or higher).

If you have previously been diagnosed with PTSD or have not been diagnosed but have suffered trauma (or ongoing trauma) and your score is in the high 30s on the PCL-5 or higher, you may have experienced some or all of the following cognitive, behavioral, and affective issues:

- You may experience strong feelings of shame, guilt, and self-blame even though you have been abused.
- You may have had difficulty with your ability to regulate strong emotions like anger.
- You may have experienced times when you engaged in self-abusive behaviors (SIBs) such as cutting, burning, and punching walls.
- You may have struggled to maintain healthy, positive relationships in your intimate, social, and occupational life. You may have abruptly begun and

ended relationships, withdrawn, been very distrustful, and found yourself looking for someone to rescue you (or looking to rescue someone else).
- You have regular bouts of dissociation where you cannot seem to stay present (spaced out) or become preoccupied with trauma.
- You may have regularly found yourself in relationships with verbally, physically, or sexually abusive partners.
- You may have struggled to find meaning in your life and maintain optimism for the future and may be burdened by hopelessness and despair (Frankl, 2006; Meichenbaum, 1994).
- You are far more likely to be self-medicating with alcohol and other drugs.
- You are more likely to be isolating yourself from peers and people with whom you were once close.

These symptoms are especially common in Type II trauma, or complex trauma (van der Kolk, 2014), or those who experienced ongoing trauma. Having spent two and one-half decades treating trauma and consulted on trauma for about the same length of time, my own experience is that a strong sense of hope and a belief that one can heal their trauma with therapy, social support, and work are the most significant factors in the healing process. An important part of this text is moving one's belief from trauma victim to survivor to thriver and finally into post-traumatic growth.

Trauma Memory and Reframing: The Story You Are Telling Yourself

People who have experienced trauma often have memory gaps, especially regarding their trauma. Long-term and short-term memory can be lost due to the victim dissociating or *going offline* during the abuse as a survival mechanism. Interestingly, however, if a particular strong sense is paired with the abuse, such as the abuser's cologne, a song, particular image, tactile sense (abuser's sweater), etc., this pairing becomes a conditioned stimulus and much like Pavlov's dogs, there is a conditioned response occurs (person is triggered) such as screaming or physical altercation (fight), a quick escape (flight), or the person freezes up (freeze). These triggers can lead the trauma sufferer to have the same type of extreme reactions as to the original traumatic event (Rothschild, 2000). People observing a traumatized person's overreaction to an interaction on the train, in the workplace, or in another venue, will typically wonder what all the fuss was about, given they see only the result and not what led up to that blowout (i.e., the original trauma).

Gregory Boyle, a Jesuit clergyman who has worked with gang members in East Los Angeles for over 40 years, opines that society has a mental health crisis regarding our judgment of the mentally ill, the homeless, the poor, immigrants, and anyone seemingly representing those who are visibly different (Boyle, 2024). He references that many elected officials, among others, simply see homeless persons milling about and react with scorn, not understanding that such people often suffer from mental illness and severe trauma, which they self-medicate with alcohol and other drugs, further compounding their problems. My experience mirrors that of Boyle, and often in the rural and remote regions of the globe where my career has taken me, I have often heard pejorative sentiments expressed toward those living along or below the margins of society. Like Fr. Boyle, people see only the result of trauma and not what led up to that trauma (e.g., gang violence, sexual assault, military service).

My own opinion is that, like Boyle's above and Dialectical Behavior Therapy (DBT) founder Marsha Linden, you are having a normal reaction to an abnormal experience (Linehan, 2015). My further opinion, based on four decades in the field and a long history of working with traumatized people, is that while trauma survivors do not want to remember their trauma and for good reason, as it's traumatic-remembering and revising our trauma experience are a key part in understanding and healing those traumas. Furthermore, the trauma survivor's memory is fragmented due to going offline in dissociation. However, while the survivor's memory is imperfect, what they tell themselves about that memory is what is so powerful, whether to heal or to hurt oneself (Meichenbaum, 2014). Regarding Meichenbaum and Linden, consider the following scenario of one of my former clients:

Promises Made and Kept

Sarah (pseudonym) was abducted as a 12-year-old and spent 6 years as a sex slave, locked in a dark, dank basement, ritually violated for that time by her captor. During her captivity, she promised herself that she would find a way to escape, make her abuser pay, and heal to the point where she could help other such survivors of long-term sexual abuse. Her captor, believing he had total control over her, began taking her on excursions. One day, he took her to lunch at a fast-food restaurant. Explaining she needed the restroom, he okayed it, but instead she diverted into the kitchen and informed the manager, who called the police. The police arrived quickly and arrested her captor. Later, she would testify against him in court, whereupon he was convicted and sentenced to many years in prison.

Eventually, through her foster mother, she found her way to my office. After she outlined her story, I inquired how she had kept alive her optimism of escape. She explained that an abiding spiritual faith helped fuel her resilience, as "God was the only one I could talk to." She further stated, "I told myself every day that I would escape, make my abuser pay, and that I would heal and help others like me." She explained she'd ticked the first two boxes and was now ready to focus on her healing. This resilient, optimistic young woman met all her treatment goals during my time with her. When I inquired what made her so confident in her ability to heal, she replied that it was the power of her belief that she could heal from years of abuse. In other words, she believed in her self-efficacy! You, too, must develop an abiding faith in your ability to heal from trauma. You do not have to do it alone, and in fact, that's why people are trained as mental health therapists, why we have support groups, faith-based communities, and workbooks like this one. Now, I do not believe healing from trauma requires a spiritual or religious belief. Atheists and agnostics can heal as well as anyone. What is required is a resilient belief in one's ability to heal their trauma.

Your Power of Belief

Once again, I will repeat the self-fulfilling prophecy mantra. That is, if, like Sarah above, you believe you can heal, then you will likely take steps to begin or continue healing. Consider the questions below.

1 On a scale of 1 to 10, with 10 being high, what is your belief in your ability to heal from your trauma? How might you increase your score by just 1 point? (Remember, belief is *very* important in healing.)
2 If you were to write a short story about your journey to post-traumatic growth (i.e., healing), what might you write? (If writing is not your interest, perhaps tell someone you trust, like a good friend or therapist.)
3 What is one small change you might make to begin your healing journey, or if you are already on that journey, what's one change you could make that will aid in your healing?
4 Self-medicating trauma pain with alcohol and other drugs is common. Have you found yourself using alcohol and drugs to numb the pain of trauma?
5 Many times, you may have heard 12-step people mention giving power over to a Higher Power or acknowledging a force greater than oneself to stop self-medicating. What does "giving control…" over mean for you? How might you go about giving over control to help guide your recovery from trauma and/or self-medication?

Remembrance for Healing

"I want to remember my traumatic experience(s)," *said no trauma survivor ever.* I understand the sentiment very well, having treated scores of survivors and consulted on trauma for 40 years. One young adult male client, a survivor of long-term childhood sexual abuse, remarked, "I have these years of awful, traumatic experiences, and you are asking me to open that door?" Like many of my former clients, he was very skeptical of my treatment approach. Interestingly, I think of the late Albert Ellis, founder of Rational Emotive Behavioral Therapy (REBT), borrowing from the Stoic Epictetus, that people are not disturbed by events but by their perception of those events (Ellis, 2011). I have found Ellis (and Epictetus) to be prescient on this matter. Every trauma survivor I can recall grew stronger after staring at their trauma in the safe, encouraging environment of the therapeutic encounter (granted, it took some time). Once I had clients talking about their trauma, writing on it, drawing, singing, and so forth, they began to lose their fear of it. One middle-aged woman expressed that her abuser no longer held power over her after 12 weeks of trauma-focused therapy. Essentially, avoiding traumatic memories, while understandable, will keep one prisoner to those memories, magnifying the pain, anxiety, and fear within your mind, heart, body, and soul, keeping you engaged in self-blame and often self-abuse (Linehan, 2015). Through the crucible of deconstructing memories, survivors come to understand it was the abuser's culpability or, in say, auto accidents, perhaps something unavoidable. Another important factor in this ingredient is the survivor believing therapy is a safe place to address traumatic memories.

Judith Herman is a prominent researcher in the field of trauma. Her tri-phasic model (1994) has become a staple in trauma treatment and one I made much use of in my approach. Phase I is about establishing safety for the client. This phase involves distinguishing between a real vs. perceived threat and involves cognitive reframing, breath, body work, and healthy risk-taking (Herman, 1994). For example, one former client had been trapped in a violent marriage for several years. However, with support from close friends and a few family members, she was able to get out of the marriage. She identified that a real threat was living with an abuser, while a perceived threat was talking about her abuse. To help her manage the perceived threat, I used self-regulating exercises such as gripping something solid and saying aloud, "I am now in a safe zone." I also encouraged her to say "Stop" when she felt her anxiety level was in the 7–10 range, on an anxiety scale of 1–10, with 10 as high. This gave her control of the situation. She also liked using a squeeze ball as that provided her with an energy outlet for her tension. Finally, I used EFT touchpoints to help lessen her anxiety, something she was initially resistant to trying. For a good example of tapping points and exhaling for the vagus nerve response, read Peter Levine's *Waking the Tiger: Healing trauma* (2011). You can also do a keyword search on EFT/Meridian Tapping points, and several websites will come up. (I make much mention of the vagus nerve throughout this workbook)

Phase II of Herman's triphasic model is remembrance and mourning, which is the largest part of treatment. In this phase, the clinician must use the safety protocols in phase I. I always had the client develop the treatment plan with me and emphasized they were in control, using the anxiety scale of 1–10, and when the level was 7 or higher, to say, "stop" if needed. Then, treatment involved discussing the trauma, journaling about the trauma (homework), creating a collage for what healing looked like, drawing for healing, healing visualization, reframing, etc.

The final phase (Phase III) is reconnection. Reconnection involves completing phases I and II and assisting survivors in reconnecting with themselves, others, and aspects of their lives they had put on hold. Examples of this phase might be practicing self-compassion (or self-forgiveness), developing an active self-care plan, listing one's strengths gained through healing (or journaling on them), making plans, such as new relationships, a new career, healthier behaviors, etc.

Consider the triphasic reflections below:

Phase I: Safety and Stabilization

1 If you were to create a safe place, what might that place look like? What would you want to fill that space with? (Perhaps list out. The space might be a physical location or simply a mental one.)
2 Now that you have created a draft of a safe space, how might you begin to create that space?
3 After you have made use of your safe space, what do you find helpful regarding your safe space?

Phase II: Remembrance and Mourning

1 Many trauma survivors speak of a loss of innocence regarding trauma. If you were to grieve and mourn your lost innocence, what practices or rituals might you employ? (e.g., memorial, obituary to lost innocence, funeral)
2 An empty chair dialogue with your younger innocent self, perhaps explaining that you are sorry for your childhood/early adulthood/etc. being disrupted by trauma. You might recount how you mourn their passing and that you will always keep them alive by honoring their memory.

Phase III: Reconnection and Integration

Now that you have graduated from treatment, consider the following questions:

1 On a scale of 1–10, with 10 being high, what is your confidence in establishing healthy relationships? (friendships and potential romantic, sexual relationships) Now, if needed, how might you raise your score by 1 point? (Remember, fluctuation of 1–2 points every month is natural.)
2 Now that you have healed your trauma, what do you most enjoy about feeling emotionally healthy? Some people might say the ability to enjoy romance again, or their ability to say "No" and set limits with others (e.g., family, lovers, friends). What might you say?
3 Regarding your healing journey, what is the most important lesson you have learned?

Some self-reflection questions/reflections: I recommend that you write out the answers to the following questions in your Trauma Recovery Journal, as then you are likely to be more committed to them.

1 If someone were to ask, *"Who are you?"* How might you answer?
2 What are 3 important facts that describe you?
3 Where does your sense of meaning and purpose come from?
4 My basic values governing my life are ______________________________.

5 Where does your courage come from?
6 Levine (2011) defines self-compassion as that understanding and nonjudgment that you would hold for a close friend. Given this, how does self-compassion work for you? Or how might self-compassion work for you?

Albert Ellis deconstructed words like "should" and "ought" and recommended that we challenge the self-judgmental emotional weight such terms place upon us. Therefore, list 3 should-type statements you commonly use and that make you feel uncomfortable, and how to reframe these statements to be more rational and realistic.

For example: "I *should* be perfect and always my very best self."

Reframe to: "I will do my best and feel okay, even when my best is less than I would like it to be."

I should ____.

I should ____.

I should ____.

Now, write these out in your Trauma Recovery Journal, and then draw a line through each "should" statement you wish to eliminate. Then, reframe these should statements as in the previous example above.

The Arms of Love Exercise

A metaphor I have used is the arms of love. So, if you were to consider the arms of love holding you in love and safety, how might you describe what that feeling is like?* How might safe, unconditional love feel when surrounding you? (write out)

Now, regarding self-compassion and healthy self-love, how might you become those arms of love? How might you begin embracing yourself in nonjudgmental acceptance, safety, and love?

*You can practice this exercise by crossing your arms over your chest in a self-hug and reframing any self-judging statement that pops into your mind. You might even make self-statements like, "I am worthy of love," or "I am loved."

My Healing Journal

Pennebaker (2004) encourages journaling for emotional growth and healing from disappointment (and trauma). Here are some reflective questions that may help guide you in this process:

1 How has your healing helped you grow emotionally, or as a friend, loving partner, parent, etc.?
2 What are three critical lessons my healing has taught me?
3 How will I continue to grow and develop from these lessons I have learned through my healing process?

The next chapter will provide strategies for strengthening your sense of safety and security. Remember, maintaining well-being is as much about habituating the practice of safety as it is safety itself.

Lessons Learned

1 What is the most important concept you learned regarding understanding and managing trauma in this chapter?
2 If you have grappled with trauma, anxiety, or ongoing stress, what lessons have these maladies taught you? (My experience is that trauma and related issues can teach us valuable lessons)
3 On a scale of 1–10, with 10 being high, how much confidence do you have in your ability to heal your trauma (or manage stress)? Score = ___/10. Okay, how can you increase your score by just 1 point?
4 The concept of self-compassion has been mentioned in this chapter. Healing trauma can take a lot of work and requires discipline and emotional support from others. Therefore, practicing self-compassion is very important in your healing. Based on your understanding of self-compassion, what's one way you can begin to practice daily self-compassion?

2 Establishing Safety and Security

At the conclusion of Chapter 1, I mentioned that habituating the practice of safety and security is as important as safety itself. I have a story to illustrate this. While completing doctoral studies, I often resided at a monastery on weekends for all-day meditation and guidance on spiritual direction and mindfulness. I was entertaining joining the monastery upon completion of my dissertation. While I eventually decided not to become a monk, my time at the monastery taught me some valuable lessons. One of the most significant lessons was in the practice of daily gratitude, which has shown strong efficacy in research (Brooks & Winfrey, 2023; Dickens, 2017).

One afternoon during spiritual direction, my superior suggested I commence a daily gratitude practice. He recommended acknowledging three things I was grateful for. That sounded all too simple to me, so I asked, "What's the catch?" He replied that the catch was acknowledging gratitude on days when I didn't feel grateful. Furthermore, he encouraged me to make this a lifelong practice, emphasizing that habituating gratitude practice was even more important than the gratitude practice itself. Sort of an example of the whole being greater than the sum of its parts. For the past 35 years, I have maintained a daily gratitude practice. My usual gratitudes are

1 I am grateful for my health.
2 I am grateful for my spouse.
3 I am grateful for this day, whatever joy or sorrow it may bring.

I was later to discover that Viktor Frankl, one of my heroes, credited gratitude acknowledgment as key to his survival in the Nazi Holocaust (Frankl, 2006). With this in mind, let's begin this chapter by acknowledging three gratitudes. In your Trauma Recovery Journal, or somewhere, write out as I did previously:

1 I am grateful for ______________________________.
2 I am grateful for ______________________________.
3 I am grateful for ______________________________.

DOI: 10.4324/9781003689232-2

Like my superior, I encourage you to verbally or in writing acknowledge your gratitudes every day for the remainder of your life. I do mine upon rising from bed (admittedly after the first sip of coffee!). Remember, healing involves habituating the practice of healing…and continuing it throughout your lifespan. Just as getting physically fit requires a lifelong approach, the same applies to emotional well-being. I also follow up with my gratitude practice with the following activities:

My workout routine, which varies during the week, consists of jogging, light weights, yoga stretching, EFT tapping points, and using Levine's vagus nerve exhale (2011). Levine recommends a sustained "voo"-sound exhale. This is used to regulate a move from the sympathetic nervous system into the parasympathetic nervous system. A few simple tips:

1 Get in a comfortable position: Sit with your shoulders relaxed, with your head tilted slightly upward.
2 Inhale deeply, drawing the breath into your belly rather than just your lungs.
3 While you exhale, make a long, sustained "voo" sound, originating from your belly. I often feel vibrations in my ankles and legs, and a warm sensation ensues.
4 After each voo exhalation, pause briefly (2–3 seconds), then continue with voo exhales. I usually do 10 voo exhales as I find that's optimal for me. I suggest that you experiment for yourself.
5 Notice any changes in your thoughts or your body after completing the exercise. I notice a warm tingling sensation that begins in my ankles and slowly moves up my legs.

Note: You can view Peter Levine (and others) demonstrating voo exhaling on YouTube by typing Peter Levine voo exhaling. Several videos will appear.

After I finish the voo exhale practice, I meditate for 30–40 minutes while taking the train to work.

Establishing Safety and Security

What does emotional and psychological safety involve? Psychological and emotional safety in counseling means feeling secure enough to trust your therapist and take healthy risks in the therapeutic encounter (Hunt et al., 2021). Granted, a violent, chaotic home is scarcely a therapeutic environment, and thus survival means subjugating one's own opinions, beliefs, values, and behaviors to those of the abuser to prevent abuse. Unfortunately, this type of protective behavior, while understandable, does significant emotional harm. Webber and Mascari define safety as the sense of feeling reasonably secure from harm to oneself or others (Webber & Mascari, 2018). With these definitions in mind, feeling safe to disclose sensitive personal information in the counseling space and, just as important, feeling secure at home, in the workplace, and in society is critical for optimal mental health. Therapists refer to the sense of feeling grounded in the present as a precursor to making sound decisions impacting one's future.

Feeling Grounding: The What and the How

When we speak of being grounded, it refers to the sense of being present or firmly connected to the ground beneath you. Grounding also can mean the sense of being connected to the present reality, as opposed to fantasizing or dissociating due to the stress of sexual, verbal, or emotional abuse. Examples of being grounded include:

- Noticing that your physical being is grounded to the floor, earth, chair, or something solid.
- Understanding and relating to the external world around you in a meaningful way (gratitude practice helps here).
- The ability to pay attention in the classroom, workspace, or another important venue.
- Ability to converse honestly and respond appropriately with peers.
- Awareness of your body's movements through space.
- The ability to carry out daily responsibilities (e.g., home, work, school) in a responsible way.

Now, the previous examples of grounding are important, but even more important is how to remain grounded when you are not feeling safe. Too often, people feel unsafe in school, at work, and at home. Trauma survivors need to practice grounding techniques to feel safe (assuming they are in a safe place!). People suffering from PTSD are always on the cusp of feeling in peril. The following are examples of how trauma sufferers and those feeling anxious can ground their being and begin to relax.

1. **Finding solid ground:** This simple mindfulness exercise is one of the most basic techniques I use. Grounding involves focusing on your feet, feeling the solid ground or floor when walking. Focus on the soles of your feet as they strike the ground or sidewalk. Notice how solid the ground or sidewalk feels as you stand, sit, or move through space. Now, describe that feeling in your mind.
2. **5 senses exercise:** Look around you and name 5 things you can see, 4 you can touch, 3 you can hear, 2 you can smell, and 1 you can taste.
3. **Special or Sacred object:** Holding a special or sacred object helps many people stay present. I have had numerous clients who held onto teddy bears; a spiritual object (e.g., crucifix, beads, special rock); a photo of a loved one; or whatever was meaningful.
4. **Body Scan:** Focus on bringing your awareness to the soles of your feet and slowly allow your attention to move up your body to your calves, knees,

thighs, midsection, chest, throat, and head. You might notice a relaxing, tingling feeling as you do this. Give yourself 5 minutes to proceed slowly.

5. **Imagining a Safe Place:** I mentioned this in the previous chapter. Visualize yourself in a place where you feel safe. (more on this)
6. **Talking with a friend:** Sharing your concerns with a trusted friend can help you feel less isolated and provide a different perspective.
7. **Meditation:** Even a brief meditation of 5 minutes can help. I prefer simply breathing deeply inward and slowly exhaling. Some prefer guided meditation and use apps like Headspace, Insight Timer, or another App. I suggest that you do what works best for you.
8. **Journaling:** Writing about how you are feeling, whether safe and secure, or in peril and insecure. I particularly encourage you to journal on your ability to move from insecurity to security, given the power of written language (Pennebaker, 2004).
9. **Movement:** Movement is healing and promotes the influx of hope molecules throughout your brain (McGonigal, 2017). Even simple movement like sustained walking across the living room floor, for say 15 minutes, can be self-soothing.
10. **Gratitude acknowledgment:** Remember those three gratitudes? Feel free to repeat them multiple times during the day. Over 35 years, I have found this simple practice is the foundation of my well-being.

Naturally, there are numerous additional grounding techniques and activities. The above list represents interventions I regularly assigned to clients and used myself. Please feel free to explore other clinicians and trainers and add their helpful suggestions to your practice.

Reflective Exercises on Safety

How safe do you feel in your living space? (or in your workspace, school, etc.)

1	2	3	4	5	6	7	8	9	10
Unsafe									Safe

Why did you assign the number you gave? How might you increase your safety score?
What does physical/emotional safety look like for you? What does it feel like?
What would you need to do to feel safe at home, at work, or by yourself?
Consider people you know whom you feel safe interacting with. What makes those people safe?
How might you begin to protect yourself?
When (or where) do you feel safest?

Note: Remember to apply self-compassion, as you are not to blame for feeling unsafe.

Exercise: Establishing Safety in Your Life

Safety is a basic human right. Unfortunately, many people feel unsafe at home, in school, in the workplace, or in their neighborhood. The following questions represent your exploration in creating a safe place for yourself. As usual, my suggestion is for you to write down the answers in your Trauma Recovery Journal or another secure location.

Establishing Safety

If you feel unsafe, how could you establish a place where you do feel safe?

Is there a particular time of day or week that you feel safe?

Have you placed meaningful objects in that environment that help you feel safe? (e.g., stuffed animals, photos of loved ones, special or sacred objects)

If you are working with a mental health professional or another helping professional, how safe are you feeling in that person and that space?

Regarding the previous question, counseling work can bring back strong feelings and reactions. How can you ground yourself safely when those painful memories emerge?

Regarding personal safety, are you safe with yourself? Do you have strong desires to self-harm by cutting, burning, or more serious abusive actions? If so, what might you do to feel safe and cease self-abuse?

Many trauma survivors I have treated have expressed the belief that somehow, they deserved the abuse, whether it was sexual, physical, verbal, or emotional (or all). Regarding self-compassion mentioned previously in this text, what might you say to a loved one or close friend if they expressed deserving current or past abuse? Then, give yourself the same counsel as to a loved one or friend (and write it down).

If you are considering self-harm (like cutting, burning, etc.), what's a healthy activity you could substitute for an abusive one? For example, some people will take a brief walk, engage in EFT tapping, a 5-senses exercise, call a trusted friend, a 12-step sponsor, etc. So, what healthy alternative can you use as a substitute to self-harm?

At this precise moment in time, are you: (Check one of the below)

___ Feeling safe
___ Feeling unsafe
___ Unsure

If you are feeling unsafe or unsure (e.g., from an abuser, self-abuse), I strongly encourage you to contact your therapist, call the national hotline (988), or make an appointment with a qualified therapist. In the meantime, here are additional activities to help yourself:

- Create a list of three to five activities you enjoy doing and then do them.
- Answer the question: "If I were to feel just 10% better, I would be doing _____." Then, do that. (This is a PRN question—as often as necessary, so ask and activate as often as needed.)

- Notice the times during the day or week when you feel safest. Record these safe times and what you were doing, and then engage in those activities more often.
- When you think safe thoughts or engage in safe activities, reward yourself with an activity or object that is healthy.
- Bill O'Hanlon (2013) recommends doing one thing differently for positive mental health. What's one healthy activity you can do each day? (Pick one you enjoy and will follow through on.)
- Listen to music that soothes you, watch films and shows that are uplifting, and listen to upbeat podcasts, as opposed to music, films, TV shows, and podcasts with themes of anger or violence that may trigger you.
- Each week, schedule a time with a supportive friend to meet in person, online, or by phone for socialization and support.

My Safe Place Visualization

My safe place visualization is a common intervention therapists use when working with clients healing from trauma. Interestingly, I created my own safe place during my turbulent childhood. Living with my grandparents across the creek from the laundromat, the manager would discard the large cardboard boxes that washers and dryers had been shipped in. I would take a box, break it down, and then use it to roll over the dense thicket behind my grandparents' garden. The saplings, sage grass, and weeds were thick enough to support my weight, allowing me to roll the length of the garden (around 100 feet), feeling temporarily safe and insulated from all harm. This was my safe space from bullies, siblings, mother, stepfather, and the challenges of a lonely, occasionally abusive, neglectful childhood. My happiest times during childhood were in that box, rolling atop the thicket behind the garden. So, create your own safe place/space. You can start below.

Visualizing Your Safe Place

I want you to imagine a safe place you create, either a physical location or the shelter of your mind. Consider that space, and then write out the location of your safe place in your Trauma Recovery Journal. Spend time in your safe place. Look around you. What relaxing images do you see? Focus on soothing sounds you can hear, allowing those happy sounds to fill the silence. Who would you invite to share your safe space, if anyone? Remember, no one comes into your safe space without your invitation.

Now, you must keep your safe space safe. If your safe space is not in your home or another physical location, I encourage you to find a space that can be private. I would suggest it not be a park or other private place where others are constantly moving through, as you lose your privacy. A former client of mine had his safe space on a large hill above his neighborhood. He would carry a small camping chair, a backpack, and water and sit at the top of the hill and gaze down into the valley below. He'd spend a few minutes in meditation, then focus on his 5 senses. He found visualizing his thoughts, whether troubling or happy, floating past as on a river, an effective way to remain emotionally regulated and grounded. Sometimes he would set a photo of his late mother, with whom he'd had a very good relationship, beside him. "She's sitting with me," he would say. He would retreat to his safe place as often as necessary, and usually that was 2–3 times per week.

Safety Checklist

As you work through your trauma, anxiety, or stress, it is important to have outside connections with others so that when you need them, your contacts are readily available. Readers involved in 12-step programs like AA already well know about this type of connection, where you always have a sponsor to contact or a local meeting to attend. My own experience is that women have a stronger network than men and make regular use of that support network. Male readers may need to work to expand their network. The network may include your therapist, doctor, 12-step contacts, house of worship, close friends, etc. See an example below:

My Support and Wellness Network: Write out names and contact numbers/email addresses/etc. in your Trauma Recovery Journal.

1 My three close friends are: ______________________________.
2 My therapist: ______________________________.
3 My spouse/partner: ______________________________.
4 My doctor(s): ______________________________.
5 My closest sibling/family member ______________________________.
6 The closest hospital: ______________________________.
7 My spiritual advisor/minister: ______________________________.
8 My 12-step sponsor: ______________________________.

If none of these contacts are readily available and I feel unsafe, I have the following options that can keep me safe until someone is available:

____

____

Examples of safe options: Calling the crisis line (988), taking a walk, working out, writing in your journal, using EFT tapping, doing voo breathing, meditating, going to the nearest emergency room, etc.

Relaxation: It All Starts with Breathwork

Many years ago, I attended a meditation workshop given by a Buddhist monk. During a question session, a participant inquired what this monk considered most important in meditation. "Is it a mantra (word or phrase in meditation), how you sit, your eyes closed or open?" were among the various options the participant mentioned. The monk nodded sagely and then replied that while there were many parts to meditation, such as the sitting position, standing or walking meditation, use of a mantra or silent meditation, and so forth, one stood above all else, that being the breath. "You can do without much of what you mention," he added. "However, you cannot do without the breath. If you don't think so, try sitting through a day-long meditation without breathing!" We all got the message! So, remember, your breath is the most important part of relaxation. When your breath is relaxed, you are feeling relaxed, your thoughts are calm, and you feel grounded and centered.

Okay, let's start with breathwork. Jack Kornfield is an internationally known meditation teacher, Buddhist monk, and clinical psychologist. He recommends meditation to reduce anxiety panic attacks, as a respite from a hectic schedule, stress reduction, and to create inner peace, among other reasons (Kornfield, 2005). He recommends:

- Rhythm: Focusing on the natural rhythm of your breath, feeling its sensation as it enters and leaves your body. Establishing a rhythm helps calm and center you.
- Allow the breath to be natural. Don't try to control it.
- Grounding: Imagine roots growing from the soles of your feet into the earth, providing sustenance, stability, and nurturing.
- When your mind wanders during meditation, gently bring your focus back to your breath.
- Loving-Kindness or Compassion Meditation: Cultivate feelings of love and compassion for yourself and others, using phrases like, "May I be peaceful," "May I be well," "May I be loving," or "May I be kind."
- Forgiveness Meditation: Explore forgiveness toward yourself and others, releasing anger and negativity with phrases like, "May I be forgiving toward myself and others."

Note: You may need to be in a later stage of healing to meditate on forgiving a former abuser. Do not force forgiveness; just let it come naturally when you are ready. Keep in mind as well that forgiveness means that you have come to peace with that person, but it does not mean you will continue to have an active relationship with them.

Tips for Practicing Meditation

- Find a comfortable posture: Sit, lie down, or use a walking meditation that allows you to relax and focus.
- Focus on your breath: Use a slow breath intake and exhale method. I often visualize a slow intake of 3 seconds and repeat on my exhale.

- Allow whatever thoughts to come into your mind without trying to block them. Instead, visualize them floating past, as on a river, since this is a more natural process.
- Many experienced meditation practitioners use a mantra, or a word or phrase that's meaningful to them. For example, "I am loved," or "I am healing," or whatever they find comforting. One Catholic friend uses his Rosary Beads while he meditates, so use what is meaningful for you.
- Do the meditation that's helpful for you. If, say, an hour is too long and you are fighting distraction, try shorter meditations. Even brief meditation of 5 minutes can help one relax. So, don't worry about what others are doing; it's about habituating a meditation practice that works for you.

Mindfulness: What Is It Exactly?

Mindfulness has become the term du jour in meditation circles and in the mental health field. I will borrow from John Kabat-Zinn: Mindfulness is awareness that arises through paying attention, on purpose, in the present moment, non-judgmentally (Kabit-Zinn, 2017). Sometimes Kabit-Zinn adds the term "and with wisdom." While he has yet to explain what he means by wisdom, I would add that wisdom implies the use of good judgment. One might argue, of course, that this entire workbook is as much a text on applying wisdom to one's life as anything else. While I expect few therapists will make use of the term "wisdom," honing good judgment is a part of all therapeutic approaches.

Now, let's expand on the terms "mindfulness" and "wisdom." Mindfulness teaches us to pay attention to our inner thoughts and how they impact our relationships with others (e.g., family, friends, colleagues, strangers) and the impact those thoughts have on our bodies and influence our behavior. Practicing mindfulness provides us with the opportunity to sit with our thoughts with intention and curiosity, absent the need to immediately jettison them. For example, while I was writing this very section of the chapter, I was experiencing a lot of challenges. My focus was good, and I was happy to be writing and creating, but the computer was acting up (continually wanting to shut down), my fingers kept mis-hitting keys, and my frustration increased, my blood pressure increased, and my negative thoughts became articulated into profanity. Ironically, writing this chapter on meditation and mindfulness was causing me significant stress, and wisdom and good judgment were left far behind! Fortunately, my wise mind, as Linehan (2015) would say, intervened. Practicing self-compassion, I acknowledged my hypocrisy, took a long moment to breathe and calm my inner lizard, and then continued. So, you see, even longtime practitioners of meditation slip up and lose our mindful focus. The important thing is to notice and name our frustration and then activate our wise mind to help us get back on track. Wise mind, in Linehan's dialectical behavior therapy (DBT), is a state of mind that balances emotional mind and reasonable mind to provide for balanced and healthy decision-making (2013). This workbook is a practical application of cultivating Linehan and DBT's wise mind.

There are a variety of ways one might think about mindfulness. I usually think in terms of water images, given years of living near the subtropical, Southern Queensland coast, the past few years. Recently, while visiting a friend on the Sunshine Coast in Queensland, Australia. My spouse, friend, and I were standing at the end of a long pier watching the ocean waves roll in and back out. The day was calm and sunny, and the waves rolling in and then out were as rhythmic as meditative breathing. While we were standing on the pier observing the waves in the beautiful natural environment, we were still solidly grounded in the here and now. Mindfulness is about the eternal present, and regardless of whether nature is gentle, sunny, and beautiful or harsh, stormy, and throwing out a violent thunderstorm, we remain grounded in the moment. Our thoughts are like nature in the sense that, at times, we can feel so peaceful and compassionate that life seems so incredibly blissful and wonderful. At others, however, when circumstances in our lives are volatile due to job loss, divorce, death of a loved one, and the myriad disappointments life brings our way, we can wonder if we'll make it through to the other side. Wisdom, however, provides us with the perspective that everything changes, whether in good times or hard times. Mindfulness, involving present moment awareness, and implementing meditation, regulating our breath, body, mind, and spirit, is our vehicle back to feeling grounded. I would also opine that any healing we do will involve regular (likely daily) practice of mindfulness-based activities. Speaking personally, I cannot imagine being healthy, optimistic and happy without my daily gratitude practice, meridian tapping, voo exhaling (vagus nerve), workouts, and meditation. If you complete this workbook and then drop your mindfulness practice, you will almost certainly regress and lose whatever gains you made through counseling work and the exercises in this and other workbooks. Therefore, while the exercises in this workbook are important, habituating some of them into regular practice is even more important (daily or weekly).

You can become more mindful by engaging in regular meditation practice several times a week. A helpful way to begin is to take short periods during regular moments of the day to practice mindfulness. For example, if waiting at the dentist's office, use that time to practice meditation, noticing how meditative breathing changes your breath, body, and thoughts. If you need to walk to deliver something to your supervisor or a colleague, focus on the sensation of walking and how your feet feel when striking the floor, sidewalk, or earth. When eating lunch, slow down and concentrate on the taste of the food, chewing slightly longer and more deliberately. If sitting in a meeting you find boring, notice how your back feels supported by the chair, how your feet feel on the floor, and be aware of your breathing as you take air into your lungs, and then slowly exhale. You may begin to notice that mindfulness may help you live life more fully and likely will increase your ability to pay attention in even mundane (boring!) meetings.

While there is no lack of resources on mindfulness, given websites, phone apps, books, videos, etc., I do recommend *Kornfield's Meditation for Beginners*

(2005) and Kabat-Zinn's *Wherever you go, there you are—30th anniversary issue* (2024). There are helpful, popular apps like Headspace, Calm, Insight Timer, and many others. My favorite mindfulness-oriented podcast is Dan Harris' 10% Happier Podcast. Naturally, my go-to books, apps, and podcasts may not fit you as well, so sample and find what works best for you. I can say with confidence that regular practice of mindfulness through meditation, present moment awareness (with wisdom), and daily gratitudes can help your emotional well-being (Kabat-Zinn, 2024; Kornfield, 2005). Habituating mindfulness practice moves us from the sympathetic nervous system into the parasympathetic, calming our hippocampus and amygdala (the Lizard Brain), and strengthening our brain's plasticity, which assists in memory, managing stress, healing trauma, and delaying dementia (Singh & Newberg, 2021).

Without question, mindfulness has been married to numerous theoretical approaches to counseling (e.g., Mindfulness-CBT, DBT, ACT, EMDR). As a long-term mindfulness-based CBT practitioner, I find cognitive therapy a natural fit for mindfulness-oriented work and integrated it into my approach long ago and found it very helpful to clients struggling with PTSD, anxiety, and ongoing stress. Many of the primary ingredients of mindfulness are cognitive behavioral in nature, "like exposure, cognitive retraining, and affect regulation," (Briere & Scott, 2015, p. 220). Now, while meditation works very well for most people, a small subset of survivors with Type II trauma (what I call "complex trauma") may find it difficult. For those with intense, intrusive memories of abuse (around 5%), meditation is not recommended (Briere & Scott, 2015). However, learning and incorporating mindfulness practices like the 5-senses exercise can provide stable grounding for people healing from trauma. Likewise, challenging and reframing self-defeating thoughts and applying self-compassion (non-judgment) can help decrease anxiety and depression (Bentley et al., 2021). Basically, habituating a mindfulness practice can assist standard therapeutic approaches (e.g., CBT, EMDR, Gestalt) as well as help to build self-compassion (Neff, 2011). Again, the habituation of healthy practices, like in this and similar workbooks, is a large part of healing.

Checking in with Yourself: Taking a Recess from This Workbook

This text is not the type of book readers should plough through from Chapters 1 to 12. Instead, I suggest taking whatever time you need, even if that means taking time away from the workbook. It is also worth saying that some chapters and exercises may fit you better than others will, and this is natural. Just as two different clients healing from trauma or managing anxiety and stress will vary in what interventions work best with them, they also progress at different rates. The important part of this text, or any such text or therapeutic approach, is to help a person heal their trauma, manage their anxiety and depression, and manage daily stress. So, if any exercises leave you feeling emotionally vulnerable, try a different chapter or set the book aside temporarily. If you notice any of the following signs of PTSD distress, please take a recess from this book. If you feel significantly distressed, contact your therapist or return to therapy if you are not in counseling with a skilled provider.

- Symptoms of intrusive, distressing memories of a traumatic event.
- If you begin having overwhelming flashbacks.
- If you experience anger, irritability, depression, anxiety, or other feelings that seem beyond your control.
- If you feel a strong urge to self-injure.
- If you begin to engage in addictive behaviors like alcohol or drug abuse, compulsive eating, or unsafe sex.
- If you begin to develop bulimia (binging and purging) or anorexia nervosa (restricting eating).
- If you begin to experience numbness and are devoid of emotion.
- If you begin to isolate yourself from social contacts.
- If life has begun to feel empty and without purpose.

Adapted from the Mayo Clinic (www.mayoclinic.org)

Should any of these signs arise, it likely represents your mind's early warning system telling you that you are over-stressing your coping mechanisms and need to take a break. Remember, taking a rest means you can then be ready to return to working on your healing when you are rested. I also encourage you to talk openly with your therapist about these symptoms, as they are signs you need the support of a trusted, trained professional. Again, if you are not currently in therapy when these warning signs come up, I would encourage you to return to counseling. In the meantime, activate your self-care/well-being plan or consider the following well-being strategies below:

- As always, a regular exercise routine (e.g., cycling, running, dancing, yoga, walking) is a validated asset in healing trauma and coping with anxiety and stress (McGonigal, 2017).
- If meditation works for you, I strongly encourage brief periods of it. I also would encourage writing in your Trauma Recovery Journal and writing down what steps you are taking to heal, as writing seems to help with following through on healthy practices (Pennebaker, 2004).
- Spending quality time with trusted friends and valued family members. Loneliness can make our anxiety and depression worse (Novotney, 2019).
- For spiritual self-care, talking with a trusted spiritual advisor may be a prudent decision. Many of my former clients were actively involved in spiritual practice.
- For others who are not spiritual, speaking with a close friend or therapist to address purpose in life is recommended. Like Frankl (2006), my belief and experience are that meaning and purpose are required ingredients for a healthy, fulfilling life.

- Remember, to develop a regular mindfulness practice. (daily or multiple times a week) that practice may include meditation, gratitude practice, meridian tapping, a safe space, physical activity (e.g., dancing, yoga, walking), and for some, spiritual readings and/or prayers, etc. Once again, developing meaningful practices is likely to be emotionally grounding and helpful in trauma recovery and anxiety and stress management.

Lessons Learned

I encourage you to answer the following questions in writing in your Trauma Recovery Journal:

1 Regarding what you have read in this chapter, what was most significant?
2 What do you understand the term "mindfulness" to be about for you?
3 What are three mindfulness-based activities you are committed to practicing for three months? (Trying out and then habituating such practices)
4 If you have made use of a mindfulness-based practice or intervention (e.g., meditation, meridian tapping, voo exhalation), how helpful has that practice been for you? Use the following 1 to 10 scale, with 10 being extremely helpful and 1 not helpful.

1	2	3	4	5	6	7	8	9	10
(not helpful)				(helpful)				(very helpful)	

5 Several mindfulness-oriented books were mentioned within the chapter. Is there a particular book you have found especially helpful to you in managing trauma, anxiety, and stress? If so, what is that book, and how and why was it helpful to you?

3 Addressing Your Trauma

When it comes to managing and healing your trauma, anxiety, or stress, it is important to understand when you are approaching the ceiling of your coping. While it's important to face your fears, it is also wise to address trauma in manageable increments. Here's a story to illustrate this point. When my oldest brother was 16, he bought a used car. Now the car was not in good shape, but it was what he could afford with his part-time job. While giving me a ride in his "new" car, I noticed an instrument that had been mounted onto the dashboard. The instrument had a set of numbers with a red line from 7 to 10. I inquired what the numbers represented, and he replied that if you ran the engine too long in the red-lined numbers, it would burn up, and your engine would need major and expensive repair work.

So, like my brother's car, running yourself too long at a high stress level can cause you to burn out as well. Now, there are various methods to use when measuring your trauma or stress level. One, the *Professional Quality of Life Scale* (ProQuol; Stamn, 2009) will be profiled in a later chapter. A quick and easy method of assessing the degree of distress you are experiencing at a particular time is the Subjective Units of Distress Scale (SUDS). SUDS scales are usually scored on a 0 (or sometimes 1) to 10 scale, with 10 representing significant distress and 1 minimal or no distress. The goal in therapy, and this workbook, is to provide readers with a SUDs scale to measure distress when triggered. The SUDS scale assessment provides a method of assessing when we are approaching the red line zone and thus understanding we need a break, need to use our mindfulness skills, take a walk, etc.

The SUDS Scale

As mentioned, the SUDS is a basic unit of self-measurement to assess your distress. The scale has 11 points, from 0 to 10, from no distress to very distressed. The SUDS scale is used in many areas of the field, especially in cognitive therapy, solution-focused therapy, EMDR, and pain management, to cite a few examples (Wolpe, 1969).

DOI: 10.4324/9781003689232-3

0 = I am completely relaxed, with no distress.
1 = I am very relaxed.
2 = I feel slight stress.
3 = I feel a little tension, but it's manageable.
4 = I feel mild distress (or anxiety).
5 = My distress is unpleasant, but I can manage it.
6 = I am experiencing moderate distress and anxiety.
7 = I am experiencing significant distress and high levels of anxiety, fear, and worry but can manage it.
8 = I am experiencing a great deal of distress with high levels of fear, worry, and anxiety. I will not be able to manage it much longer.
9 = My distress is so great that it is affecting my thoughts and feelings, and I am not managing it well at all.
10 = I am experiencing extreme distress and feel very anxious and panicked, and have extreme tension in my body. I cannot manage this level of distress.

I would encourage readers to make use of the SUDS scale while reading through this workbook. If your SUDS score is in the 7–10 range (remember, the red line, like my brother's car), I encourage you to consider taking a break. You may wish to review the mindfulness exercises in the previous chapter to ground yourself.

Now, considering the SUDS scale, what is your current SUDS score? _____/10

What are the reasons for your score? ______________________________

What's one intervention you might use to lower your score by 1 point?

____

Remember, SUDS scores can change quickly. The desired change is in the more manageable direction (i.e., lower scores). SUDS scores are effective in calculating your distress level and then taking action to lower your distress. The more skilled you become at de-stressing, the more confident you will feel. Practice patience and self-care, as distress reduction takes time.

Dissociation

My experience in the mental health field is that my patients/clients fear dissociation as much as any triggered response. I expect this is a conditioned response to over-dramatized Hollywood films, which bear scant resemblance to the reality of dissociation. The DSM-5 TR defines dissociation as a disruption in the normal integration of consciousness, memory, identity, emotion, perception, body representation, and/or motor control (American Psychiatric Association, 2022).

Film, TV, uninformed talking heads on the internet, and the media have exaggerated dissociation to an extreme and reinforced the belief that it is something very bizarre. While dissociation is concerning, it is a common response to trauma triggering and likely is the mind and body's way of shutting down your perception as a means of self-protection. I very much prefer DBT founder Marsha Linehan's approach, emphasizing that you are having a normal reaction to an abnormal experience (2015). The reality is, it's the traumatic experience(s) that are abnormal and not the trauma response (e.g., dissociation, flashbacks, startle response). Now, let's distinguish between the types of dissociation.

Normal dissociation is the most common type. (Pardon the term *normal*) Everyone experiences dissociation, such as tuning out a boring meeting, lecture, movie, or your least favorite in-law! This type of dissociation involves briefly losing touch with one's surroundings, but there is scarcely anything to be anxious about, absent your boss or spouse's animus.

Trauma-related dissociation is the most common type encountered in trauma therapy. This type commonly occurs when a person has been traumatized. (e.g., auto accident, physical or sexual assault, war zone) As a result of the trauma memory (the "neurons that fire together, wire together" saying), your hippocampus remembers, and, thereafter, whenever it perceives danger, it shoots cortisol into your brain via the amygdala, causing significant distress and often dissociation (Herman, 1992). Thus, trauma-related dissociation is a learned response that gets reinforced. In trauma terms, this type of dissociation causes the blinking red hypervigilance that becomes stuck in the on mode. Emotional regulation through therapy and practicing intervention techniques (as in this workbook) is to re-regulate trauma survivors and thus turn that button off.

Dissociative disorders, such as dissociative identity disorder, dissociative amnesia, and depersonalization, occupy a different place in the mental health lexicon and represent a more serious, persistent issue. In this workbook, we shall focus on normal dissociation and trauma-related dissociation, as these additional types would require a separate workbook. Because normal dissociation is not so serious, apart from a bad grade in geometry or a nasty look from your boss, the heavy focus will be on treating trauma-related dissociation.

Treating Trauma-Related Dissociation

Identifying Ways I Dissociate

Please check any of the following examples of dissociation that occur to you.

__ Feeling like I have left my body.
__ My mind blanks out momentarily.
__ I have memory lapses.
__ I feel as if I am observing myself from outside my body.
__ I feel like I am simply on autopilot.
__ I feel numb both physically and emotionally.

Regarding the above, when and under what circumstances do you experience these dissociative behaviors that you have checked? Do you experience any additional dissociative behaviors not on the list? If so, list them in your Trauma Recovery Journal.

My experience in treating trauma dissociation is that healing involves the mind, but also the body, breath, and spirit. My further experience is that simple, easy-to-use grounding interventions work best. The important concepts are quick strategies to break away from dissociation and return to the present. Here are some examples:

5-Senses Approach (from Chapter 2): To recap, what are:

5 things you can see right now?
4 things you can hear?
3 things you can feel?
2 things you can smell?
1 thing you can taste?

Body-Oriented Interventions

Clapping your hands loudly, stomping your feet, slapping your thighs, snapping your fingers, and holding onto something solid (e.g., a desk, bed frame, solid chair) represent a few of these types of interventions.

Vagus Nerve Voo Exhale

As in Chapter 2, practice Voo exhales for 6–9 seconds, then catch your breath for 2–3 seconds, and then repeat the Voo exhale. Repeat 5–10 times. This intervention taps into the parasympathetic nervous system and helps reset your emotional regulating ability.

Light Stream Technique

Francine Shapiro (1996) especially emphasized this technique when she developed EMDR:

1 First, ask the client where in their body they feel stress at that moment.
2 Then ask what color they most associate with healing.
3 Ask them to imagine a column of that light coming down from the ceiling through the part of their body where they feel distress.
4 Encourage them to allow that light to bathe and permeate their body for about a minute and feel its soothing ability.
5 After a minute, ask how they feel. (Suggestion: use the 0–10 SUDs scale to assess improvement, with 10 representing feeling much better).

Flashbacks and How to Manage Them

A flashback occurs when a traumatized person becomes triggered by a trauma-related memory, like a scent, scene, sound, or experience, and relives a traumatic memory. Flashbacks may involve intrusive memories but may also occur via reliving certain emotional or physical sensations from the traumatic event. Flashbacks are often fragmented and intense, leaving the person experiencing them feeling confused. Trauma sufferers, especially those with PTSD, commonly experience such flashbacks (van der Kolk, 2014). So, remember, flashbacks are very common among trauma survivors. I encourage readers to remind themselves that flashbacks are the mind and body's way of saying, "wake up and heal yourself." Remember, flashbacks are the mind and body's normal response to abnormal, traumatic experiences (Linehan, 2015).

Flashbacks can affect people in a variety of ways. Some flashbacks are brief and mild, while others can last longer, making a person lose awareness of their present surroundings. During a flashback, the person may not be able to distinguish between the flashback and reality, causing increased anxiety and distress. Flashbacks can occur in children as well as adults, and younger children may act them out as opposed to verbally describing them (van der Kolk, 2014). Sometimes, traumatized children will inflict upon others the trauma that was inflicted upon them. For example, while I was working in an inpatient psychiatric center, a youth climbed into bed with a peer and attempted to sexually assault him, something his older brother had done to him, and yet he did not know what he was doing when interrupted.

Here are some examples of flashbacks: While watching a sexual assault scene in a film, Sarah suddenly sees her stepfather climbing into bed with her and screams before running out of the theater to the shock of the audience and her friends. Sun-Mi gets a whiff of her male colleague's cologne, and it takes her back to a date rape she experienced in college, as her assailant wore the same cologne. She rushes to the bathroom, enters the stall, curls up, and cries for several minutes.

Flashbacks can occur at any time of the day or evening, as triggering events are unpredictable. Flashbacks may involve explicit memories of former abuse or brief fragments of a traumatic experience. Flashbacks impact the mind, body (nerves), respiration, and a person's behavior. As the mind perceives a threat, cortisol is released, activating the fight, flight, and freeze reaction administered by the hippocampus and amygdala. People experiencing flashbacks often report hyperventilation, sweating, catastrophic thinking, trembling throughout their body, or feeling entirely numb, among various responses (Herman, 1992; van der Kolk, 2014).

Addressing and Managing Flashbacks

Remember, flashbacks are common among trauma survivors and are communicating an important message to you: "Heal yourself." Remember, as Linehan states, you are having a normal experience of an abnormal experience (2015). To heal and manage flashbacks, we must face and reframe them as steps toward healing. In this way, consider the following questions focused on describing your flashbacks. Please use your Trauma Recovery Journal to answer the questions:

1 Describe your most recent flashback and what you experienced.
2 Was this most recent flashback the same or very similar to those in the past?

3 What conditions or triggers led to the flashback?
4 Consider the flashback. How did the flashback look, hear, smell, feel, or taste? (some flashbacks impact all 5 senses, while others only 1–2.)
5 Who was involved in your flashback?
6 Regarding coming out of the flashback, what were 5 things you could see, 4 you could hear, 3 you could smell, 2 you could touch, 1 you could taste? (Remember the 5 senses grounding for managing flashbacks and their aftermath, and make regular use of them.)
7 Beyond the 5-senses grounding exercise in the previous question, what other methods can you use to ground yourself during and after a flashback? (e.g., hold something meaningful/sacred; holding onto something solid like a desk, chair, clapping your hands; stomping your feet)
8 What emotions, thoughts, and body sensations did you experience as you completed this exercise? What helped you manage any triggers and sensations experienced?
9 When your flashback has passed, you may need to use additional interventions: For example, box breathing (breathe in slowly for 4 seconds, hold your breath for 4 seconds, then slowly release for 4 seconds, then repeat until your breathing is normal again); taking a slow walk for 5–10 minutes; paying special attention to your feet walking across the floor, street, sidewalk, etc.; and using Linehan's "I am having a normal response to an abnormal experience" mantra as the story we tell ourselves is powerful (Brown, 2011).
10 SUDS scaling: On a scale of 1 to 10, with 10 representing "very distressing," what score would you assign the flashback? (they can vary significantly) Now, how might you lower your distress score by just 1 point? (Think about your preparation through counseling, mindfulness practice, self-compassionate self-talk, etc.)

Replay and Review Flashback Technique

Another approach to addressing and reducing flashbacks is the Replay and Review Technique (formerly the DVD Rewind Technique for those of us seniors). Consider your flashback(s) as something you can replay and review, just as if using a laptop or other computer device. You can review your flashback in brief segments and control the stop, start, and rewind buttons.

Before reviewing a traumatic flashback, pair it with a positive memory of an event you have experienced. For example, one former client paired her flashback with her walking on the beach during a rainstorm (a resident of the Pacific Northwest, she preferred stormy coastal days over sunny beach days!). Thus, another narrative opportunity for writing in your Trauma Recovery Journal:

The positive memory I will use is ________________________________.

When I replay and review this positive event, I review it with my 5 senses (what I see, hear, smell, and taste):

____.

When I rewind this positive event, I see, hear, feel, smell, and taste:

____.

If I were to pair these positive images with my flashback, the top three I would select would be: ______________________________.

The flashback I am going to use is ______________________.

When I fast-forward this flashback to review what occurred during the event, I experienced (What I saw, heard, smelled, felt, tasted, etc.):

____.

When I review the flashback, I experience ____________________.

When I pair the flashback with positive images, I experience __________.

On a SUDS scale of 0–10, with 10 high, what was your score? ___/10. Now, how might you reduce that distress score by 1 point? (Hint: Continue the replay and review on flashbacks and pair with more positive images. Your distress score is likely to fall over time.) Just as flashbacks are natural and common for trauma survivors, addressing them actively will naturally help you reduce them and possibly eliminate them, or at least make them rare.

Addressing Flashbacks in the Mind, Body, Breath, and Spirit

Trauma treatment has become very holistic and moved beyond merely addressing thoughts (van der Kolk, 2014; Shapiro, 1996). This next exercise will focus on managing and hopefully reducing flashback distress (and hopefully reducing flashbacks). In your Trauma Recovery Journal, address the following:

1 **Mind**: A staple of cognitive therapy is reframing negative thoughts. For example, instead of thinking, "I'm a complete failure for having this flashback and will always be a victim," think, "I am having a normal reaction to an abnormal experience. I survived my trauma, and with treatment and ongoing work, I will heal my trauma, and flashbacks will no longer be problematic." So, what's an example of a negative, distressing thought you have regarding your flashbacks? Okay, what is a more reasonable, positive reframe for your negative thoughts regarding your flashback?
2 **Body**: Because we have nerves running throughout our body, we feel anxiety throughout our body. Thus, we must address the body to heal trauma. Every trauma client I treated who made progress also did bodywork. Some examples of bodywork are yoga, Pilates, massage, EFT/meridian tapping points, regular workout routines (4 times per week for, say, 20–30 minutes), dancing, walking, etc. As meridian tapping points may be new to some readers, I have offered a photo representation of them. The tapping points, which correspond to acupuncture, are generally believed to have originated in China, being first mentioned in documents dating to 100 BCE (White &

Ernst, 2004). The practice of acupuncture, of course, would be much older, perhaps dating to 6000 BCE (White & Ernst, 2004).

3 **Breath:** Our breath is the life force within each of us. Our breathing is also another of the signs we are relaxed or upset, depending on our respiration rate. Box breathing is so effective that even Navy SEALs are trained to use it to stop panic attacks. Box breathing involves the following: (1) Breath in slowly through your nose for a count of four; (2) Then exhale slowly out of your mouth for a count of four; (3) Then breathe in slowly through your nose for a count of four; (4) Then exhale slowly out of your mouth for a count of four. Repeat as long as it takes to slow your respiration. As you slow your respiration, your thoughts will be calmer. Box breathing could become very important in managing dissociation and flashbacks and anytime you are triggered.

The other breathwork is meditation. Meditation is slow, regulated breathing through the nose and then exhaling slowly out the mouth. Many meditation practitioners use a mantra, which is a brief saying they repeat over and over (Ex.: "May I be well," or "May I be filled with loving kindness"), or for some, it involves a religious expression, such as "I in Christ" on inhale and "Christ in I" on exhale, or "Hare Krishna." I use silent, mindful meditation and do not fight the distractions, simply allowing them to float past as if on a river. Meditation is more helpful after a dissociative experience as a means of calming oneself.

(**Note:** I will provide more detailed steps on breathwork in a couple of pages.)

4 **Spirit:** Spirit can represent many things to many people. It can be a religious or spiritual belief, while for others it's love for their family or something else. When I refer to spirit, it's about what the client/patient/reader finds meaningful to them, much like how the term "Higher Power" in 12-step programs means different things to different people. As one former client in treatment for complex PTSD opined, "The purpose in my life is to maintain the purpose in my life."

Detailed EFT/Meridian Tapping Points

Now, I have listed 11 tapping points that I was taught in professional EFT training many years ago. If you search the internet, you will see there are different numbers of tapping points. I am including those points I was taught, use myself, and have taught past clients and trained others to use. The tapping order does not seem to make a difference as well. If you have been taught more or even fewer tapping points and that works for you, then continue tapping those points to help self-soothe anxiety. When you tap, simple touch/tap lightly for 1–2 seconds.

With that being said, here's the tapping order I use with basic information:

1 Touch the side of the hand (karate chop): The outer side of the hand between the wrist and the base of the little finger.

2 Top of the head. Just place the palm flat on the top of your head.
3 Eyebrow: (EB): The beginning of the eyebrow, near the bridge of the nose.
4 Side of the eye (SE): The bone on the outer corner of the eye.
5 Under the eye (UE): The bone directly below the pupil on the cheekbone.
6 Under the nose (UN): The bone directly under the nose.
7 Chin point (CP): The crease between the bottom lip and the chin.
8 Collarbone point (CB): About two inches below and to the side of where the collarbones meet.
9 Under the arm (UA): About four inches below the armpit, under either side of the body.
10 Gamut between ring and tiny finger (GS): The slight valley between the small bone of the ring and the tiny finger. (**Note:** For some reason, I cannot find a drawing of this pressure point. However, as I was taught it, I am including it.)
11 Chest center (CC): Place your hand on the very center of the chest. (Another point not on the diagram.)

Now, I find that doing my daily tapping has been very helpful in calming and emotionally regulating my emotions and anxiety. Most of the people I have treated for trauma have also found some degree of value in the EFT/meridian tapping. I usually experience a warm, tingling sensation that starts in my ankles and then travels upward toward my knees. Most of my former clients have reported similar experiences, although in different locations on their bodies. Admittedly, a minority of clients have expressed experiencing no change from the tapping. What I learn is that tapping helps calm me, and most people I have worked with regarding managing triggers, dissociation, anger, and even chronic pain (Levine, 2011). What I learn from my experience in using EFT tapping in practice is that while it seems to help most people self-soothe, some derive little or no benefit from this intervention. This experience is another reason I have offered numerous methods for self-soothing (e.g., Voo exhaling, box breathing, mindfulness meditation, 5 senses calming).

The tapping points are illustrated on the following page (Figure 3.1).

EFT, or meridian tapping, draws on the ancient Chinese practice of acupuncture, which teaches that the body's energy travels along specific pathways. When stimulated, these pathways (nerves) tap into the parasympathetic nervous system. EFT tapping has demonstrated effectiveness in treating PTSD among military veterans and shows promise in reducing general anxiety (Bach et al., 2019). I have made extensive use of this in treating PTSD clients, and most have found it helps soothe their anxiety. I also use it on myself every morning and have found that the procedure has a calming effect on me.

I do wish to point out that while tapping points have been used for centuries, there is a considerable amount of argument about why it works, much as in the debate regarding acupuncture. Traditional Western medicine providers will argue that meridians are not scientifically validated,

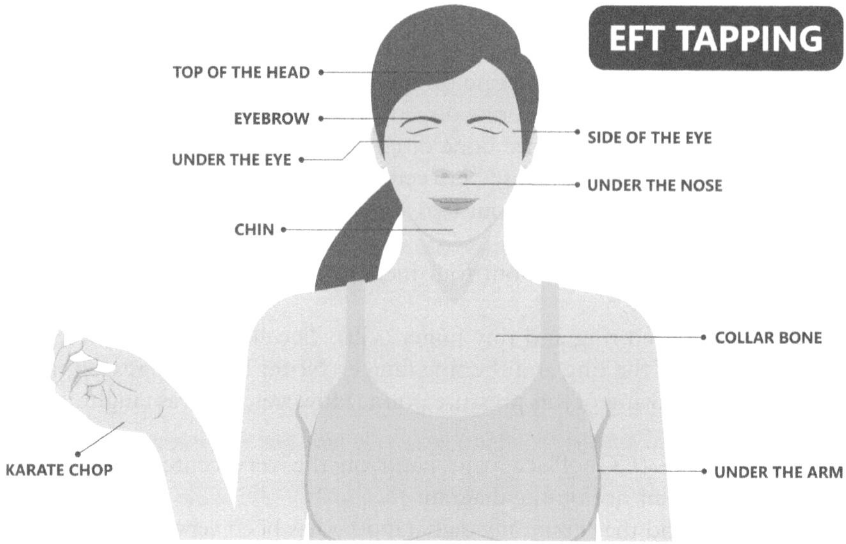

Figure 3.1 EFT/Meridian Tapping Points.

while Eastern healing professionals will assert otherwise. My perspective is that I am less concerned with the why of EFT/meridian tapping and more interested in the fact that it has worked for me and most of my clients in reducing PTSD symptoms (e.g., anxiety and flashbacks). My own belief is that, like the Voo exhale, yoga, massage, body movement, the polyvagal nervous system, composed of hundreds of thousands of nerves threaded throughout the body, likely is stimulated and thus helps the person grappling with PTSD, anxiety, stress, etc. by serving as a type of reset button via the parasympathetic nervous system. Peter Levine makes a similar point in his excellent book, *Waking the Tiger: Healing Trauma* (2011). Levine also makes regular use of the Voo exhale as well, something I have also used in my trauma work and, likewise, practice each morning. As an aside, people undergoing trauma treatment may be wise to ask their therapist(s) if they themselves use the interventions they treat clients/patients with.

I use the EFT tapping each morning after my daily workout and after my gratitude practice, and thus I feel relaxed when I use it. Then, I sit down in a comfortable chair and touch three rounds of my 11 EFT points (some people touch more pressure points, others less) for a total of 33 touch points. Thereafter, I engage my Voo exhale, performing 10 exhales, each lasting around 6–9 seconds. Then, I go into my 30-minute meditation and thereafter listen to my favorite podcasts while traveling on the train to the campus I work at, some 40 minutes north of my home. I make use of my mindfulness routine daily, and it has had a profound calming effect on me. Once again, experiment and find what works for you in healing trauma triggers, anxiety, and stress.

12 **Breath:** There are two types of breathing I have included. The first is what is known as "box breathing," which I mentioned briefly just a couple of pages ago. Box breathing is very effective in stopping or managing a panic attack as it targets slowing respiration. In fact, box breathing is so effective at regulating respiration that the Navy SEALs train their soldiers in using it (Kumar & Utteker, 2025).

See box breathing instructions below:

a Find a comfortable position: Sit or lie down in a quiet place.
b Close your eyes or keep your eyes open. (whatever is most comfortable)
c Inhale: Breath in slowly and deeply through your nose for a count of four, filling your lungs.
d Hold your breath for a count of four.
e Exhale: Exhale slowly and completely out of your mouth for a count of four, releasing all air from your lungs.
f Hold again: Hold your breath for a count of four.
g Repeat: Repeat the cycle of inhale for a four count, hold your breath for a four count, exhale out your mouth for a four count, and then hold for a four count, for as long as it takes for you to calm and center your respiration.

The second type of breathing is what we refer to as meditation. Meditation breathing is more regulated and rhythmic than box breathing. Box breathing is also used for brief periods of time, while meditative breathing may be done for extended times (say, an hour or even several hours). I have maintained a daily Zen-style meditation practice for 35 years, and it is a staple of my daily well-being routine. Now, there are many variations of meditation. Here's the one I practice:

a Sit or lie down in a comfortable position.
b Close your eyes or keep them open, depending on your preference.
c Inhale: Breath in slowly and deeply through your nose, filling your lungs.
d Exhale: Exhale slowly and through your mouth.
e Thoughts: Do not try to force thoughts from your mind; rather, simply visualize them as floating past on a river. Accept all thoughts and then watch them float away.
f Continue the inhale-exhale for say 5 minutes. Practice this micro-approach to meditation and eventually work up to 15 minutes per day.

Note: Many use a mantra, or repeated word or phrase that helps them focus (i.e., "May I be kind," "May I be loving," or "May I be well"), while others use koans, or contradictory sayings: Example: "What is the sound of one hand clapping?" Others use walking meditation and focus on the feel of their feet making contact with the ground or noticing their 5 senses as they walk (I use walking meditation occasionally). My recommendation is that readers experiment and then use what works best for you.

13 **Spirit:** This word often carries religious/spiritual overtones. Some readers of this workbook are religious, others are spiritual but not religious, some are agnostic, and others are atheist. All these philosophical types can use the work spirit in ways that are congruent with their values. Friedrich Nietzsche's famous saying is, "he that has a why can endure almost any how." I will use a more inclusive variation: The person with a why can endure almost any how. Your why is essentially your purpose and meaning in life, or, as Arthur Brooks, director of the Happiness Project at Harvard University, believes, meaning in life involves identifying what you are willing to die for, as it clarifies one's significance and purpose (Brooks & Winfrey, 2023). For our purposes, our why might be our family, spouse, children, spiritual life, country, etc. So, reflect upon and complete the sentences below in your Trauma Recovery Journal:

My why (meaning/purpose) is life is ____________________________.

What brings meaning and purpose to my life is ____________________.

What I am willing to die for is ________________________________.

What brings happiness and fulfillment to me is ____________________.

If I were to make one change in my life, that change would be

____.

Note: If you do not know the answer to one or any of the above questions, how might you begin to find out? Answers to some of these questions may take extended thought and time. It is also fair to say that your answers to these similar existential questions will likely change over time.

Addressing Nightmares

One of the more distressing symptoms of trauma, especially sexual trauma, is managing nightmares, or as some call them, night terrors. Many of my clients in trauma recovery experienced occasional, if not regular, nightmares. As the conscious and subconscious are connected, what occurs during conscious times (e.g., traumatic experiences) can manifest in our dreams. Often, the experiences in the dream state can be disturbing, given that sleep is such a vulnerable time and likely because we feel passive in dreams. During my undergraduate years, way back in the early 1980s, I took a workshop in lucid dreaming. My most helpful takeaway from the workshop was that we can be active participants in our dreams. I realized this meant that with my traumatized clients, I could prepare them to be active participants during their nightmares.

Not long after the training, a young male client came to see me at the university health center where I was working. He was a survivor of childhood sexual abuse perpetrated by his stepfather. Each night when he heard his stepdad's footsteps on the stairs, he would wonder whether his stepdad was going into the master bedroom to be with his mother or if he was coming into his own bedroom. Over time, the most problematic part of his healing was his nightmares. In those disturbing dreams, he was being chased down a long, dark hallway, pursued by a shadowy figure whose footsteps would echo throughout the endless hallway. Terrified, I would wake up from the nightmare in a cold sweat. He eventually came to me for treatment after attending a workshop I had presented on the campus.

I explained lucid dreaming to him, and he was very skeptical, but feeling desperate, he was willing to try it. I started treatment by having him sit and watch me standing before him and stomping my feet while he was imagining being back in that nightmare, in that dark, long, gothic hallway. Using scaling questions, I had him say "Stop!" when the score became 7 out of 10. We spent an entire session on this, and his score dropped from an 8 to a 2. I continued with this approach, eventually standing behind him, stomping my feet while he reclined in his chair with his eyes closed. I began to have him imagine himself turning to face the pursuer, resulting in his eventual turning in his chair to face me. We practiced this for a full session, and his score dropped from 9 to 3, and then finally to 1. I predicted to him that he would soon be able to turn and face the pursuer in his dream. I furthermore predicted that when he faced his pursuer, he would lose his fear.

He made a lot of progress but continued to struggle during nightmares, something understandable given his abuse history. I continued to phrase his eventual success, opining, "When you are ready, you will turn and face your pursuer, and that dream will lose its power over you." After each session, I would articulate, "You are a little stronger and your nightmare a little weaker." Then, one afternoon, he came to the session with a wide smile on his face. I knew even before he spoke that he had been successful in facing his nightmare. He explained the process of turning to face the figure chasing him, and when he did, the figure was this young, friendly-looking character who, out of breath, said, "I have been trying to catch up and tell you how proud I am of you for surviving a horrific childhood!" That was the last session we had together.

Suggestions for Facing Your Nightmare:

1 Practice during waking time: Manifest what you wish to dream about. In my former case, I had him focus on facing his fear (his pursuer) and then turning to face it in his dream.
2 At 2–3 points per day, tell yourself, "I will face and lose my fear in my dreams by confronting them." (Again, I suggest you write these down.) This involves confronting your fear vicariously and setting an intention to overcome it.
3 Now, should you awake feeling anxious from a trauma nightmare, be sure to practice grounding techniques like the 5-senses grounding (5 things you see, 4 you hear, 3 you can touch, etc.) or simply by holding a favorite object

or grasping something solid like the bedframe or a nightstand. Focus on your body's contact with that solid object, the feel of that surface, and describe that tactile sensation to yourself out loud. For a follow-up grounding technique, clap your hands, rub them together, stomp your feet, etc.

4 Remember, planning to change the outcome of your dream is also a part of success. So, just as coming to counseling for healing represents success, planning to manage and defeat your trauma nightmares is a type of success as well.
5 Finally, nightmares, like dissociation, are not weird nor evidence of a severe mental disorder. Once again, to paraphrase DBT founder Marsha Linehan, you are having a normal response to an abnormal experience. Your unconscious is basically saying to you, "Please pay attention to me. You need to heal."

Adapted from Maren and Holmes (2016)

Exercise: Revising your Trauma Nightmare

1 Describe your trauma-related nightmare in your Trauma Recovery Journal by answering the questions below. Include as much detail as possible, including dream details, like what's happening, your feelings during the nightmare, and any sensations you noticed (e.g., what you saw, heard, smelled, could feel, and tasted). If you are having multiple trauma-related nightmares, then make a separate entry to address additional nightmares. Include your reaction to the nightmare (i.e., how you felt, your actions, and how the nightmare ended).
2 What triggers occur during the day that lead up to your nightmares? Examples might include reading or viewing (the internet, TV, video, film, news, etc.) upsetting information reminiscent of your trauma(s), an argument with your spouse/partner, boss, or colleague, or something upsetting a colleague discloses to you.
3 Many patients in PTSD treatment articulate that their nightmares have provided them with information that helped them address and heal their trauma. If applicable, how has your trauma nightmare helped you address and heal from your trauma?
4 How have your nightmare(s), or addressing your nightmares, provided perspective on your trauma?
5 Now, write a paragraph about how you would like your nightmare to be resolved. Include what actions you can take to resolve the nightmare. Regarding resolution, what helpful information have you learned from past or current therapy, information from this workbook, or somewhere else, that will help you resolve your nightmare(s)? Practice self-compassion, as trauma nightmares are often healed gradually when addressed. Remember, your subconscious wants you to heal, and that's why it's replaying your nightmare(s) (write down this important fact).
6 Scaling to grade for improvement: 0–10 Nightmare Distress Scale, with 0 = no distress and 10 = extreme distress. Grade your improvement over time.

Your Trauma History

There are many variations on a trauma inventory. The following represents you listing your trauma event, the age when the trauma occurred, and a brief description of the trauma. The important concept is to acknowledge your resilience in surviving the trauma and continuing to persevere despite that trauma.

Event	Age	Brief Description

Surviving a fire
Witnessing an unexpected death
Witnessing a violent death
Surviving an auto accident
Surviving a natural disaster (tornado, earthquake)
Surviving a robbery
Surviving combat
Being exposed to a war zone
Surviving childhood abuse (physical, sexual)
Survivor of date rape
Surviving domestic abuse
Surviving torture
Surviving sex trafficking
Surviving serious alcohol and drug abuse

The second part of the above list addresses the resilience you developed to survive these ordeals, the courage to heal, and then to move forward in your life (Nugent et al., 2014).

My Resilience Record

Once again, you are encouraged to write out answers in your Trauma Recovery Journal.

1 Regarding the traumatic experiences from your past, what are some of the positive traits you developed to survive and thrive after those events?
2 Describe the resilience and determination you demonstrated in the aftermath of your trauma.
3 What is the most important lesson you have learned in surviving your trauma(s)?
4 Many trauma survivors see themselves as lacking courage, even though survival requires courage. In what ways have you demonstrated courage during and beyond the post-trauma period?
5 Viktor Frankl wrote extensively about meaning as critical to trauma recovery. Where does your meaning in life come from?
6 How has your sense of personal meaning helped you survive and recover from trauma?

7 Nobody wants to be forced to learn from traumatic experiences, but this is required of people who experience trauma. So, what have you learned from surviving trauma?
8 What strengths have you developed in response to addressing your trauma?
9 Who are the people who provided emotional support through your trauma recovery?
10 Now that you have survived trauma(s), in what ways are you a stronger, more resilient person?

Writing Your Trauma Timeline

A common method in trauma recovery (and addiction treatment) is to draw a trauma timeline. The trauma timeline can be completed on a sheet of paper (such as legal size), poster-size paper, or cardboard. You can make it as long and detailed as necessary. Many people begin their trauma timeline when they were in utero, as their mother may have experienced trauma due to abuse, an accident, substance abuse, depression or anxiety, etc. Otherwise, begin at birth with a horizontal line running to the present.

Next, list any personal trauma that occurred above the line (e.g., loss of home, parents' divorce, injury, illness). Below the line, record events that happened to loved ones. The below-the-line events are ones you either witnessed directly or, if not, still significantly impacted you (births, deaths, etc.). You can write brief narratives about the event; post photos, memorials, drawings of yourself and others, and anything you feel is important to include. You can also add to the line whenever you like.

Depending on where you are on your healing journey, you may wish to write your Healing from Trauma Timeline. You could include all your healing points, including the diligent, dedicated work you have put into reclaiming your life (e.g., via therapy, ongoing practice, new relationships, advocacy work). Both the trauma timeline and the healing timeline can play important roles in acknowledging hurts and in healing from those wounds.

When You Are Ready, Here's a Three-Part Question to Address in Your Healing Journal

1 What did you learn about yourself from completing the trauma timeline?
2 What did you learn from drawing your healing on the trauma timeline?
3 If you were to continue your trauma healing timeline for, say, 5 years beyond the present, what might post-traumatic growth (i.e., your healed self) look like?

Writing My Healing from Trauma Story

Without question, writing about your trauma can be a very challenging and painful experience. However, avoiding one's trauma causes even greater suffering in the long term and is not therapeutically effective.

Writing about your trauma and especially journaling about your healing from trauma is very therapeutic (Sloan et al., 2023; Pennebaker, 2004). Putting your trauma in narrative form is a type of exposure therapy that provides the opportunity to separate past trauma from a more grounded, safer place. Writing also provides a concrete method to lessen your fear and reduce your sensory responses to trauma triggers. As trauma creates fragmented memories due to dissociation, journaling creates a complete story whereby you write about managing and healing your trauma. My experience in treating clients' trauma is that writing about healing tends to help trauma survivors become more committed to the healing process. Writing also helps the trauma survivor reclaim their life story. I recall one mid-30s female who remarked, "Journaling about my trauma story helped me get my life back."

There are many ways to write about your trauma history. Perhaps starting by describing the who, what, where, when, and how of your trauma. Then, difficult as it will be, include the worst of your trauma experience(s), including the resulting losses from trauma (e.g., people, innocence, emotional and physical health, self-medication). Then, write about your healing journey from trauma, including overcoming fear, progress you have made in therapy, and beyond, new, healthy relationships, and the freedom that comes when conditioned fear (trauma) no longer rules your life. Include your experiences in post-traumatic growth and how you now view your life as meaningful, purposeful, and fulfilling again.

Here Are a Few Suggested Steps for Writing Your Trauma Recovery Journal

1. Write at a time when you will be less interrupted and prone to distraction.
2. Practice self-compassion, meaning you write free of self-judgment. Remember, self-compassion is how you would speak to or write about a close friend.
3. Write what needs to be written, but do not hurry. Take the time you need, whether that is 5 minutes or an hour at a time.
4. Prioritize your writing time, as healing is a top priority, much like food, water, and sleep.
5. Read what you have written, as this provides you with the benefit of self-reflection.
6. Make sure you have a well-being plan to manage the distress that writing about the trauma healing may cause. (e.g., in therapy, talking with a trusted friend, taking a long walk in nature, healing meditation)
7. Journal about the pain, but even more important, focus more on your healing. Journaling on your progress is a concrete method of acknowledging success, as this facilitates healing (Pennabaker, 2004).
8. Write about anything related to your healing, including dreams, small successes, setbacks that precede progress, and anything that seems relevant.
9. When you have decided you have completed your healing from trauma journal, write a formal letter to yourself outlining your accomplishments

and successes. Within the letter, include a reward for the hard work and success you have achieved, then sign the letter. I also suggest you keep the letter and re-read it. Do not forget to reward yourself with something you enjoy (e.g., ice cream, coffee with a friend, going to a film).

10 Keep your journal in a secure location (perhaps locked). Some former clients have found freedom in burning or burying their journal(s), while others preferred to keep their journal available. One young former client put together a memorial service with readings, music, and a eulogy and then burned the journal (cremation), representing the death of her traumatized self. This is an individualized process, so do what you find meaningful.

Lessons Learned

Contemplate and answer the following self-reflective questions in your Trauma Recovery Journal:

1 Regarding manifestations of trauma triggers (e.g., flashbacks, somatic concerns, hyperventilation, nightmares), which of these is most problematic for you? (Some may be equally problematic, of course.)
2 Of the various interventions covered in this chapter (e.g., box breathing, meditation, Voo exhaling, 5 senses intervention), which have been or which do you believe would be most helpful for managing your triggers?
3 Regarding your recovery from trauma, what has that healing process taught you? (Remember, even a little healing is still healing.)
4 Solution-focused therapy has a popular intervention called the miracle question (de Shazer, 2010). The miracle question goes like this: If a miracle occurred while you were asleep and your trauma was healed, what might be different about your life? What might be different in your relationships with others? What would be different in how you feel about yourself? What would your family and close friends notice as being different from you? Now, how can you begin to create this miracle? What steps can you take?

4 Self-soothing Interventions When You Are Triggered

A trigger is an experience or memory that intrudes into your thoughts and reminds you of a past event. For people with a trauma history, trigger events set off the hippocampus and adrenal glands and activate the release of cortisol, resulting in a hyperarousal state. People who are hyperaroused are said to be triggered and subconsciously and consciously look to assess safety versus being unsafe. For trauma survivors, those with PTSD, they are dysregulated. That is, they overreact when faced with something reminiscent of their trauma. Triggers can be scents of their abuser, a whistle they recall from prison, a uniform similar to their abuser, foods they ate right before the abuse, or an aroma they smelled during their abuse (Matsakis, 1994). Triggers may lead to flashbacks, anger outbursts, dissociation, numbness, or a panic attack. In the previous chapter, there was a checklist of triggers that might lead to flashbacks (or dissociation). Identifying flashbacks and developing an awareness of them is a key step in learning how to manage them (also covered in Chapter 3).

The focus of this chapter will be on self-soothing interventions for situations when trauma survivors are triggered. There is no question that everyone is triggered at times. There are positive triggers, such as the pleasant odor of our favorite cookies baking in the oven, the aroma of fine coffee brewing, or the smell of vanilla. Then, there are the triggers trauma survivors dread, such as those precipitating a flashback (e.g., smell of past abuser, seeing the abuser at a family gathering).

Managing and Soothing Triggers

When you learn to manage your triggers, you begin to lose some of the fear associated with them. Managing triggers means you will be able to strategize ways to address them and to self-soothe so that the discomfort is lessened. Here is a list of ways to identify and manage your triggers:

1 **Recognize Trigger Warning Signs**: Pay attention to physiological reactions, increased heart rate, hyperventilation, sweating, and negative or catastrophizing thoughts. These symptoms are often the first warning signs of being emotionally triggered.

DOI: 10.4324/9781003689232-4

2. **Taking a break:** When you are triggered and experience the above symptoms, take a brief time out (if able), or take a deep breath and pause (count to 5 or so), before you react.
3. **Ask for a momentary delay**: Before reacting and speaking words you cannot rewind, consider saying, "I'm sorry, but I need to think about your statement briefly." (Note: This statement has saved me a LOT of regret.)
4. **Utilize grounding techniques**: Remember the 5 senses intervention (5 you see, 4 you smell, etc.), clapping hands, stomping feet, or grasping something solid (e.g., a table, signpost, favorite object)
5. **Reframe Self-Talk**: Basically, what's the story you are telling yourself?" (Brown, 2010). **Remember the three Cs**: **Catch** that negative thought (From, "I'm a total loser,"), **Challenge** the thought (i.e., "I have had many successes like graduating from college, holding a steady job"), and then **Change** the negative belief: ("Okay, so I have human setbacks, but I am still healing and improving").
6. **EFT/Meridian Tapping**: Remember those 11 tapping points, and make use of them. I have used these to help severely traumatized clients self-soothe when triggered.
7. **Remember, it's the breath**: To stop hyperventilation, use Box Breathing: inhale slowly through your nose for a count of 4, then hold for a count of 4, then exhale out your mouth to a count of 4, then repeat as long as needed. After the panic passes, meditative breathing becomes a method of emotional regulation: Slow, rhythmic inhaling through your nose, followed by slow, rhythmic exhaling through your mouth for several minutes or until you feel calmer and more grounded. Don't try to block out any thoughts, just allow them to float out of sight.
8. **Practice Self-Compassion**: Self-compassion is how you would advise a close friend who was being overly self-critical. So, remember reframing above (the story you are telling yourself). If we spoke to others the way we talked to ourselves, we'd be very lonely people. So, practice realistic, but self-compassionate self-talk.
9. **Peer Support**: Healthy friends are essential for optimal mental health. Who are your three go-to friends when you need support? If you do not have go-to friends, you need them. My trauma treatment approach always included making healthy friendships. See the next step.
10. **Creating healthy friendships**: Naturally, the 21st-century method is to meet people online, and then in person. Or join a gym, a support group, a social or hobby club, a community choir, etc., to meet people with whom you share a common interest.
11. **Professional Help**: Continuing to see your therapist. If you have completed counseling and are in post-traumatic growth, regularly attend your 12-step meeting, other support group, or, if needed, return to counseling for a brief check-up.
12. **Practice, Practice, Practice**: Remember, just as there is no stopping point to physical fitness, there is no stopping point to emotional well-being. This

workbook represents part of an ongoing well-being practice, as opposed to an endpoint well-being mindset.

13 **Journaling or Empty Chair:** When the trigger is past, and you have managed it with something from this list (perhaps more than one from the list), consider writing a brief paragraph in your Trauma Recovery Journal on your success in managing the trigger—even if you believe you managed the trigger poorly, what was one thing you did well? For example, perhaps you remembered to ask for a break, explained you needed to think for a moment before responding, used the EFT/ Meridian tapping, etc. An option for journaling is a brief empty-chair conversation with yourself (@5–10 minutes). Speak to the self who was dealing with the trigger and then explain what you did well in the moment and how you might improve next time. Then switch chairs and let your triggered self-speak with you about progress made and challenges that still need work.

Remember, it was not your choice, nor was it your fault, that you were traumatized. You get the choice, however, of how to address your triggers. Avoiding triggers is impossible as they manifest in our 5 senses. What you can do, however, is to habituate a practice of managing the triggers when they occur (as in the previous steps). Here's a prediction: the more you work on your trigger management plan and face your triggers, the more you reclaim the part of your life that trauma stole (Meichenbaum, 2014).

Now, I do not wish to understate the challenge of recognizing, managing, and healing our trauma triggers. Addressing trauma triggers can be stressful, challenging, and anxiety-provoking work. "I'm pleased that I was traumatized and now have this great opportunity to heal from them," is a statement no person surely even thought, much less articulated. So, self-compassion, in this case, might sound like, *"It sucks that I was traumatized, dysregulated, and now have these triggers that create fear, anger, and dissociation for me! However, I will heal them, become stronger, and help others like me."* Healing trauma triggers will take time, so be patient and self-compassionate.

Managing My Triggers

The following exercise is to help you manage your triggers by writing. When we write our commitments down, we are more likely to remember and practice them (Pennebaker, 2004). So, once again, answer the following in your journal. (You may need to address multiple triggers.)

1 I will choose to manage my trigger of __________ (name trigger) by ____
____

(List ways you can manage your triggers, like the previous suggestions, or other methods you learned in counseling or through your own experience)

2 I will choose to practice remaining present when triggered by using the grounding techniques in this manual or another. For example, my grounding techniques include:

____

(List 5-Senses grounding, clapping hands, stomping feet, holding a special/sacred object, grasping something solid, etc.)

3 Now that you are actively practicing managing your triggers, answer the following questions:

I was feeling ______________ (name the emotion) when triggered by __________________ (name the trigger). I chose to address the trigger by ______________________ (cite what strategy used to manage trigger). When the ____________________ (cite trigger) began to decrease, I felt ____________ (the emotion) and then I ____________________ (explain what you did to manage the trigger).

4 SUDS Scale for Trigger Management: 0= minimal distress, 10= extreme distress.

When I was triggered, my SUDS score was initially _____ (cite score), but when I began to manage my trigger(s) by the 5-senses, or clapping hands, Box Breathing, etc., my score became ____ (cite score). Next time, I will lower my SUDS score by 1-point by _________________ (cite how/ways you will improve by 10%)

Remember, healing usually involves micro-steps before you begin taking big steps. Success often is slow before it becomes fast.

Narrative Exercise for Managing Trauma Triggers

A narrative exercise for managing trauma triggers involves creating a detailed account of a traumatic event, then reflecting on it to identify patterns, emotions, and coping mechanisms. This process is common in trauma-centered therapeutic approaches (e.g., MCBT, EMDR, ACT) and helps the client in trauma recovery reprocess traumatic memories, reduce emotional intensity, and build resilience.

Steps in the Narrative Trauma Management Exercise

1 **Just the Facts:** Start by writing down the factual details of the traumatic event: who, what, where, when, and how.
2 **Emotional Processing:** Provide details regarding the thoughts and feelings experienced during the event, and how they changed over time.
3 **Identifying Triggers:** Reflect on the narrative to identify potential triggers regarding specific people, places, situations, or sensations that elicit strong emotional or physical reactions.

4 **Develop Coping Strategies:** Develop strategies for managing triggers when they arise, such as grounding (e.g., 5 senses, holding a special object) and seeking professional or peer support.
5 **Reauthoring:** Reflect on how the trauma experience(s) have shaped your life and revise your thinking to include how you will heal and how that healing will promote a healthier, more resilient you. (i.e., Post-Traumatic Growth)
6 **Professional Help:** If you have not worked with a qualified trauma therapist, you need to do that, as otherwise this experience will certainly trigger you in ways you may not be able to manage alone. If you worked with a professional and made significant progress and feel you can continue with this exercise, then continue.
7 **Self-Monitor your Anxiety:** Remember the SUDS Scale 0–10, where 0 = no anxiety, 10 = high anxiety. So, what's your SUDS score before starting this exercise? (or any trauma healing exercise). Ok, check your score as you proceed with this exercise. If your score reaches the 7–10 red zone, perhaps take a brief break. Then, when ready, proceed slowly. Check your SUDS score when you have finished to assess change.
8 **Practice Self-Compassion:** Remember, talk to yourself and write a narrative about yourself, articulating in a manner as you might to a dear friend. How might you speak and write to that loved one? I expect you would use a kind, encouraging tone, not a harsh, critical one. Remember, you cannot shame yourself into healthy change.
9 **Physical activity:** Physical exertion and body movement represent key methods that humans use to move stress out of their bodies (McGonigal, 2017; van der Kolk, 2014). So, set a schedule to walk, cycle, jog, swim, or whatever activity you enjoy for 20 minutes at a time, at least four times a week.
10 **Mindfulness:** Represented by regular walking or sitting meditation. Even 5 minutes of meditation can help manage stress and trauma (Levine, 2011).

Narrative Trauma Healing Exercise

Writing about your trauma and subsequent recovery can be a creative, healthy way to rewrite the trauma story and promote healing (Glass et al., 2019; Pennebaker, 2017). I strongly recommend even brief written entries in your Trauma Recovery Journal, as writing down successes has a way of making them more operational and helps with reprocessing and thus lessens our fear and trauma. The entries below are examples of reprocessing trauma, with a fictitious person narratively recounting their auto accident. This is the type of narrative exercise I have assigned trauma clients when they are ready to face their trauma. We discuss the exercise, and when they are ready, they agree to write about it. After they write about the traumatic event (to the best of their memory), they then read it aloud to me in the session. Now, when they read it, I always remind them they can stop anytime if they are feeling overwhelmed or triggered. Sometimes it takes several attempts before clients can read their narration aloud in session. So, write out your version of what healing looks like for you, and when you are ready, read it out loud to yourself.

The Facts Entry

It was a Saturday morning, and I was very excited as I had plans for taking a long hike through the hills above the city. I ate a healthy breakfast of eggs, toast, and hash browns, drank coffee, and then called Jane, a new girlfriend who was joining me on this hike. I left the house around 10:00 AM to pick Jane up at her apartment.

About 15 minutes later, while driving down Civic Avenue, listening to the jazz radio station, my car was suddenly violently blindsided by a truck driver who ran a yellow light. Although I was seriously injured with broken ribs, a broken right leg, and a dislocated shoulder. I was fully conscious, although in considerable pain, before being medicated. The paramedics arrived soon thereafter, and I recall loud sirens and red and blue lights flashing all around.

The paramedics worked quickly on me and put me on a stretcher. The paramedics were calling out my pulse and blood pressure and asking questions such as, "What's your blood type?" I was taken quickly to the nearby hospital's emergency room and prepared for surgery to stop internal bleeding. Due to being concussed, my memories are fragmented, and bits and pieces are missing from my recall of the event. Parts of the accident still seem shrouded in a fog.

Thoughts and Feelings

It was a Saturday morning, and I was looking forward to taking a long hike with my new girlfriend, Jane, through the rolling hills above the city. I was in an upbeat mood, having just completed a large work project. I was particularly excited about having the following week off from work. Monday, I was booked for a flight to visit my family across the country and was thinking of all the fun activities I would have with my family.

Before leaving, I ate breakfast and drank a cup of coffee, then called Jane to see if she was ready for the long hike. Around 10:15 AM, I was driving on Civic Avenue when a maroon car ran through a yellow caution light and slammed into me. I had no time to react and take defensive maneuvers to avoid the collision. Despite the airbag and seatbelts, the violence of the collision left me with broken ribs, a broken right leg, a dislocated shoulder, and a concussion. The paramedics seemed to arrive very quickly, and there were flashing red and blue lights everywhere. They put me on a stretcher and rushed me to the hospital. I recall the loud siren for the entire journey.

Being concussed, my memories are fragmented, but I recall being wheeled into the ER, placed on an operating table, and hearing snatches of medical terms from doctors and nurses while wondering if I was going to die due to internal bleeding. Several hours later, however, I awoke in the recovery room. A kind-looking nurse informed me I made it through surgery in good standing and was expected to make a full recovery. I recall feeling very confident in the presence of this kind, hopeful woman.

Now I am well on the road to recovery, as physical therapy has helped me regain my complete leg strength. My ribs are no longer sore, and I have begun hiking again now that the cast is off my leg. I remain very fearful of traffic, especially when I am in the vicinity of Civic Avenue, where the accident occurred.

Final Draft: The Worst Moments

I was so shocked and disoriented right after the accident. I was in great pain from numerous broken ribs and my leg. I knew I had internal bleeding and wondered if the ambulance would get to me in time. I kept thinking of my family and how I would get word to them or how they might cope if I were to die from my injuries. When the paramedics arrived, I was struck by their focused, professional manner. Yet, something also bothered me; it was as if I were just another person in trouble for them. I suppose it was like an assembly line for them; I was just the latest broken toy that needed repair.

The Concluding Paragraph

Now I am in recovery mode. Physical therapy has helped me rebuild strength in my damaged leg. I remain fearful of traffic, especially when driving, but I am making progress. For a few months, I refused to even ride in a car and took the train to work. Through work with a trauma counselor, my SUDS score regarding the accident has dropped from a 10 score to a 3. Driving seems safe again, and I am gradually inching closer to driving on Civic Avenue, where the accident occurred. The panicked thoughts and hyperventilation have ceased after several sessions, and my life seems normal again. My counselor believes that I will be ready to drive on Civic Avenue very soon.

Writing can be an innovative, creative method of healing one's trauma. By engaging in this narrative exercise, trauma survivors can gain a deeper understanding of their trauma and its impact, develop effective coping strategies, and begin to facilitate the healing and recovery process (Pennebaker, 2017). What my former clients have expressed regarding narrative approaches to therapy is that they control the narrative, especially concerning how healing their trauma experience(s) has helped them become an emotionally stronger person. One former client remarked, "I sure as hell would never have wanted to be raped. No one would. However, my recovery from this awful, traumatic experience has helped me become a stronger person and a really strong advocate for victims' rights."

Suggestion: How I Have Showed Courage

This workbook, and all similar books, represent ongoing training and practice models on healing trauma. No question, it is unfair that you have been hurt, wounded, and traumatized, whether it be a single event like an automobile accident or ongoing trauma represented by childhood sexual and domestic abuse. My experience as a longtime trauma counselor-therapist, clinical supervisor, international trainer, consultant, and professor of counseling is that survivors seldom give themselves credit for surviving and moving through their trauma history into healing. My experience is that self-compassion also involves acknowledging our strengths and personal growth, especially when it involves post-traumatic growth. Given that so much of this workbook involves narrative self-reflection on the reader's part, I encourage you to complete the following narrative exercise.

Ways I Have Demonstrated Courage

List the ways you have demonstrated courage in surviving, healing your trauma, and even thriving due to the personal growth you have made:

I have demonstrated personal courage by (list three ways or more)

1 ____

2 ____

3 ____

In writing in your Trauma Healing Journal, list as many ways you can think of. *This is not a time to be modest*, but rather for you to unabashedly brag about your courage, tenacity, resilience, determination, and utter refusal to let trauma define and rule your life. Then, when you finish your courage list, write a letter to yourself praising you for your courage, being a positive role model, and becoming a stronger person. I am reminded again of the Japanese term "kintsugi." It literally translates to "golden joinery" and involves mending the broken pieces with lacquer and then highlighting the repair with gold, silver, or platinum. So, let's write our Kintsugi Letter. Below is an example of how you might write your Kintsugi Letter:

Dear Self:

I am writing you this letter because I know you've been through a lot with your trauma and subsequent recovery. I know there have been times when you felt lost, scared, and alone, and when you blamed yourself for what could not have been your fault. I want you to know, however, that I see you, understand you, and that I love you, even when it seems otherwise.

I'm sorry for the times I let you down, the harsh words I spoke to you, and not always believing in your resilience. I'm sorry for the pain and guilt you carried and for the times I didn't offer you the love and support you deserved.

Most important of all, I'm incredibly proud of you. You've demonstrated incredible courage, resilience, and emotional strength, even when life seemed overwhelming. You've overcome challenges that would have broken many others, and yet you're still here, still growing, and still learning.

I want you to know that you are worthy of love, kindness, and forgiveness. I encourage you to forgive yourself for past mistakes and to release the shame and guilt that you've been harboring for so long. You did the best you could have under the circumstances, given the knowledge and resources you had at the time.

Moving forward, I promise to be kinder to you. I will be a better listener, validating your feelings and celebrating your successes, both large and small. I will prioritize your well-being and nurture your spirit.

I believe in your ability to heal your trauma, move into post-traumatic growth, and be an example to others of the possibility of healing. I believe in your ability to create a life filled with meaning and purpose. Most importantly, I want us to travel this journey together.

With all the love and support,

Yourself

Yourself.

This letter is just an example of how a courageous letter to yourself might be written (and a love letter to yourself). So, write your letter and adapt it to your specific needs and experiences. Be as specific as needed and make sure you give yourself credit for the hard work and growth you have made in your healing.

Lessons Learned

Use your Trauma Recovery Journal to answer these questions:

1 The most important intervention or concept I learned from this chapter is ________________________________.

2 The most important lesson I have learned regarding healing from my trauma is ________________________________.

3 The technique or intervention that seemed most helpful was ________________________________.

4 The most difficult exercise in this chapter was ________________________________.

5 The most challenging part of my healing journey has been ________________________________.

6 The most uplifting part of my healing journey so far is ________________________________.

5 Managing Trauma When It Arises

The title of this chapter is a bit unusual as every chapter in this workbook is about managing or coping with trauma's aftereffects. No question, there is also overlapping information between the chapters, but some degree of repetition is likely unavoidable and helps habituate new interventions to manage trauma triggers. As I mentioned in Chapter 1, there are many exercises in this workbook, and some will seem more applicable to you than others. While I encourage you to complete as many of the exercises as possible, I realize that would take considerable time and effort. Once again, if you need to take a break anytime while proceeding through the chapters, please feel free to do just that. Taking your time to complete the exercises and then reflecting on what you have learned about your trauma and healing is likely wise.

Procrastination

Everyone procrastinates, no exceptions. Successful people, however, do not procrastinate indefinitely. They plan to address the issue and then act on that plan. My own experience, both personally and in counseling traumatized clients, is that procrastination can be therapeutic, provided one does not delay addressing their trauma for too long. Thus, this chapter will focus on managing procrastination, breaking up traumatic memories and triggers into smaller, more manageable parts, and the use of self-reflective exercises to assist you in being successful in moving through recovery. Everything in this workbook, and specifically this chapter, is about helping you to be at least 1% healthier (or 10%, 20%, etc.).

People avoid dealing with their responsibilities for various reasons. My experience is that writing down ways to address issues of concern helps us plan to deal with whatever responsibilities we need to deal with. As a trauma counselor, my approach is for clients to practice in session to be able to manage for the rest of the week when they are not in session. The reasons actors, musicians, dancers, athletes, and others practice are so that they will be more prepared when following through with desired behavior matters. The reality is that the more you practice addressing and dealing with your triggers, the

DOI: 10.4324/9781003689232-5

more effective you will be in managing, and later possibly, eliminating them. Perhaps even more important, your anxiety (fear) will be lessened each time you face that fear.

Okay, so let's practice breaking overwhelming tasks into smaller tasks. Naturally, use your Trauma Recovery Journal to scribe in:

One traumatic trigger I have been avoiding is:

____.

The reason I have been procrastinating on addressing this trigger is:

____.

One way I could begin to address this trigger is through

____.

The supports I need to address this trigger are (list all that are major):

____.

What is the scariest part of addressing this trigger?

____.

If I could address managing the smallest part of this trigger, I would be doing:

____.

Albert Ellis, the rational emotional behavior therapy (REBT) founder, believed that people were not afraid of addressing, say, their trauma triggers, but were instead fearful *of the idea* of addressing their trauma triggers. If you find you agree with this statement, what makes facing the idea of your trauma triggers so difficult?

____

____

The Miracle Question

The Miracle Question is a technique developed by Steve deShazer (2010), co-founder of Solution-Focused Therapy. I have used this question extensively in therapy, as I find it helps clients focus on a future time when the struggles they are having with triggers, anxiety, depression, etc., are not a problem.

The Miracle Question: Imagine that tonight, while you are asleep, a miracle occurs, and as a result, the issues that have plagued you regarding trauma triggers, anxiety, nightmares, etc., are no longer a problem. What would you notice being different about your life? What might others notice that is different about your life? How might you help make the miracle a reality? In your Trauma Recovery Journal, write a brief paragraph addressing this miracle using the previous questions as a guide.

Separating a Traumatic Memory into Smaller Sections

Procrastinating on addressing traumatic or unpleasant experiences may provide short-term relief, but over time, the anxiety worsens (Meichenbaum, 2014). An additional complication with avoiding behavior is that it is reinforcing, and thus, you begin to avoid more often. An extreme example of this is people with agoraphobia (AKA shut-ins), as they fear leaving their home due to uncertainty beyond their abode. Treatment of agoraphobia involves systematic desensitization, whereby the patient/client is exposed to the stressor by degrees, beginning with the least disturbing thought, then working up the phobia hierarchy (Meichenbaum, 2014).

Select a traumatic memory that is no greater than a 5 of 10 on the SUDS scale. For example, your boss says to you, "We need to talk about some things. Can you see me at 1:00 PM?" You expect to be fired, but it turns out the boss just needed to ask basic questions about staffing. (Note: This type of anxiety issue is one that many clients have recounted in session.)

What preceded the traumatic event:

____

____

Regarding the traumatic event, what is the first thing you recall?

____

____

During the event, what were your thoughts about what was happening?

____

____

What happened next?

____

____

What happened after that?

____

____

How did the event end?

____

____

What are the most important facts about the event?

____

____

What thoughts were you having during the event?

____

____

What were you feeling during the event?

____

____

What thoughts do you have about it now?

____

____

What feelings do you have about it now?

____

____

What ongoing impact has this event had on your life?

____

____

What significant lessons have you learned about this event by completing this exercise?

____

____

The Purpose of a Traumatic Memory

If you are reading this workbook, you have likely experienced a trauma, perhaps even been diagnosed with PTSD. As you have just addressed how to break traumatic memories into smaller parts, it is also wise to consider what function traumatic memories play. On the surface, this previous sentence seems odd. You might be thinking, "Traumatic memories play the role of making me miserable!" While you likely feel a good deal of discomfort regarding memories of your trauma, evolution has shaped your brain in a manner that trauma memories serve a concrete purpose. The brain's early warning system, the hippocampus and the amygdala, activates our early warning system to help us survive (for example, in prehistoric times, to escape something like a saber-toothed cat). Those traumatic memories were likely to remind us of the danger. Unfortunately, fear can become generalized to overreacting to a perceived threat, even if that threat exists only in our minds. (i.e., the boss says, "Let's talk at 1:00 PM." You get all anxious only to discover she offers you a promotion.)

What I treated clients with PTSD, I coached them via the Marsha Linehan philosophical approach (2015), meaning they are having a normal reaction (trauma memories) to an abnormal experience (e.g., auto accident, sexual assault, robbery at gunpoint). Like in a previous chapter where I recounted working with a client having trauma nightmares, the nightmares were saying to him, "Pay attention and heal me!" Your traumatic memories are telling you, "You need to heal your trauma."

Self-talk Regarding a Traumatic Memory

Suzi was sexually assaulted by a boyfriend during her freshman year of college. Her boyfriend claimed she gave consent by entering his room with him after a date. Suzi is having a mishmash of conflicting emotions, questioning whether she sent mixed messages and buying into her ex-boyfriend's narrative. She feels guilty and has frequent flashbacks about the assault but remains confused regarding culpability, given her jumble of emotions. She decides to seek counseling after an experience at the campus bookstore when she is triggered by watching a movie where a woman is raped by her boyfriend. She ends up running from the movie theater, crying, and then having a panic attack before calling a close female friend, who comes to spend the night with her.

Rescripting and Revising the Dominant Narrative

Narrative therapy uses a technique called rescripting and revising (White, 2007). In rescripting, the therapist and the client deconstruct Suzi's dominant narrative that she was somewhat to blame for being raped and revise the script. Her therapist explains that in narrative therapy, the survivor is not the problem; the problem is the problem (i.e., rape and rapist). In revising, the client, Suzi, rewrites the script to be more realistic. Here's her revised narrative:

"During the first term of my freshman year of college, I had my first boyfriend. He was cute and seemed nice, and we began dating. After a few dates, we went to see a movie on campus. We went back to his room afterwards, had a couple of drinks, and began kissing. Things progressed pretty far, but I told him I did not want to have sex. He persisted, however, and pinned me and raped me. He covered my mouth with his hand, and there was nothing I could do. When I said, "You raped me!" he was full of denials, expressing that since I entered his room to make out, I must have wanted it. I felt so guilty and confused. I began to be afraid of dating and turned down other guys who asked me out.

"My counseling experience has helped me understand I was buying into society's dominant script that if I were raped by my boyfriend, I must have wanted it. My ex-boyfriend and the rape were the problem, not going into his room, not having two alcoholic drinks, and not me owing him because he paid for the movie. I am now exploring options, judicial and otherwise, including becoming a counselor to help other survivors rewrite their guilt scripts and to provide advocacy. I feel much healthier now that I have realized that societal male power and control of women are the problem, not me."

Now, in your Trauma Healing Journal, write out the dominant narrative that has kept you feeling anxious, depressed, or otherwise sad. Then, revise and rescript that narrative into one that is more realistic and healthier (as in Suzi's story above).

The Problem with Dissociation

Bessel van der Kolk (2015) recounts vivid examples of dissociation in his popular book on trauma. Through actual examples (using pseudonyms), he cites numerous examples of dissociation, primarily through sexual abuse. In many examples, well-intentioned people accidentally trigger those with PTSD, resulting in sometimes shocking behavior on the part of the traumatized person. Dissociation, as previously noted, is a method of protecting oneself from perceived threat and injury (Herman, 1992).

Dissociation is a survival strategy imprinted in our brains since prehistoric times. The more severe your trauma (i.e., long-term sexual abuse), the more likely you are to dissociate. Dissociation can also be based on boredom, enjoyment, fantasy, an escape from mundane circumstances, etc. For example, during a boring meeting, do you daydream? (Most people do!) In general, how often do you use your imagination as an escape? Have you ever watched a film and then realized you couldn't recall significant details? These examples all represent examples of dissociation, although not due to trauma. Dissociation is a normal response to undesirable circumstances, be those circumstances traumatic (abuse), boredom (dull meeting), or an uninteresting movie (just blanking out).

When I Dissociate

In your Trauma Recovery Journal, cite four situations that trigger you to dissociate:

1 ____

2 ____

3 ____

4 ____

How We Can Manage Dissociation

Now that we have established that dissociation is common, the next step in the process is to understand when and why we dissociate. As you have gotten this far in the workbook, you have read a lot about trauma triggers. Coming to understand triggers and how to manage triggers can be very helpful in preventing or stopping dissociation. For example, several examples of grounding techniques were offered in a previous chapter (e.g., 5 senses, clapping hands, stomping feet, holding sacred object). Grounding exercises can help you stop dissociation.

The stop and rewind technique is a popular intervention used in trauma therapy to reduce the emotional impact of traumatic memories. It involves visualizing the traumatic event from a detached perspective and then rapidly "rewinding" the memory in one's mind. This process is believed to help reconsolidate memory fragments, decrease emotionality, and reduce or alleviate PTSD symptoms (Muss, 1991). Here's how the stop and rewind intervention works:

1 **Safe Space Visualization:** The therapist helps the client create a mental image of a safe and calming place. (or use a visualization the client has previously created)
2 **Film Analogy:** The client imagines watching a movie about their traumatic event, starting before the event occurred and ending after it's over.
3 **Rewinding:** The client then imagines themselves as a character in the movie, rapidly rewinding through the event from the end to the beginning.
4 **Replaying:** This process of watching and rewinding may be repeated multiple times, potentially at different speeds, until the memory evokes less emotional distress.
5 **Future Rehearsal:** If the trauma involves a future situation (e.g., driving, heights, dating), the client may imagine themselves confidently navigating that situation.

Behaviors Resulting from Untreated Dissociation

There are many consequences of untreated dissociation. Here are some of the common ones:

1 Blunted affect and finding little pleasure in activities that formerly provided enjoyment.
2 Thinking errors, like all-or-nothing thinking (i.e., all is wonderful, or everything is awful, or "I am a complete loser," despite ample evidence to the contrary).
3 A shame-oriented view of oneself, manifested in negative thoughts regarding oneself (e.g., "I am a bad person," "I am ugly," "I am dumb").
4 Withdrawal from close social contacts.
5 Sense of lethargy (feeling constantly weary).
6 Sense of physical and emotional numbness.
7 Compassion fatigue, or the inability to care about people and social situations (e.g., homelessness, poverty, crime victims) that one previously cared about.
8 A sense of emotional burnout, resulting in lethargy, blunted affect, numbness, sleep disturbance, etc.

How many of these symptoms have you experienced because of ongoing dissociation? No question, you may have needed to dissociate to survive whatever trauma(s) you needed to survive. The problem is that dissociation can become a primary coping response and lead to personal difficulties as problematic as the trauma itself (van der Kolk, 2015).

During high school, I was a passenger in a vehicle that was involved in an accident. I was riding in the back seat of the car, with my brother in the front passenger seat and a friend at the wheel. Suddenly, a semi-truck ran a stop sign and was rapidly approaching to T-bone us. Fortunately, the driver saw it happening and immediately turned us into the ditch, saving us from serious injury or worse. During this harrowing experience, it seemed everything had slowed down in some surreal, cinematographic manner, as if I were in a movie theater watching a scene from a film. While I was wearing my lap belt (it was the late 1970s), my head struck the window hard, leaving me dazed. Somehow, I cannot recall how I managed to extract myself from the damaged vehicle and hold a conversation with a police officer, although I have no memory of this. Now, my response was likely the combination of concussion and dissociation. Later, in conversation with my brother, who had been riding in the front seat, I began to recall fragments of before and after the accident. Interestingly, my brother had more anxiety in the accident's aftermath, while I experienced far more emotional numbness. Years later, while a graduate student in a counseling program studying traumatic experiences, I learned my experience was relatively common. Interestingly, I did not experience any residual fear of driving or riding in motor vehicles, something I attribute to my fragmented memory. However, my brother did experience what was likely an acute stress disorder (under 30 days). Fortunately, he recovered fully, eventually becoming a paramedic and regularly dealing with many automobile accidents over a 40-year career and saving many lives.

Ways I Avoid Potential Trauma

As we have seen, dissociation is a common trauma coping mechanism but can lead to ongoing difficulties. Put a check mark by all the behaviors you use to avoid potential trauma.

___ Stare blankly into space
___ A general sense of confusion and disorientation
___ Regularly escape into daydreaming
___ Separate myself from my body
___ Feeling like I am watching myself from outside my body
___ Regularly avoid social situations of even minor conflict
___ Feeling like you are acting on autopilot
___ Feeling detached from the world around you
___ Significant memory gaps regarding any upsetting experience

Now, put a check mark beside any of the arousal and/or behavioral responses in the list:

___ Difficulty concentrating
___ Regularly body jerking upon awakening
___ Your blood pressure and pulse are elevated when facing any conflict
___ Using alcohol or other drugs to cope with trauma memories
___ Feeling confused much of the time
___ Engaging in risk-taking activities you might have avoided pre-trauma
___ Engaging in compulsive behaviors (e.g., how you walk, objects needing to be in particular places, counting and checking)
___ Ongoing nightmares (violent themes, being chased, being persecuted)
___ Repetitive self-soothing behaviors such as rocking back and forth, rubbing legs, arms, etc.

In your Trauma Recovery Journal, describe how, when, and where you use these ways to avoid or dissociate.

____

____

What do your answers suggest to you regarding how you avoid traumatic experiences or memories of your trauma(s)?

____

____

Addressing Trauma-Related Dissociation

Once again, your dissociative responses to trauma were adaptive during and in the aftermath of the trauma and helped you survive. However, as previously noted, dissociating and avoiding behaviors can become troublesome and almost as problematic as the trauma itself (van der Kolk, 2015). Below are some basic strategies to help reduce avoidance. After each strategy, write in your Trauma Recovery Journal how you used this strategy and how this strategy has been helpful to you.

1 To reduce avoidance behaviors, identify the trauma memory or trigger. You do not need to go into excessive detail, just simple identification.
   A significant trauma trigger of mine is: ______________________
   ____.
2 How I go about avoiding this trigger is: ______________________.
3 To address trigger memories, I can engage in safe, enjoyable activities like the following:
   ____.

4 Having read about mindfulness-based activities in earlier chapters, I can use them (e.g., box breathing, meditation, EFT/Meridian Tapping, My Safe Space Visualization, etc.)

Cite 2–3 such activities: ______________________________.

5 For readers currently working with a therapist, you likely have been taught to use prolonged exposure to manage trauma triggers, anxiety, memories, etc., by breaking down the trauma into smaller, more manageable segments. Remember, proceed slowly, as any improvement is improvement:

(**Note:** If you have not worked with a therapist, I recommend you do so before trying this step.)

____

____

Facing Your Most Common Triggers

In your Trauma Recovery Journal, list the five triggers you attempt to avoid most often. Start by listing the most disturbing triggers (or most feared), then list the least common or feared triggers.

1 ______________________________

2 ______________________________

3 ______________________________

4 ______________________________

5 ______________________________

In the following exercise, select three strategies/interventions you can use on each of these triggers to manage the pain or desire to avoid them. For example, if you are triggered by the smell of a particular deodorant, cologne, or aftershave your abuser wore, you might:

9 Buy that same aftershave, deodorant, or cologne and spray or apply it to something you like (like a favorite blanket, sweatshirt, towel) to change your association with that smell. Repeat and track your decreasing SUDS score (1–10 scale, with 10 being high and 1 being low on discomfort).

10 Buy a bottle of that cologne, aftershave, or deodorant and gradually smell it as you also hold a special or sacred object. Repeat and track your SUDS score as with the previous items.

11 When your SUDS score is regularly 3 or below, buy a bottle of the cologne, aftershave, or deodorant and smash the bottle or crush the deodorant. (This might also be a type of reward for the progress you have made.)

Addressing the Triggers That Lead to Avoidance

Identify three actions that help you manage each of your avoidance triggers. Complete this exercise using your Trauma Recovery Journal:

Trigger 1. ____

a ____

b ____

c ____

Trigger 2. ____

a ____

b ____

c ____

Trigger 3. ____

a ____

b ____

c ____

Trigger 4. ____

a ____

b ____

c ____

Trigger 5. ____

a ____

b ____

c ____

Now that you have listed possible actions you can take to manage your triggers, start at the bottom of your list (Trigger 5) and do what you have written. Work on that trigger. (Record in your Trauma Recovery Journal)

Write what happened when you did what you said would work on trigger 5?

____

____

Now, repeat the above with Triggers 4 and 3. Eventually, you will go all the way up to Trigger 1. Now, in your Trauma Recovery Journal, write out what this exercise has taught you about your triggers and the power they have over you. Then, write how you have taken back that power by engaging in this exercise (and other exercises in this text).

____

____

What I Have Learned about Dissociation

What have you learned about yourself and dissociation by completing the previous exercises? What are your dissociative triggers and avoidance behaviors? Through using this chapter (and workbook), what progress have you made in identifying, managing, and addressing dissociative behaviors? As usual, record these in your Trauma Recovery Journal:

____

____

Self-injurious Behaviors (SIBs) and Ways to Reduce and Stop Them

Perhaps the most concerning trauma-related behaviors are self-injurious behaviors (SIBs). SIBs are a set of non-suicidal self-injurious behaviors involving deliberately harming one's own body, such as by cutting or burning oneself. This type of self-injury is a harmful method of coping with emotional pain, anger, sadness, isolation, and numbness. While self-injury may bring about a temporary sense of relief from physical and emotional tension, it is usually followed by guilt, shame, and the return of painful, traumatic memories. SIBs are usually non-suicidal, but it's possible they can escalate into fatal self-harming, so learning to manage and eliminate them is very important.

Symptoms of SIBs Can Include

1 Scars, often in patterns.
2 Fresh cuts, scratches, bruises, bite marks, or other wounds.
3 Using a match, lighter, or other instrument to burn the skin.
4 Keeping sharp items used for self-injury on hand.
5 Wearing long sleeves or long pants to hide self-injury, even during summer months.
6 Frequent reports of accidental injury.
7 Behaviors and emotions that change quickly and are impulsive, intense, and unexpected.
8 Difficulties in relationships with others.
9 Talk of helplessness, hopelessness, or worthlessness.

Forms of Self-injury

10 Cutting, scratching, or stabbing with a sharp object are common methods.
11 Burning with lit matches, cigarettes, or heated, sharp objects such as knives.
12 Carving words or symbols on the skin.
13 Self-hitting, punching, biting, or head banging.
14 Piercing the skin with sharp objects.
15 Inserting objects under the skin.

Treatment for SIBs

Years ago, I treated a young adult who likely had experienced the worst form of traumatic experience imaginable. When she was 12, she was kidnapped and kept in captivity as a sex slave for 5 years. She was held in a dank basement with only basic food and water essentials. Each evening, she was sexually violated by her captor. During these horrible years, she informed me she kept hope alive by two thoughts: one, as a girl raised in a religious household, she prayed daily and talked to God. Secondly, she vowed that one day she would escape and then make her captor pay for his crimes. As her captor believed he had total control over her, he began to take her on outings. Amy (pseudonym) bided her time, her mind preparing for an escape. Then, while having lunch with her captor at a fast-food restaurant, she informed her captor that she needed to use the restroom. Her captor, believing he had total control, allowed her to walk to the restroom alone. However, she quickly diverted into the kitchen and informed the manager regarding her situation, whereupon he called the police, who arrived quickly and arrested the man. Later, she testified against him in court. He was convicted and given a long, well-deserved prison sentence.

She came to therapy with me on the recommendation of her foster mother, who knew me through my work and who was adopting Amy. I offered her a female therapist, but she stated a preference to work with me, trusting her foster mom. Amy proved to be an incredibly motivated, focused client, determined that she would heal her trauma. She acknowledged struggling with dissociation (very understandable!) and SIBs. She would cut herself with a sharp knife, stating it relieved the pressure but also left her feeling ashamed and defeated, two feelings she loathed. She disclosed being triggered by a certain cologne or deodorant her captor wore. She reported it was a popular deodorant and aftershave. I explained prolonged exposure, which she was aware of from previous therapy. Obtaining that aftershave, I gradually exposed her to it. I offered that anytime she felt her anxiety was in the 7–10 SUDS scale range, for her to say "Stop!" I also collaborated with her on healthy behaviors to replace the SIBs (and to give up cutting) and to check in with her foster mom, a very supportive middle-aged woman. Over something like 12 weeks, Amy met every treatment goal, including significant dissociation reduction and elimination of SIBs. I was then able to get her into a PTSD support group that the clinic ran, and she was a faithful attendee.

Now, Amy's story took far more work than what is recounted above, given her trauma triggers and self-loathing remained with her long after her escape. Key factors in her healing were her self-fulfilling belief in her ability to heal and her future goal of becoming a therapist and treating PTSD victims like herself, especially those traumatized by sexual violence. Thus, Amy had clear, tangible reasons for wanting to heal, and her foster mother provided the day-to-day emotional support she had previously lacked. There is little question that Amy's motivations and the newfound support and encouragement at home were critical assets in her healing work with me.

My Self-injurious Behaviors

Now, if you have not worked on SIBs with a therapist, I suggest you do that before trying this exercise. If you have completed therapy, use this exercise to continue to be free of SIBs. As always, use your Trauma Recovery Journal:

1 I engage in (or previously engaged in) the following SIBs due to anger, frustration, anxiety, or numbness:

____

____

2 Healthy behaviors I have/or could substitute for the above SIBs are (e.g., delaying behavior by taking a walk, checking in with a trusted person, meditating, or praying, wrapping yourself in a cozy blanket, listening to soothing music, box breathing, doing yoga poses):

____

____

3 Expressing Yourself: Sometimes, especially in trauma recovery, memories and emotions can seem overwhelming. While not an exhaustive list, I have used the following with clients in trauma recovery: writing a healing journal, writing poetry on healing pain, painting on healing trauma, creating a healing collage, singing, chanting, and playing a musical instrument. Now, what creative expressive outlets have you used to help heal trauma pain and refrain from self-abuse:

____

____

4 Physical exercise is an effective method of addressing stress and anxiety. Examples are swimming, walking, jogging, dancing, cycling, and yoga.

What are your three go-to physical activities to manage self-abuse urges, anxiety, or stress? List in your Trauma Recovery Journal:

a ______________________________, b ______________________________,
c ______________________________

5 Should you relapse and start self-abusing, you need to return to therapy. Should you begin feeling hopeless and/or in crisis (i.e., suicide), please call your local crisis line or the national hotline 988. Remember, everyone needs support at times, and it takes strength to admit we need help and even more courage to make that call for assistance. As a young undergraduate who was struggling across the board, going to counseling certainly turned my life around (and who knows, may have saved it!).

Remember: The urge to relapse and engage in self-abuse is a temporary one. That's why you need a go-to plan like the one above. Make sure you have a written go-to plan to delay and stop SIB behavior. Should you relapse, practice self-compassion statements and behaviors like, "Relapse happens, but I can re-enter treatment and stop SIBs"; "Trauma recovery is a marathon, not a sprint, and takes much time and work"; "I am proud of the healing work I have accomplished, but there is more room for growth, and I will grow and heal fully in time." Compassionate self-talk is critical to keeping yourself from engaging in harsh self-statements and judgments. Just as with people who are quitting smoking, there is that occasional strong, albeit brief urge to light up. However, interrupting that urge by calling a friend, taking a walk, box breathing, etc., can help keep you safe until that urge passes, and it will pass.

Prolonged Exposure Therapy (PET)

Prolonged exposure therapy is an efficacious treatment approach for PTSD that helps clients process traumatic memories and reduce avoidance behaviors (Foa & McLean, 2016). The core thesis is that the brain has learned to associate sounds, sights, smells, tactile sensations, etc., with the danger of past trauma. PET helps clients gradually and safely begin confronting their triggers until the brain learns they are no longer dangerous. In PET, there are two general approaches to exposing the client to their triggers.

Types of Exposure

Imaginal exposure is the first type and involves repeatedly recalling and describing the traumatic event in detail to a trained therapist to process the memories and emotions associated with the trauma.

Steps in Imaginal Exposure

1 The client verbally recounts the feared event or memory in detail, including what they saw, felt, and thought, for an extended session (30–50 minutes).

2 The client usually recounts the traumatic experience in the present time for more engagement with the experience.
3 The goal is to fully engage with the emotional and sensory aspects of the trauma memory to diminish the fear response over time (extinction).
4 The therapist guides the process, asking questions to help the client stay focused on the emotions that arise, as opposed to avoiding them, to facilitate healing insights and reduce anxiety.
5 The therapist provides support and encouragement, asking for any needed details, and supportive language ("I am here with you," "You are getting stronger," etc.).

The second type is called **in vivo exposure** and involves gradually approaching and confronting feared situations, objects, people, and activities. For example, for someone who avoids crowded places after a traumatic experience, a therapist might suggest they visit a busy shopping center at a non-peak time, eventually progressing the client to more crowded shopping periods.

In Vivo Exposure

1 The therapist creates a phobia (fear) hierarchy with the client, from least to most frightening.
2 The therapist has the client confront the least anxiety-provoking situations on the list.
3 The therapist repeats the process, gradually moving up the hierarchy to more fearful situations, as the client becomes gradually less frightened. (SUDS scale 0–10).

The ultimate goal of PET is to assist clients in functioning normally again by processing traumatic memories and diminishing the fear and anxiety associated with trauma-related triggers. By confronting these memories and anxiety-provoking situations in a systematic, safe, therapeutic way, the overwhelming fear gradually subsides, allowing the client to move forward with their lives.

Case Example: Imaginal Exposure

Jenny is a 35-year-old earthquake survivor and has been experiencing PTSD symptoms for three years. Jenny consistently avoided thoughts and images related to the carnage she had experienced in the earthquake. To help fill the gap, she began spending an increasing amount of time at work and isolating at home to reduce anxiety-provoking situations.

Jenny worked hard to fill her time with various obligations at work, meaning long hours, while at home, reading numerous books and watching comedies to keep herself calm. She also worked hard to convince coworkers and herself that the earthquake had not affected her emotionally. Over time, however, she began having nightmares, causing her to lose valuable sleep each night.

A friend recommended she consult a therapist to address the nightmares, but she feared confronting her traumatic memories would send her into a panic attack. The avoidance of her traumatic memories only worsened them.

Jenny eventually sought treatment from a therapist specializing in trauma treatment. First, the therapist informed Jenny about the SUDS scale, with 10 as very high anxiety. He informed her to say "Stop!" anytime she felt overwhelmed, which he suggested would be in the score range of 7–10. He also taught her box breathing and explained simple grounding exercises of clapping hands, stomping feet, and the 5-senses grounding. Her therapist put her through several sessions of imagined exposure, where she provided a detailed account of what she witnessed during the earthquake. The therapist prompted her to begin at the point of the earthquake and describe where she was during the earthquake, who she was with, and what she was thinking and feeling. With each recounting, the therapist asked Jenny to provide more sensory and emotional details about the experience to decrease her anxiety related to confronting the experience. By facing her traumatic memories, Jenny's fear began to significantly decrease. Her SUDS score dropped from an initial 10 score in session one to a 2 score after five sessions. Her nightmares eventually stopped, and she began to socialize with friends again.

The second example illustrates using in vivo exposure therapy with a client.

Case Example: In Vivo Exposure

Juan is a 25-year-old graduate student at the University of the West Coast. During his first semester, he was robbed at knifepoint in the train station at the edge of campus. Although he survived the ordeal without physical injury, he began to experience traumatic memories and developed severe anxiety. Previously an excellent student, he began skipping classes and isolating in his apartment. His academic advisor noticed his absences and intervened, referring Juan to a therapist at the University Counseling Center. The therapist recommended a treatment protocol of gradual exposure. Juan is initially hesitant, as he does not want to face his traumatic memories. The therapist explains they will practice in the therapy room, and when Juan feels ready, the therapist will accompany him to the train station where the robbery occurred. The therapist explains to Juan that when he (Juan) feels the anxiety is too high, he is to say, "Stop!" He also illustrates grounding techniques like box breathing, 5 senses, stomping feet, holding a special object, and the like.

In the first role-play, Juan's SUDS score is 10. During the 50-minute session, the therapist and Juan did three role-plays. In the first one, Juan stops the role-play at the station. In the second, he gets up to the robber pulling out the knife. In the third role-play, Juan hands over his money. Juan's score has dropped to 7, and while the score is still high, the therapist encourages and praises Juan for his success. In session two, Juan begins at 9, and after three role-plays where he completes the entire traumatic reenactment, his SUDS score drops to 5. Juan feels noticeably more confident. In session three, Juan begins at 5, and after three role-plays, his SUDS score is down to 2. The therapist inquires if Juan is ready to visit the train station where the robbery occurred. Juan hesitates but then says yes. The therapist has Juan meet him at the Counseling Center, and they walk over to the train station. When the train station is visible, Juan says his SUDS score is 10. The therapist inquired if Juan would like to stop or continue. Juan hesitates and then decides to continue, and they get to the platform where the robbery occurred when Juan asks to leave the site. The therapist praises Juan for getting so far so quickly. They plan to try again in the following session. In the next session, Juan begins with a 9 SUDS score. However, while he must stop twice, he makes it to the platform where the robbery occurred. He looks around and then explains where the robbery occurred. He reports a SUDS score of 5, smiles, and tells the therapist he'll ride the same train tomorrow. He successfully does this, with a SUDS score of 2. Juan then has a last session with the therapist, where the therapist and Juan recount his success.

Prolonged Exposure Caution

Now, once again, if you have been traumatized and have not worked with a trained therapist, do not try this next exercise on your own. My experience with PET is that it works very well, but it also requires gradually facing your trauma, something I do not recommend you initially do on your own, absent previous treatment. The therapist's presence also provides important emotional and safety support for anyone who is traumatized.

Practice: Prolonged Exposure Therapy

In your Trauma Recovery Journal, answer the following questions regarding your trauma. Use the Imaginal Exposure. (*Remember: only attempt this exercise if you have been through treatment.*)

Imaginal Exposure

Before answering the questions, what is your SUDS score on a 1–10 scale (10 = high)

Pre-SUDS score = ___/10

1 Briefly, but thoroughly describe what happened.
2 Who was there?
3 Where did this occur?
4 When did it occur?
5 Now, review what you have written, either silently or speaking aloud. Repeat 5 times.

Post SUDS score after completion = ___/10

For in vivo exposure: Attempt post-treatment and after completing the previous Imaginal Exposure exercise. Then, I recommend you complete the exercise with a therapist. Or, if you have completed therapy and are continuing to extinguish fear, have a trusted friend accompany you for emotional support and encouragement.

Real-Life Exposure

Pre-SUDS score = ___/10

1 If you were involved in an automobile accident, your friend drives you toward where the accident occurred, monitoring your SUDS score. Starting SUDS score: ____/10.
2 As you come closer to where the accident occurred, use box breathing, meditation, and positive self-talk ("You have come so far…", and "I can take a break and then re-try").
3 You decide that with a SUDS score of 10, to reverse course and talk and get support from your friend. Your friend encourages you, pointing out the progress you have made, and then asks if you would like to continue or try again tomorrow. Your SUDS score has dropped to 7, so you ask to continue.
4 You get to where you can see the street where the accident occurred and ask your friend to turn around. You ask for a 10-minute recess, and then you and your friend recount your progress. Your SUDS score drops to 7 again. You ask your friend to drive you to the place of the accident. Your SUDS score goes to 9, but your friend's gentle, supportive statements of, "I'm right here with you, and you are doing great." You make it to the accident scene and then past it. You and your friend celebrate, as your SUDS score is now 4. You have your friend drive past the accident location four times, and each time your SUDS score drops, eventually ending at a score of 1.

Post SUDS score= ___/10

5 You and your friend go for a delicious lunch together as a reward.

Remember: Any progress you make is progress. It's common and very understandable to stop, take a break, and then keep trying. Make sure you have supportive people in your life to encourage you on your healing journey, as emotional support and encouragement make success more likely. Then, treat yourself to a reward (e.g., lunch, coffee with a friend, favorite ice cream). My strong reminder is that you do not neglect healthy emotional support from trusted family and friends. Isolation from human support is a recipe for disaster. There is a reason, after all, that humans have evolved as social creatures.

The Empty Chair Exercise

The empty-chair technique was developed by Jacob Moreno (2020). Fritz Perls, founder of Gestalt Therapy, was trained by Moreno and adapted the exercise into his approach, and the intervention is often called the Gestalt Empty Chair Exercise (but was originally from psychodrama). In the empty-chair technique, a person speaks to an empty chair as if someone they have unresolved feelings toward were sitting in that chair (or if speaking to their younger or future self, inner critic, etc.). This intervention offers an opportunity to explore and express emotions in a safe, controlled manner, potentially leading to increased self-awareness, emotional growth, and resolution of internal conflicts or relational issues. Typically, a therapist has a client address their unresolved issues to the absent party and then switch chairs and play the role of the absent party.

The empty chair works in the following manner:

1. Identify the absent person: For trauma survivors, this might be the person who hurt you, if you are ready to speak to that person's empty chair—but only if you feel ready. If not, perhaps select someone else you wish to talk with. For example, you might express compassion to your younger self or respect to your future self for the courage to heal. You decide.
2. Setting the scene: Place an empty chair before you, representing the person (parent, abuser, friend, younger/older self, etc.).
3. Begin with the dialogue: Speak to the empty chair, expressing your thoughts, feelings, needs, or whatever needs to be expressed. Take whatever time you need.
4. Switch chairs: Move to the empty chair, taking on the perspective of the non-present person.
5. Respond to the dialogue: Now, respond to your own prior statements as if you were the other person, or if it's your younger or future self.
6. Return to the original chair: Move back to your original chair and verbally reflect on the dialogue and any insights gained.

Empty Chair Example

Jen-Li is an adult survivor of childhood domestic abuse. Her father was physically and verbally violent to her mother. Her mother was then, in turn, physically and verbally violent to Jen-Li and her siblings. In her late twenties, at the suggestion of a friend, she decided to work with a therapist to heal her trauma. Over time and through therapy, she desires to forgive her parents and decides to begin with her mother. After practicing during the session, she informs her therapist that she wants to have an empty-chair conversation with her mother. The therapist sets out an empty chair.

Jen-Li: "Mother, I have been very angry with you for many years. You were very abusive to my siblings and me. You used to slap us around after my dad abused you. You called me awful names and treated me as your punching bag, and I hated you for it." She pauses and tears up. "But I also know you had a lot of pain in your marriage and that dad was a very abusive man. I want to express that while his treatment of you was abusive, that was no reason to hurt your kids. Still, I have learned to hold compassion for you and to tell you that I forgive you. I'm sorry I could not tell you while you were alive…but wanted to say it now."

She nods, and the therapist suggests she switch chairs. Jen-Li takes the chair where her "mother" was sitting.

Jen-Li, as her mother: "I wish that I could take back all the hurtful things I said and did to you and all my kids. I was hurting so badly, and I turned the anger from your father onto you kids. I have no excuse…I am sorry. I am grateful for your forgiveness and wish I were still alive, where we could have a real mother-adult daughter relationship. I did love you but was so wounded I could not properly express it. I also felt that my own dreams were crushed by both your father's and family's expectations. I wanted to go to college and become a teacher, but my parents told me I had to give up my dreams and marry your dad."

In this scenario, the empty-chair dialogue is brief due to space issues. I would also express having observed many empty-chair conversations in my career, and they do not all go so well. I have witnessed raw anger toward the empty chair, animus that the client was unable to express toward their abuser. Yet, even in these more evocative moments, expressing that hurt was necessary in the client's healing journey. I also hold empty-chair conversations with loved ones from my past, including my younger self and future self. I have found these conversations to be both an emotional salve and a practical way to address my hopes, fears, and to fill that void when I am alone and far from home.

The Empty-Chair Technique: Practice

So, let's begin by imagining you speaking to your future self. Your future self is in post-traumatic growth, and you want to take the time to express your love and respect for the courage, persistence, and work you did to reach that desired place. Select a time when you have some privacy and set out two chairs. Then, following the previous directions, speak to your future self for whatever time is necessary. Then, when finished, switch chairs and let your future self-speak directly with you.

Okay, in your Trauma Healing Journal, what did you learn from the empty-chair technique?

____

____

Now, you may decide to speak to your abuser, but the caution is that it can be very emotionally difficult to have that conversation, even in an empty-chair mode. I recommend addressing the abuse issue in therapy before holding an empty-chair conversation with a past or current abuser, as such conversations can be triggering. Before Jen-Li's empty-chair conversation with her abusive mother, for example, she completed counseling with a skilled therapist. Then, feeling she was prepared, she held an empty-chair conversation with her mother. My advice is to put in the therapeutic time and then hold the empty-chair conversation.

Lessons Learned

In your Trauma Recovery Journal, answer the following questions:

1 How have the exercises in this chapter helped you address your triggers?

____

____

____

2 What is the most difficult aspect of facing your trauma?

____

____

3 Who are the people supporting you in your healing journey? (list 3–4)

____

____

4 Steve deShazer's miracle question was mentioned earlier. A variation on it is, "When you are healed, what will your life look like then?" (Or "What does it look like now that you are healed…or healed enough?")

____

____

5 This was a very challenging chapter, as it required directly facing your trauma(s). So, how were you able to gather the courage to face your trauma(s)?

____

____

Remember: Facing trauma requires persistence and a lot of bravery.

6 Regaining Trust and Developing Self-compassion

Negative Beliefs and Self-talk

As humans, we hold personal beliefs about ourselves and others around us. Our beliefs are the way in which we make sense of the world around us and how we make sense of ourselves. Our beliefs can impact on us how we think about ourselves, how we behave, and the choices we make. For survivors of trauma, negative self-talk tends to be very negative, self-denigrating, fearful, and at times, anxious. Aaron Beck's cognitive behavior therapy (CBT) focuses on negative schemas (2019) and Albert Ellis' rational emotional behavior therapy (REBT) on irrational beliefs (2011). Both theorists well understood the link between our self-talk and our well-being and behavior. Basically, the more rational our self-talk, the healthier and better adjusted we are emotionally, cognitively, and in our behavior. My own experience in providing counseling to clients in trauma recovery, dealing with depression, severe anxiety, and stress shows such clients tend toward very negative self-talk. Therefore, it is very important in the healing process that we monitor and revise our self-talk on a regular basis to attain good emotional well-being. If we spoke to others using the type of language we speak to ourselves, we'd likely have no friends. So again, remember to use self-compassion in our inner dialogues.

Beliefs Regarding My Trauma

Ongoing experiences with trauma can impact our identity, worldview, beliefs, health, and sense of meaning and purpose. When meaning and purpose erode, we are vulnerable to depression, anxiety, burnout, and even suicide (Frankl, 2006). People who have experienced significant trauma often come to believe they deserve their trauma ("I had it coming," as one survivor said in session). Thus, self-blame and criticism become some of the more intractable residual beliefs trauma survivors must overcome to heal. Survivors may come to view themselves as damaged, worthless, ugly, and many other unpleasant things. The more we tell ourselves that we are worthless, bad, evil, ugly, etc., the more likely we are to believe it. In this chapter, we will spend a lot of time challenging and revising negative core beliefs.

DOI: 10.4324/9781003689232-6

Your negative schemas guide and organize those negative concepts and result in negative, self-defeating talk. They help to maintain a sense of homeostasis, even if it is an unhealthy balance (Ellis, 2011). Our strongest and most enduring schemas are those that get reinforced regularly. Thus, telling yourself you are ugly and damaged, and then socializing with people (e.g., family, friends, and colleagues) who reinforce these negative schemas, is likely to keep you from healing. Perhaps a key reason the cognitive approaches to counseling are the most efficacious likely lies in the reality that if we change our self-beliefs for the better (through counseling, daily practice, ongoing focus, etc.), we tend to feel better and act more rationally. Negative beliefs about yourself are key to the maintenance of PTSD, just as healthy beliefs and behavior are key to healing trauma (Briere & Scott, 2015).

While healing from trauma requires work (in counseling and on our own), personal support (e.g., family, friends, spiritual support), self-compassion practice, physical activity, cognitive restructuring, etc., the most critical element lies in your belief that healing is possible (Briere & Scott, 2015). As my high school counselor was fond of expressing, "If you think you can, you're right, at least to some extent. If you think you can't, you're absolutely right." So, believe in the possibility of healing, work the steps (counseling, resources like this workbook, emotional support, etc.), and you will heal…at least to some extent. (If you believe you can't heal, you're likely *not reading* this book.)

The Three Cs to Healing Negative Beliefs

Cognitive therapy focuses on noticing unhealthy thoughts/beliefs (catch it), challenging the negative belief ("What's the evidence for the belief?"), and then changing the belief ("The evidence does not support my negative belief"). Because we tend to believe what we tell ourselves, we must evaluate the efficacy of our self-statements. I recall a colleague telling her students, "I do not believe everything I think, and neither should you." On a recent podcast, I heard a Buddhist monk articulate something to the effect that "the mind is a jungle, and I never go in alone." He went on to elaborate that he sought the advice of his teacher and the Buddha to meditate properly and release toxic negativity. This case of Scott illustrates the three Cs below.

The Case of Scott

Scott is a 28-year-old engineer at a large company. He has long struggled with his self-concept, believing he is unattractive. His negative core belief (schema) has its origins in a verbally abusive family where his father, a popular, successful CEO, often expressed that Scott was homely and dim-witted, and voiced that he longed for a son who was a handsome, winner type, as such people are more successful. Consequently, Scott has struggled with depression and anxiety, given that he feels so inadequate. A friend at work eventually suggests to Scott that he might go for therapy. After months of indecision, he finally makes an appointment. After the intake, he is assigned to Katrina, a therapist who explained the three Cs of cognitive therapy. She points out to Scott that his self-talk is very negative and that it is making him depressed and anxious. She explains that when he tells himself, "You're ugly," she wants him to catch that thought, challenge it ("What's the evidence I'm ugly?"), and then change his belief into something more realistic ("Okay, I'm not movie star handsome, but someone will find me attractive"). Katrina assigns him the homework of applying the 3 Cs three times per day between now and the next session.

The following week, Scott returns and reports that he has been doing the homework daily. Katrina inquires how the three Cs' homework has impacted him. He replies that it's been difficult to accept the premise that someone might, for example, find him attractive. Katrina explains that, as he's spent his life believing he's unattractive, it will take time and practice before his negative core belief changes to become more realistic and positive. She spends the session having Scott revise several negative self-statements (e.g., "I'm a loser"). She continues the assignment the following week but suggests he reframe negative self-statements to more healthy, realistic statements three times a day.

In the next session, Scott reports that revising negative statements now feels more natural, as he's been doing it for a week. He admits feeling a little odd, however, that after a lifetime of suffering verbal put-downs from himself and others, the practice still seems a little inauthentic. Katrina continues cognitive revising practice during the session, and Scott makes some progress. For homework, she continues the assignment of having Scott revise five negative self-statements per day.

Next week, Scott comes to the session with a sheepish smile. He offers that he is beginning to believe his revised self-statements and is feeling better. Katrina asks for details, and Scott says, "Maybe I'm becoming more emotionally fit." Katrina offers that becoming cognitively fit is akin to becoming physically fit in that there is no stopping point, explaining that cognitive revision of negative self-statements is a lifetime assignment. Like physical fitness, cognitive-emotional health takes daily, lifelong work.

Cognitive Revision Example (3 Cs)

Catch Your Negative Statement: "I'm dumb."

Challenge it: "I have been promoted at my job, so some people found me capable."

Change it: "Okay, I'm successful and planning to be more so. I reject the dumb label."

Note: My experience is that many clients and others view cognitive reframing as just saying nice things to yourself. While it's true that it involves being more self-compassionate, it's also about checking the evidence for our negative schemas and then revising our self-statements to be more realistic. Just as the food you put into your body impacts your health, what you tell yourself regarding your self-worth will impact your emotional health and well-being. Like physical fitness, emotional fitness and health require a lifetime of work, as there is no stopping point for emotional well-being, just as physical fitness requires ongoing workouts.

3Cs Practice

In your Trauma Healing Journal, consider three common negative self-statements you make and complete the following cognitive revision exercise (three Cs):

Catch Your Negative Self-Statement: ______________________________.

Challenge the Negative Self-Statement: ___________________________.

Change the Negative Self-Statement: ______________________________.

Catch Your Negative Self-Statement: ______________________________.

Challenge it: ____.

Change it: ____.

Catch Your Negative Self-Statement: ______________________________.

Challenge it: ____.

Change it: ____.

Commitment: The Hard Part Exercise

Now, starting day one (today), take the oath: "Starting today, I will begin challenging my negative automatic thoughts three times per day for the rest of my life."

______________________________ ___/___/___

Name Date

People Who Have Betrayed Me: Acknowledging and Releasing Bitterness and Coming to Forgiveness (when you are ready)

Who among us has not been hurt by the actions or inactions of someone? Perhaps a parent constantly criticizing you growing up, a friend who let you down, a colleague who betrayed you, or a spouse or partner who had an affair, or maybe a close family member or friend who abused you. These wounds can leave lasting feelings of resentment, bitterness, and anger, and occasionally even hatred. I have counseled clients in their 60s who held bitterness toward a family member, former friend, or colleague for several decades. Unfortunately, that anger and bitterness will typically end up being turned against oneself to one's own detriment. In my wife's tradition, there's an old Yiddish expression: "Before you embark on a journey of hatred and revenge, dig two graves."

No doubt, some people may well have earned your anger by their actions. However, if you hold onto that pain, you will likely be the one who pays the greater price. You may wish to consider the powerful and difficult act of forgiveness. But what is forgiveness? In my experience, there tends to be a lot of misunderstanding about forgiveness.

What Is Forgiveness?

Forgiveness means different things to different people. However, it typically involves an intentional decision to release the resentment and anger held against a third party. The act that hurt or offended you might always be with you, and in serious issues like sexual abuse, such is understandable. Working on releasing that anger, which people often turn inward, can be a transformational step toward self-healing. Forgiveness is actually about freeing oneself from the bondage of destructive anger and is not about saying "Oh, everything is fine and okay now," as that's a lie and will only compound your pain. Working on genuine forgiveness, meaning forgiving the person but without excusing the act, can lessen anger's grip on you. It may even help liberate you from the control of the person who harmed you. Sometimes forgiveness might even lead to feelings of understanding, empathy, and compassion for the one who hurt you—not because their abuse was okay, but because you realize the abuser may have been in pain themselves.

Forgiveness does not mean forgetting or excusing the harm done to you. It does not necessarily mean making up with the person who caused the harm. But forgiveness can bring a type of peace and resolution that allows you to focus on yourself, helps you release the anger and bitterness that keeps you enslaved, and frees you up to move forward in the healing process. Forgiveness can be liberating, but it does not mean that you and your abuser will be socializing together, as that is likely unhealthy in most cases.

The Effects of Holding onto Anger

If you continue to hold onto anger, you may:

1 Bring that anger and bitterness into new relationships.
2 Become so consumed by past hurts that you cannot enjoy the present.
3 Find yourself feeling irritable, anxious, and depressed.
4 Lose important relationships with family and friends due to lashing out in anger.
5 Self-medicate with alcohol and other drugs, leading to addiction and poor health.

How Can I Begin to Achieve a State of Forgiveness?

1. Identify what needs healing and who you want to forgive.
2. Recognize the value of forgiveness and how it can improve your life.
3. Many trauma survivors tend to blame themselves for past abuse that they could not have prevented. Begin by forgiving yourself, and that starts with practicing ongoing self-compassion.
4. Acknowledge your pain from the harm done to you, recognize how this anger affects your emotions and behavior, and then work to release that anger.
5. If you have not done so, I strongly recommend seeing a therapist.
6. If you have been to therapy, consider joining a support group.
7. Meditate on (or pray, or both) how to heal your wounds and send out meditations of loving kindness to those in your life. (Sending meditations out to a past abuser may be a later step, if at all.)
8. Trauma survivors have had their boundaries violated by commission (i.e., sexual, physical, or verbal abuse) or accidentally (i.e., auto accident). For sexual, physical, and verbal abuse survivors, setting limits in new relationships is critical for healing.

Setting Healthy Boundaries with Others

To establish healthy boundaries, you must first understand your own needs (e.g., collegial, friendship, emotional, sexual) and limits through self-reflection and experience. This is likely to take practice, especially if you have a long history of abusers violating your boundaries (as that's what abusers do). Healthy boundaries start with clear communication and the use of "I" statements, focusing on your feelings, observations, and needs as opposed to blaming others. Remember, be clear and consistent, as we are basically training others on how to respect our boundaries; otherwise, we are training them on how to *disrespect* our boundaries.

Basic Steps to Setting Healthy Boundaries

1. **Self-Reflection:**

   Identifying your needs, values, and limits regarding emotional, sexual, and physical needs. What types of behaviors make you feel safe and respected, as opposed to unsafe and disrespected?
2. **Clear Communication:**

   Express yourself clearly yet kindly using "I" statements to explain your thoughts, feelings, and needs without being apologetic or overly emotional.

   Example: Instead of "You make me so mad when you interrupt me!" Instead, try, "I feel hurt and disrespected when I'm interrupted and would like to finish my thought."

3 **Consistency:**
Be consistent in setting limits with others at home, at work, and in social situations. Remember, consistency, not perfection.

4 **Consequences:**
Consider appropriate actions when a boundary is crossed or violated. This might involve ending a conversation, a temporary or permanent break from the relationship, or extricating yourself from an unhealthy relationship.

5 **Respect Others' Boundaries:**
Be understanding of others' needs. Ask questions to clarify their needs and demonstrate you value their autonomy. Basically, if you disrespect others' boundaries, it's unlikely they will respect yours.

Setting Healthy Boundaries Practice

In your Trauma Recovery Journal, answer the following question:

I feel validated and respected in a relationship when ____________________.

The way I can establish healthy, respectful relationships, as in the previous question, is by ____.

A healthy disagreement involves

____.

An unhealthy disagreement involves

____.

I know when to take a break from a relationship when

____.

I know when to resume a relationship when

____.

I know when to end a relationship when

____.

The most difficult part of establishing and maintaining healthy boundaries is

____.

The most rewarding aspect of establishing and maintaining healthy boundaries is

____.

Narrative: Write a brief paragraph in your Trauma Recovery Journal that addresses how you will establish and maintain healthy boundaries in personal relationships (e.g., marriage/partnerships, close family, close friendships, and work colleagues).

Example: I will establish healthy boundaries with my family, close friends, and work colleagues by owning my opinions, behaviors, and feelings using "I" statements ("I feel validated when…"), expressing my honest opinion when asked, and demonstrating my respect for others' boundaries by inquiring about their needs and personal space when I am unsure.

What If I Am Having Difficulty Forgiving?

1. If you are having difficulty forgiving someone who abused you, then you're human. So, practice self-compassion and tell yourself something like, "Understandably, I'm angry with my abuser."
2. Ask yourself, "How has my anger helped? Then, how has my anger hurt me?"
3. Reflect on times when someone forgave you. How did that feel?
4. Seek out a therapist or spiritual guide to assist you on the forgiveness journey.
5. Journal on your forgiveness process (Trauma Recovery Journal).
6. Be patient, as forgiveness is a process that comes with work and time, much in the manner of grief resolution.
7. Remember, forgiveness does not always mean reconciliation. (nor is it necessarily desirable or even possible).

The Miracle Question Applied to Forgiveness

If I were to wake up tomorrow and I no longer harbored anger toward the person who hurt me, how might my life be different? What would likely be better? What would others in my life notice being different about me? Finally, how might I begin to create this miracle?

The Empty-Chair Forgiveness

You remember this from a previous section. The key part here is being ready to talk directly to someone who has hurt or disappointed you. Be aware; sometimes, we need to speak with our younger self and express compassion and forgiveness toward ourselves. After all, holding onto our anger and hurts most often hurts us more than anyone else. I recommend caution regarding empty-chair conversations with past abusers (abusers who committed sexual assault, ongoing domestic abuse, bullying, etc.). Once again, I suggest you have completed therapy, or are currently involved in therapy, before completing this exercise, as conversing with a former abuser can be traumatic if not adequately prepared.

Practicing Self-compassion

Self-compassion means treating yourself in the manner you would want a loved one treated (Neff, 2019). Thus, that's remembering the three Cs exercise (Catch negative self-talk, Challenge that negative self-talk, and then

Change that negative self-talk into something more rational and realistic). Self-compassion is essentially about being gentle on yourself. Listed below are some basic examples of practical self-compassion:

Gentle and Reassuring Self-Talk

"It's okay, everyone makes mistakes."
"This is a painful moment, and suffering is a part of life."
"Making mistakes is part of my learning journey."
"May I be kind to myself during this moment."
These types of statements provide self-acceptance.

Acknowledging Present Moment Emotions

Allow yourself to experience those unpleasant emotions, such as anger, sadness, or frustration. Perhaps frame feelings by the statement, "I'm noticing that…"; e.g., "I'm noticing that I'm feeling angry" or "I'm noticing that I'm experiencing sadness."

Nurturing

Nurturing is represented by small acts of self-kindness, like a coffee break with a friend, a special food snack, or giving yourself a small reward for continuing the healing journey.

Comfort Your Body

Engage in physical acts of self-care, such as dancing, yoga, walking, or basically any type you enjoy, as movement is a healing action (McGonigal, 2017).

Behavioral Examples

Permit yourself to take a short break when working on a task, especially if the task is frustrating. Then, return to the task after the break.

Give yourself a gentle hug or take a brief 5-minute meditation.

Take a short walk outside, or if at work, a short walk wherever you can.

Ask a friend or trusted colleague for a check-in.

Complete the following self-compassion sentence stem:

"I show daily self-compassion in daily life by…"

The above might be a good daily reminder, especially when you are in treatment for healing trauma.

Daily Gratitude Practice

Closely related to practicing self-compassion comes habituating a practice of daily gratitude. In an earlier chapter, I strongly recommend acknowledging daily gratitudes. I start my day by acknowledging three gratitudes. Examples of gratitude acknowledgment are listed below:

1 I am grateful for my health.
2 I am grateful for my spouse/partner/close friend/or what and who you are grateful for.
3 I am grateful for the ability to heal my trauma and anger.

As my monastic superior instructed me, acknowledge daily gratitudes every day for the rest of your life. Most especially, acknowledge them on the days you do not feel grateful; the habituation of daily gratitudes and the daily practice are even more important than the gratitudes themselves. The more you acknowledge your gratitude, the better your mood is likely to become, especially on difficult days.

People Who Have Hurt Me

In your Trauma Recovery Journal, complete the following sentence stems. Write and complete sentence stems for significant people who have hurt you.

I was hurt by ____

____.

Because of this hurt ____.

Example: *I was hurt by my brother, who sexually abused me. Because of this hurt, I have never been able to have a long-term loving relationship with a man.*

Now, complete the following sentence stems regarding the healing process. Like the previous exercise, write as many complete sentences as you need.

I can begin to heal my hurt/abuse by ______________________________.

Because I have begun to heal my hurt/abuse my life is better because ____.

Example: *Because I have begun to address the sexual abuse by my brother, I have begun the healing process through therapy and self-reflective exercises like meditation/prayer, the daily three Cs exercises, yoga/Pilates/running/etc. and through interactive self-reflection, like using my Trauma Recovery Journal/this workbook/other resources.*

Self-forgiveness

Forgiving others is typically a significant part of healing. However, you must come to forgive yourself as well. Many survivors of trauma, especially sexual abuse, blame themselves even though there likely was nothing they could have done to prevent the abuse (i.e., a child abused by an adult). The act of self-forgiveness can help lessen the impact of negative self-criticism and internal storm you may be turning against yourself, reduce thoughts of revenge against your abuser and other targets of anger, and potentially end obsessive thoughts about your abuser. Once you forgive yourself, your mind becomes more peaceful and open to healing yourself and to beginning new, healthier relationships.

Self-forgiveness Practice

On a scale of 1–10, with 10 being high, what is the level of anger you harbor against yourself for the abuse? (or the trauma, accident, etc.) Use your Trauma Recovery Journal here as well.

My self-anger score is ___ out of 10.

What did you give yourself this score?

___

___

What could you do to reduce your score by 1–2 points?

___

___

How might you begin to forgive yourself? What are some steps you could take?

___

___

How might forgiving yourself help you heal your trauma?

___

___

At this point, are you ready to begin forgiving those who hurt you? Yes ___ No ___

If you are ready to forgive, what will you do?

___

___

At this point, what have you learned about self-forgiveness?

___

___

If you were to advise a close friend on self-forgiveness, what advice would you provide?

____

____

Empty-Chair Forgiveness: Hold a conversation with yourself. The theme is self-forgiveness. Set out two chairs and put your younger self in one chair, and speak directly to your younger self, expressing forgiveness. Then, switch chairs and allow your younger self to thank your current self for forgiveness. Talk with your current and younger self regarding how forgiveness feels, what you have learned in the act of self-forgiveness, and how you can maintain this healthy self-affirming practice.

Trust

People who have been abused often report a loss of trust, especially if they were abused by caregivers like parents, extended family, close friends, and others. Many trauma survivors are isolated from peers as a means of creating perceived safety zones, when in fact they compound their sense of pain and lose potential sources of emotional support. This next section explores our sense of trust.

What Does Trust Mean?

Reflect on the following questions and write your responses in your Trauma Recovery Journal:

1. What does it mean to be able to trust someone?
2. In what ways do I trust myself?
3. In what ways do I trust my own judgment regarding romantic partners, friends, and colleagues?
4. If I were to define trust, I would define it as ____________________.
5. In what ways am I a trustworthy person?
6. How do I know that I can trust someone? What are the signs?
7. If a loved one were to seek my advice on how to begin to trust someone, I would answer ____________________________________.
8. Three people I trust are ________________, ________________, and ________________.
9. Someone I would like to trust is ____________________________.
10. If I were to begin to trust the person in the previous sentence, how might I start?

Reflections on the Previous Trust Exercise

Regarding the previous exercise, answer what you consider the most important question/answer in your Trauma Recovery Journal.

The most important question/answer from the preceding exercise on trust is:

____.

1 The reason I selected this question/answer is ____________________.

2 What does my answer suggest about my view of trust?

____

____.

3 What does my view of trust suggest about me?

____

____.

4 Having completed the trust exercises, what I would most like to change about my view of trust is ____________________________________.

5 How I could go about changing my view of trust is ________________.

6 What scares me the most about trusting others is _________________.

7 The way I could address my fear of trusting others is ______________.

8 If I were to begin to trust some people, how might my life be different?

____.

9 The reason some people trust me is because _____________________.

10 So, if others can trust me, then I can begin to trust others because

____.

Challenging My Beliefs about Power and Control

A common desire in life is exerting power and control over what happens to us (Rosenbloom & Williams, 2010). However, the reality in life is that so much is beyond our control. Viktor Frankl knew a lot about the loss of control, having lost his entire family (spouse, kids, in-laws, etc.) in the death camps of WWII. However, he emerges from this hellish experience with a firm belief that releasing control and instead focusing on the power of choice is the most significant change one can make (Frankl, 2006). He goes on to write that relinquishing perceived control (i.e., false control) and instead realizing our power lies in our choice is what leads to living free of fear. Frankl posits that the power of choice is the one thing no one can ever take from us, not Nazis, abusive persons, or unreliable family members. After his remarkable survival, he created what he called Logotherapy, or a therapy of meaning. In this next section, the focus will be on relinquishing power and instead focusing on actual choices (the power within). Admittedly, when our trust has been betrayed through abuse and trauma, relinquishing perceived power can be difficult. Like all healing examined in this workbook, recovery is a developmental process requiring work, patience, time, self-compassion, discipline, persistence, emotional support from loved ones, and, of course, therapy.

My Beliefs about the Power of Choice (and Relinquishing Control)

In your Trauma Recovery Journal, explore the following questions:

1. What does the term, *the power of choice*, suggest to me?
2. As per Frankl, the power to choose my attitude in each situation is the one commodity no one can ever take away. How might this recognition improve my life?
3. In what situations in my life at present have I given up my power of choice?
4. In what situations in my life at present have I explored my power of choice?
5. How might you begin to use the power of choice more effectively?
6. Reflecting upon past power struggles in your family, career, etc., in what ways might the power of choice have assisted you?
7. Consider a current power struggle (or conflict). How might a focus on your choice(s) as opposed to winning the power struggle or conflict lead to greater fulfillment?
8. How might you begin to let go of the need for power and control to focus on your personal choices?
9. When you were growing up, did you believe you had some degree of choice? How has this childhood-era belief influenced your life? Regarding the previous question and your answer, how might you wish to change that long-held belief?
10. Viktor Frankl wrote that the one thing that nobody can ever take away is one's ability to choose one's attitude in any situation (2006). What do you think about Frankl's belief? What has been your experience regarding choice?

Self-affirmations: Reminding Ourselves of Our Talents and Capabilities

When I was in high school, the popular TV show *Saturday Night Live* began. The hour-long show featured many popular, talented comedians and actors. One of the skits was a silly take on positive affirmations ("...and gosh darn it, I like myself!"). Taken to extremes, even healthy actions can become trivialized, if not downright skewed and unhealthy. However, like daily gratitude practice, affirmation can be very beneficial to our well-being and recovery.

The following represents a sample list of affirmations. Select a few (say 3–6) to say out loud. Then, write down these affirmations in your Trauma Recovery Journal. I would further suggest meditating on these personal affirmations to solidify your belief in them. Remember, cognitive therapy works well because we tend to believe what we tell ourselves (Beck, 2019; Ellis, 2011). So, make your self-talk healthy, compassionate, and rational.

1. I am a very loving person.
2. I am full of compassion toward others.
3. I am a successful person.
4. I live a purposeful life.
5. I am worthy of love from myself.
6. I am worthy of love from others.
7. I respect my own and other people's boundaries.
8. I am capable of growth and change.
9. I can heal my trauma and disappointments.
10. I am an attractive person.

Note: You may add affirmations to this list. The most important part of this exercise is to acknowledge these affirmations out loud.

Regarding the affirmations list, which of the affirmations resonates most for you? How might you strengthen your belief in affirmations that resonate less for you? For example, let's say that you do not view yourself as a successful person. Thus, the "I am a successful person" statement is difficult for you to accept. If being successful means being a multi-millionaire, then 99% of the population is unsuccessful. What becomes important for one's health, then, lies in defining success on your own terms. See the reframed statement below:

For example, the evidence that I am successful is:

The reframed statement: I am well educated (or a skilled tradesperson), have a successful marriage/partnership, have close friendships, have a career I enjoy, etc. Remember, to heal, you will need to call into question many unhealthy statements and messages you may have received from society and significant individuals in society.

Steps to Take

1. In your Trauma Recovery Journal, list the people who have hurt or betrayed you (you may wish to list pseudonyms for more privacy). You may or may not choose to cite how they hurt or betrayed you.
2. Now, begin considering the previous information on forgiveness, what it is and is not.

3 Practice self-compassion by revising negative self-statements, forgiving misunderstandings at home and in the workplace, and through meditation/prayer and writing in your journal.
4 Remember the Three Cs, as negative self-statements will emerge. When they do, use the Three Cs to refute them.
5 Habituate daily gratitude practice.
6 Remember that forgiveness is not the same as saying abuse is okay. It's about self-healing and unlocking those chains of destructive anger.
7 Use of the empty-chair exercise, miracle question, etc.
8 Post positive messages where you will see them regularly, like on the refrigerator door, your office wall, on your cell phone, your bedroom mirror, etc.
9 Each day, acknowledge one small success you have had. Remember, large success is often composed of small achievements.
10 At some point each day, face the mirror and say these three words out loud: "I am loved." The more you say these words, the more you will believe them, and the more likely you will express love toward others.

Lessons Learned

Consider and address the following questions in your Trauma Recovery Journal

1 What is the most important lesson you learned from this chapter?

2 How I can begin putting that important lesson in action in my life is by

____.

3 I can begin to forgive while setting healthy limits by

____.

4 One way I can start showing self-compassion is by ________________.

5 If I were to forgive myself, I would start by ____________________.

7 Addressing Trauma Symptomology

Negative Self-talk, Social Isolation, and Incongruent Emotional Expression

Although self-talk was explored in Chapter 6, this chapter will take a deeper dive into self-talk and how it impacts trauma, anxiety, stress, and social relationships. What we tell ourselves goes a long way in paving highways to healing and personal growth or leads to cul-de-sacs that build frustration and leave us mired in unhealthy, self-defeating behaviors, negative emotions, and ruminating cognitions, leading to a vicious cycle of continued traumatization (Briere & Scott, 2015; Ellis, 2011).

Persistent Negative Emotions

Persistent negative emotions are those emotions that have become entrenched in the mind and body due to long-term traumatic experiences (van der Kolk, 2015). Naturally, there is a spectrum of emotionality that traumatized people will express to greater or lesser degrees. Some of these emotions featured in this chapter are fear, anger, rage, depression, guilt, shame, helplessness, sadness, and grief. Clearly, anger in all its various states is a common emotion expressed by trauma survivors, due to having been violated, but also due to hyperarousal (emotional dysregulation). The emotions targeted in this chapter are not the complete list impacted by trauma, anxiety, and stress, but they are common and problematic ones that trauma survivors experience. A key component of healing from trauma is the ability to self-regulate out thoughts, emotions, and respiration. The focus of the workbook is on holistic healing of trauma and managing anxiety and stress through mind, body, breath, and spirit. This chapter will address negative thoughts and emotions and how to revise and regulate them (something touched on in the previous chapter).

More than 20 years ago, I attended a talk delivered by Dr. Bessel van der Kolk. One of the more interesting things he had to say about healing trauma was that the body had been ignored too long in trauma treatment. He went on to express that while the brain sends messages to the muscles and organs, those muscles and organs also send messages to the brain. Therefore, while our thoughts can distort threats, even create them, because we feel them throughout our body due to the complex polyvagal nerve system running throughout the body, the body must not be ignored. In his popular book

DOI: 10.4324/9781003689232-7

The Body Keeps the Score: Brain, Mind, and Body in the Healing of Trauma (2015). Another interesting part of his informative presentation was that the brain and the mind were not the same but rather overlapping, yet separate entities. While this latter point is a discussion for another book, it has remained in my mind ever since.

Here's an important question to entertain: in what part of your body do you feel your emotions? When I am surprised by something unpleasant, I feel my surprise and disappointment in the pit of my stomach. Often, I have asked clients, inquired of students, and asked participants in my professional trainings this same question. People have given me a variety of answers, with the stomach area being popular, but also the neck, back, and chest as common answers. Cappachione (2001) suggests that emotions are a form of energy stored inside our bodies. My further experience is that these emotions are often *trapped* in our bodies. One woman who came to me to treat her panic disorder explained it this way: "When I'm stressed, it's like I'm mashing the gas pedal to the floor!" To heal trauma, we must recognize what emotions have been impacted, inflamed, or embedded in the mind and body, and then begin to treat them holistically, as van der Kolk suggested (2015). As cognitions and emotions are strongly linked and then carried throughout the body via the vagus nerve center, emotional regulation is a significant part of trauma healing (Briere & Scott, 2015).

Start Where the Dysregulation Starts: Fear

Fear is perhaps the most misunderstood emotion we have. I write this because in the absence of fear, Homo sapiens would be simply one more extinct species (Harari, 2024). Fear, or anxiety, is what motivates a student to study for her chemistry exam and propels us to complete a project so that we can keep our jobs and support our loved ones. Having spent extended time in the saltwater crocodile territory in remote northern Australia, fear is what kept me from venturing into the billabongs they inhabit, thus preserving my life. This, something Harari explains far more eloquently than I, is the upside of fear. So, remember, extinguishing all fear is not the goal, but rather, extinguishing unrealistic fear is the goal.

Then there is that other, deeply ingrained fear emanating from the seed of pain and abuse. Perhaps we grew up in a household of violence, where we learned to keep constant vigilance of the abuser's moods. We then become conditioned to act to please the violent party (usually a parent) and thus are constantly on the verge of being triggered into anger, panic, or dissociation. This is where the genesis of much PTSD lies. People who are unfortunate to spend their formative years living in such oppressive, abusive, emotionally warping conditions are very likely to have skewed emotional reactions to basic disagreements because they are consciously and unconsciously asking themselves this most basic question of human evolution: "Am I safe or am I in danger?" In addition to racing heart rate, cortisol hyperarousal, tense muscles, and negative thoughts begin racing through the mind. Respiration is quick and shallow, and you may feel queasy in the abdomen. If you find yourself experiencing these types of behaviors regularly (say weekly), you are experiencing traumatic fear.

Questions Regarding Fear

1 When conflicts arise at home, work, or in social situations, how often do you feel quick, intense anger, negative emotions flooding your thoughts, a rapid heart rate, muscle tension, and hyperventilation? (Check one, and record it in your Trauma Recovery Journal.)

Seldom ___ Occasionally ___ Regularly ___ Often ___

2 When in the above state, I express my anger by (complete the sentence).

____

____

3 When my angry state passes, I feel (complete the sentence)

____

____

4 How might you begin to manage the times when you feel triggered by someone or something unpleasant?

____

____

5 Miracle Question: Six months from now, you awake, and you are more emotionally regulated, having healed your trauma. What might your expression of anger look like now? How would you feel different about your thoughts, respiration, heart rate, and anger level? What might family, close friends, and colleagues notice being different about you?

____

____

6 Now, how might you create a more emotionally regulated you? What would you want to start doing? Stop doing? Keep doing?

____

____

7 It is essential that you credit yourself when you successfully manage your anger and subsequent anger. Briefly list 2–3 recent experiences when you were able to regulate your anger and frustration when triggered.

____

____

8 What was different about the situations when you were successful in regulating your emotions?

____

____

9 What's one thing you can do differently that will help you regulate your emotions and manage your behavior differently when triggered?

____

____

10 The Empty Chair Conversation has been previously mentioned in this workbook. Sit facing an empty chair and have a conversation with your fear. Speak honestly but using the "I" type statements modeled in this workbook, as that's owning your emotions, thoughts, and behaviors. Speak to your fear for as long as necessary and then switch chairs and have your fear speak to you, also using "I" statements. What is your fear trying to teach you? What did you learn from the conversation with your fear? How might this information help you in your healing process? (Naturally, record in your Trauma Recovery Journal).

One of the difficulties with fear is that humans have a natural reaction to shrink from fear. However, if fear is ignored and the strategy becomes avoidance, then the anxiety becomes magnified, and more avoidance is required (Meichenbaum, 2003). Anxiety in PTSD is much like a balloon in that fear builds the pressure, and as one former client exclaimed, "I feel like I'm going to explode!" This former client's approach was to use dissociation, then avoidance, and self-medicate with alcohol to numb the pain. He came to me after experiencing a panic attack, triggered by a loud argument with a co-worker. He was transported by ambulance to the local hospital, presenting classic panic attack symptoms like hyperventilation, a racing heart rate, shortness of breath, chest pain, and thoughts that he was dying. The ER doctor treated him and then referred him to our clinic. He was a blue-collar worker, having never gone for counseling, and was very skeptical that it would alleviate his condition. I listened patiently and then suggested he might give it three sessions. Reluctantly, he agreed. The steps below represent a good deal of the treatment plan I developed for him:

1 Recognize the early warning signs that a panic attack is coming. His first warning was anxiety-based thoughts, followed quickly by a racing heart rate and then hyperventilation.
2 First, address your respiration, as it's the fastest way to begin to calm yourself. I recommend the box breathing technique (also called 4-Square Breathing): Breath in slowly through your nose for 4 seconds, then hold your breath for 4 seconds, then exhale through your mouth for 4 seconds,

and then breathe in through your nose for 4 seconds. Repeat as often as needed. Box breathing works so well; special forces like the Navy Seals use it (Kumar & Uttekar, 2011).

3 Next, catch the anxious thought(s) and use the cognitive reframing like the 3 Cs: Catch the thought ("I'm dying!"), challenge the "I'm dying!" thought ("Perhaps it's just a panic attack."), and then change it ("Okay, I'm panicking, but box breathing will help me calm down, after Navy SEALs use it").
4 Then, use a mindfulness-based grounding technique like the 5 senses, a brief meditation (silent or through an App), EFT tapping/touching, taking a short break from whatever you are doing, etc.
5 After you have calmed down, write in your Trauma Recovery Journal what you have learned about managing panic attacks. Remember, continue to apply that learning, and you will have more success in managing and even preventing panic attacks and general anxiety.

Use other strategies mentioned throughout this text in managing anxiety and panic attacks. Some people will need prescription medication to help them manage severe anxiety, at least temporarily. I am not anti-medication, as it is necessary for some, at least for a while, but more people can learn to address and manage anxiety (including panic) through more natural means like box breathing, cognitive reframing (the 3 Cs), 5 senses, and meditation. As a counselor long schooled and experienced in MCBT, I strongly recommend you identify and practice disputing and managing negative automatic thoughts through techniques like cognitive reframing/3 Cs. In your Trauma Recovery Journal, list the most common and problematic negative thoughts that tend to cause you anxiety. I call the list the Top 10.

The Top Ten Negative Thoughts that Cause Me Anxiety and the Strategies I Use to Manage That Anxiety

Consider those thoughts that cause anxiety or even panic in your mind and body. Keep this list in your Trauma Recovery Journal and edit it as necessary. In addition, record what technique(s)/intervention helps you manage each anxious thought on the line below the thought.

Example: Negative Thought: "I'm ugly, and nobody will ever want to be my partner."

Reframe: The 3 Cs: Catch it: "I'm ugly"; Challenge it: "I may not be a glamorous actor, but much is attractive about me, like my smile"; Change it: "I find my smile and sense of humor attractive. Therefore, I reject the ugly label."

Remember: You must begin to define yourself on your own terms to be emotionally and even physically healthy. Do not ignore constructive feedback, but be ready to distinguish between healthy and unrealistic standards. So, list your Top 10 negative thoughts you will challenge by using the 3 Cs below. (Use your Trauma Recovery Journal.)

Top Ten Negative Thoughts That I Will Challenge by Practicing the 3 Cs

1 ______________________________

2 ______________________________

3 ______________________________

4 ______________________________

5 ______________________________

6 ______________________________

7 ______________________________

8 ______________________________

9 ______________________________

10 ______________________________

11 ______________________________

12 ______________________________

13 ______________________________

14 ______________________________

15 ______________________________

16 ______________________________

17 ______________________________

18 ______________________________

19 ______________________________

20 ______________________________

Expressing My Anger

Trauma survivors often experience explosive anger over what outsiders will view as small issues. Explosive outbursts are the result of trauma, particularly long-term trauma (van der Kolk, 2015). Survivors of trauma often vent their anger and frustration onto family, friends (until they lose them!), co-workers, animals (pets especially), and inanimate objects (Capacchione, 2001; Meichenbaum, 2003). Many people wrongly assume that those who displace their anger onto others suffer no consequences. My own experience of four decades in the field is that people with explosive anger often experience trouble across several fronts of their lives. They experience employment instability due to inappropriate anger expression, multiple divorces or romantic partnerships ending, legal issues due to domestic violence, barroom fights, etc. In fact, most ex-convicts I have counseled were survivors of domestic abuse. I do not mean to imply that past trauma is any excuse for inflicting verbal, physical, or sexual trauma on anyone, but rather that many of those traumatized turn and inflict that trauma on third parties, and the cycle of violence and trauma continues.

Matsakis (2002) notes several reasons why trauma survivors are particularly predisposed to explosive anger:

1 You have a type of free-floating anger that's close to the surface and is easily triggered by comments or behavior.
2 You bottled up the anger, and it keeps building until you explode over something seemingly trivial.
3 You are angry at the lack of understanding or empathy of others.
4 Your primary method of managing the anger is self-medicating with alcohol and/or other drugs.
5 You isolate yourself from others and consequently are lonely and angry.
6 You have not addressed the root cause of your anger (trauma), and you continue to be triggered and reactive.

I would recommend you consider how many of these reasons apply to you and use techniques like cognitive reframing (3 Cs especially), 5 senses, box breathing, taking a short break from the triggering situation (and after 5 minutes returning and addressing the issue when emotionally regulated). Be aware also of how explosive anger has hurt you, because all the former trauma survivors I worked with were justifiably angry. However, using anger as a weapon on a third party is not justified (actual danger excepted).

How My Anger Has Wounded Me

Anger is, in most cases, a typical human emotion. Joy and boredom are also emotions, albeit less problematic than anger. In your Trauma Healing Journal, list five ways your anger has wounded you and those around you.

1 ______________________________

2 ______________________________

3 ______________________________

4 ______________________________

5 ______________________________

What do your answers teach you about the way you express your anger? Also, how might you use this information to express yourself in more constructive ways? See the next exercise.

Ways I Can Express My Anger in a Healthy, Appropriate Manner

Now, consider the following possibilities regarding constructively expressing your anger. Check any item that you would consider:

___ When someone makes a rude comment to me, instead of striking back with a rude comment, I walk away or own my feelings and express to myself, "I felt that was a rude comment."
___ When triggered by a comment or behavior, instead of letting my anger build into rage, I take an emotional time-out and do a couple of minutes of box breathing, meditation, or simply a walk until I calm down.
___ Instead of avoiding the issue, I seek out a trusted friend or colleague for advice on how to address what upset me.
___ Instead of plotting revenge on others, I calm myself and then hold an empty chair conversation with that person to gain a different perspective.
___ Instead of holding a grudge against family members, ex-friends, or colleagues, I accept an honest apology to free myself from anger.
___ When I do argue with a loved one, friend, or co-worker, I own my thoughts, feelings, and opinions by using "I" statements as modeled in this workbook.
___ I practice self-care by using emotional regulation techniques like box breathing, meditation, 5 senses, EFT tapping/touching, etc.
___ Instead of directly expressing my anger in constructive ways, I place guilt on others to get my way.

Now, record in your Trauma Recovery Journal which of these mindful interventions you are committed to using when triggered. Be aware that constructively expressing anger is a lifelong practice, much like emotional and physical fitness. Recognize that even the most emotionally healthy, self-regulated individuals occasionally express their anger inappropriately. So, work on being your better self, taking responsibility by apologizing when you are not, and working on your anger management plan.

Depression and Subsequent Guilt

It is very common for trauma survivors to experience feelings of guilt when unable to regulate their anger and frustration (van der Kolk, 2015). I witnessed this firsthand when a former client first publicly screamed at me in the clinic hallway after I held them accountable for coming to their session intoxicated. The additional complication was his blowing nearly a year of sobriety, something he had put much effort into by attending weekly AA meetings and completing addiction treatment. His wife's filing for divorce that week triggered him, and he went on a drinking binge and blew a lot of hard work. Later, after his sponsor and I met with him, he was very remorseful, realizing how he'd failed to work on his treatment and aftercare plan, part of which was to ask for help when he was feeling vulnerable. Anyone would naturally be sad in the wake of a divorce, but he went completely off the rails with his behavior. His depression left him barely able to care for himself, and a relative had to take him in for a brief period. He also returned to the clinic for addiction treatment and started over again on day one of sobriety with his AA chapter.

Consider the following questions regarding depression:

1 What led to the depression?
2 How was the depression related to your trauma treatment? (or your anxiety or stress)
3 Did you consider self-harm by burning, cutting, or other self-inflicted abuse?
4 Did you consider suicide? Did you make a suicide plan?

Depression is a mood disorder and is common for those in treatment for PTSD and related conditions. Depression can have biological, social, and psychological factors (Beck, 2021). If your depression has reached the point where you are considering it, especially if you have a suicide plan, call Lifeline, the national suicide hotline, by dialing 988.

A Suicide Intervention Plan

1 Have you considered suicide?
2 Call the national number (Helpline's 988).
3 Then, if not currently in counseling, make an appointment with a mental health professional.
4 Seek additional support through your close family and friends. If you are estranged from family and feeling you have no friends, ask your therapist to make that isolation a part of your treatment plan. Teaching people how to make healthy friendships became a significant part of my counseling work.
5 Logotherapy founder Viktor Frankl made establishing meaning/purpose in life a part of his therapy with patients. Answer the following question (and record it in your Trauma Treatment Journal): "The meaning and purpose in my life is:" ____."
6 Frederich Nietzsche opined that the person with a why could endure almost any how. So, if you lack an answer to the previous question, consider this follow-up one:

   "I could go about discovering my why in life by ____________________."

If someone were to ask you what this workbook is about in the thumbnail sketch fashion, I would encourage you to consider the best answer being, "The workbook is all about understanding and/or establishing a why in one's life." Absent a why, healing trauma, managing anxiety and depression, achieving and maintaining sobriety, and reaching out for help if feeling suicidal are all about having a *why* in your life. So dear reader, find your why and keep it close at hand. One former client posted the why of his life on his bathroom mirror. "This way, I won't forget it," he said.

Guilt and Shame: The Terrible Twins

Far too many of my former clients have expressed guilt and shame for their traumatic experiences, despite the reality that they could have done little or nothing to prevent them. Guilt is what we feel after having done something against our personal values, while shame is what we feel when our misdeeds are discovered by family, friends, or the media. For example, one client of mine was driving a car while intoxicated when he had a wreck that killed one of his passengers. He came to therapy feeling overwhelmed by guilt, but he also felt shame for what he put his family through, being arrested, jailed, and incarcerated, before being paroled. Guilt and shame, however, are all too common emotions in trauma survivors.

Unpacking Feelings of Guilt and Shame

If you feel guilt or shame for the trauma inflicted upon you, complete three responses to the following incomplete statement regarding guilt and shame:

"My trauma has caused me to feel guilt and shame because..."

1 ____.

2 ____.

3 ____.

Self-compassion Intervention on Guilt and Shame

Now, regarding the previous questions above, pretend you are holding an empty chair conversation with Guilt and Shame.

Ask the Guilt and Shame Twins:

1 "What constructive lessons are you trying to teach me?"
2 "Given that I was abused by an adult/someone more powerful, in what way was I responsible for the abuse and subsequent trauma?"
3 "If the traumatic event(s) occurred again, how would you suggest I act differently?"
4 "In what way do you see guilt and shame messages being helpful to me?"

Healing My Shame Beliefs

Now that you have unpacked your guilt and shame, let's address healing that guilt and shame. Record your responses in your Trauma Recovery Journal.

1 If I were to begin healing my guilt and shame, I would be doing

____.

2 I could start healing my guilt and shame by

____.

3 If a loved one was wracked by guilt and shame due to being traumatized, I might offer compassionate counsel by expressing

____.

4 I could begin taking the advice I wrote in completing the previous sentence by

____.

5 The miracle question has been mentioned in previous chapters. If a miracle occurred and you were no longer plagued by guilt and shame, what would be different about your life?

____.

6 What would family and close friends notice as being different about you after this miracle occurs?

____.

7 Now, how might you begin the process of creating this miracle?

____.

8 A popular song from long ago went something like "breaking up is hard to do." Sometimes, of course, breaking up is necessary for personal growth. So, how might you break up with guilt and shame? (Consider it a personal growth opportunity.)

____.

9 When you have broken up with the guilt and shame twins, how will your mood and level of optimism change?

____.

10 Changing habits and releasing old wounds, guilt, shame, anger, etc., can take time and work, and patience is a necessity in the healing process. Given this, what's one thing you can do differently to facilitate breaking up with guilt and shame and facilitate the healing and personal growth process?

____.

Remember Your Healing Companions: Mind, Body, Breath, and Spirit

Anyone who has worked in the field of addiction treatment will tell you that relapse is a common occurrence. The same maxim holds in treating trauma, anxiety, and major stress: clients will relapse and regress when it comes to their healing process. The most important concept to remember is that any progress, regardless of how incremental, is still progress, and you must acknowledge this. In fact, I like to consider the Stages of Change when working with traumatized clients (or clients with any issue):

1 **Precontemplation:** The person is unaware of the problem, even though others are aware of your problem (e.g., alcohol, other drug abuse, temper).
2 **Contemplation:** Contemplation is the first step of any 12-Step program. The person finally admits to having a problem, begins to consider making changes, but is not ready to commit to change. Change is usually not possible until the person progresses to the contemplation stage.
3 **Preparation:** The person decides to make changes and plans on taking action soon, often within the next month. They begin with small changes.
4 **Action:** The person begins making significant changes. For example, they seek addiction treatment, begin attending 12-step meetings, and talk with their sponsor weekly. These changes may last 6 months to 1 year.
5 **Maintenance:** Person completes treatment and maintains sobriety for over one year, continues attending 12-step meetings, meeting with a 12-step sponsor, etc.
   (Prochaska et al., 1992)
6 **Relapse:** The person relapses, but having experienced sobriety for over 1 year, re-enters counseling, contacts her 12-step sponsor, and applies lessons learned from the past year of abstinence success. Relapses are very common in addictions treatment and send the person back to an earlier stage. Previous work and learning, however, can assist the person to get their sobriety back on track (Prochaska et al., 1992).

With the above in mind, consider these mind, body, breath, and spirit interventions when addressing guilt, shame, anger, depression, relapse, etc.

1 **The Mind:** A staple in your recovery is cognitive reframing, usually represented by the 3 Cs of Catch it (the negative thought, "I'm a loser"), Challenge it ("What's the evidence for me being a loser?"), and then, Change it ("Okay, it seems as if I have a good job, a stable marriage, and close friends, that I'm not a loser.").

   Here's a second framework for cognitive reframing. Albert Ellis (2011) developed the **A-B-C-D-E** approach to disputing unhealthy beliefs, particularly guilt and shame.

Here's the A-B-C-D-E Unhealthy Beliefs Refuting Approach:

A= the activating event that caused my shame: For example, "I was raped by my boyfriend."

B= the subsequent belief caused by the trauma's aftermath: that belief being "I must have asked for it." (**Note:** This very belief has been reinforced by many in society as a means of victim blaming.)

C= the consequence of the belief: "I'm depressed and hate myself."

D= disputing the belief and consequence: "Hey, I was violated, and it wasn't my fault!"

E= new effect: "There's nothing wrong with me. What's screwed up is a society that shapes men to see women as prey! I'm going for counseling, considering pressing charges, and joining a women's advocacy organization."

2 **The body** is a key component of healing, as nerves run throughout the body, and we feel our anxiety in our bodies. Consider the EFT/Meridian tapping points, the 5-senses exercise (5 things I see, 4 I hear, 3 I smell, 2 I can feel, and 1 I can taste), or the tactile sensation of holding and describing a special/sacred object:

> Okay, I am holding my meditation beads. They are of rough wooden composition, and moving them while I talk feels comforting, as they ground me in my daily spiritual practice. I can meditate on healing as I work the beads.

3 **The Breath:** Breathwork is our life force. For general grounding, many of us use a **sitting or walking meditation**. I know people who use a mantra as a focal point of their meditation. A mantra involves the repetition of a phrase, sound, or word like "Be here now," or "May I be well," or whatever is meaningful to that person. I use silent meditation, whether when sitting or doing a walking meditation. When my mind wanders and the outside world intrudes (e.g., ungraded papers, not written chapters, details my spouse gave me that I forgot) I view them as just floating past like on a river. Occasionally, I might say to myself silently, "I am noticing I am distracted by..." and it floats past. Meditation has demonstrated strong efficacy in reducing anxiety and depression, and even as little as 5 minutes a day helps with emotional regulation (Fincham et al., 2024). So, breathe in slowly for 2 seconds, hold for 2 seconds, and then exhale slowly for 2 seconds, and then start the process over.

Regarding a walking meditation, you might consider saying (out loud or silently) the word "healing" as you take each step. A variation on this could be saying, "I am" as one foot touches the ground and then "healing" when the other foot contacts the ground. My walking meditations are usually one hour, but they can be any length you desire.

Some people use a headset or earbuds and download a guided meditation while engaged in sitting or walking meditation. Basically, it's what works for you, so experiment with various meditation practices and find what works best for you. Remember, when your mind wanders or whenever something else distracts you (a noise, someone's loud music, a horn honking, etc.), focus on your breath.

Voo Exhale: Remember the voo exhale. Purse your lips, tilt your head upwards, and then let out an exhale for 6–9 seconds, making a voo sound. Then, rest for 2–3 seconds (or whatever's comfortable) and make another voo exhale for 6–9 seconds. Each day, I complete 10 voo exhales. The voo exhale is another method of tapping into the vagus nerve system, which, when stimulated by voo exhaling (or EFT/Meridian tapping, or sustained movement), helps calm and regulate our emotions.

4 **The Spirit:** The spirit component to me is my why or the meaning and purpose in my life. The spirit is what ties me to my loved ones, friends, and colleagues, as well as adversaries and people I struggle to get along with, and all other living creatures. My spirit also has a *spiritual* component, as I believe in a Higher Power beyond myself. That Higher Power has a consciousness and is a being and a non-being, is omniscient and ever-present, loving and nonjudging. For some of you, my spiritual aspect resonates, while for others, your spirit is your meaning and purpose. Use whatever healthy strategy that works for you in self-soothing, attaining mindfulness, and practicing self-compassion, etc.
5 **Physical Activity:** Regular physical activity, such as walking, jogging, swimming, cycling, and yoga, helps manage and reduce depression and anxiety. Stanford health psychologist Kelly McGonigal often says sustained movement for 15 minutes or longer is like receiving a constant IV drip of hope molecules (McGonigal, 2019). So, what's important is that you engage in the movement activity you enjoy, as it increases the likelihood you will continue with the activity. McGonigal recommends 20 minutes of sustained movement four times per week. Remember, movement is a key component of healing trauma and managing anxiety, depression, and stress.

Healthy Communication: Asking for Our Needs to Be Met

Ask any therapist who counsels couples, and they will tell you that communication breakdowns are the biggest detriment in a relationship. My own experience certainly has proved this true, as a long line of clients have walked into my various offices across the globe and informed me that their spouse, partner/in-law/sibling/boss/ etc. does not listen to them. When I have inquired whether they communicate this disappointment to whoever supposedly doesn't listen, the most common response is, "Well, no, of course not!" Essentially, the clients are saying the other party is not meeting their needs. Part of the problem is that the frustrated party may not have explained its needs to the other party. Admittedly, sometimes the other party remains unable to meet whatever needs are articulated, but asking in specific terms offers the best chance for success.

To effectively ask for your needs to be met, it's important to identify your specific needs first, then communicate them clearly and respectfully using "I" statements to express ownership and the importance of the need. Furthermore, select a time when you feel calm and when your partner (or whomever) is not distracted. It's usually wise to ask, "Do you have a few minutes?" or "Would now be a good time to talk?" Here are some basic steps for asking for your needs to be met:

1 **Identify your needs**

  a Identify the specific need(s). For example, "I need to feel heard more often" or "I need more help with the house chores."
  b Take responsibility and consider what you can do to meet some of these needs for yourself.

2 **Communicating your needs**

  a Pick a good time to address your needs to your loved one. For example, do you feel calm? Does your partner seem to be in the headspace to have a serious conversation?
  b Use "I" statements: "I would like to express how much it hurt when you didn't acknowledge my mother's death," as opposed to "You just don't value our friendship!" You-statements are gasoline on a fire in any relationship! Avoid them.
  c Be specific. Clearly state the actions or behaviors you desire. For example, "I need one night where we just have a conversation," instead of, "You jump online every night and ignore me."
  d Be assertive but be respectful: "I would like us to have a date night," not, "You just don't prioritize me."

3 **Listen to your partner** (or child, friend, colleague, etc.)

  a Empathize. That is, try to understand the other person's perspective, even when you disagree. This involves you actively listening, even if that is difficult.
  b Listen without judgment. This is likely the hardest part of two-way communication. What I have usually taught clients is to practice the conversation beforehand, using deep breathing pauses, should the other party express something unpleasant.
  c Clarify. Sometimes we misunderstand what is being said. So, if you are unclear what the other party is saying, ask for clarification. "Help me understand. You would like me to…"

4 **Flexibility**

  a Be ready to compromise. When I provide mediation, both parties must compromise to resolve the conflict. Now, be aware of your boundaries. If one partner gives 90% while the other gives only 10%, that solution won't work. Seldom is any issue 50-50, so how far can each party bend? Basically, both parties must negotiate this, and it may take ongoing practice. Find the workable ratio.

5 **Know your options**

   a Know your boundaries. Be clear about what you will and won't compromise on your needs. I'd suggest one self-reflect on this and make a list of non-negotiables. In a marriage or partnership, daily "I love you" statements (with real meaning, not AI-like rote statements!) may be one.
   b Taking a break. Even the best communicators will struggle to communicate effectively at times. If the conversation is breaking down, consider taking a recess and trying again later (say in 15 minutes, an hour, etc.). However, do come back and complete the conversation.
   c Compatibility...or not. If your major needs consistently go unmet despite communication efforts, counseling, and compromise (on your part), it potentially is a sign of fundamental incompatibility.
   d Exit the relationship. If you have tried all the options and your non-negotiable needs remain unfulfilled, leaving the relationship is a realistic option to create the life and partnership you desire.

Active Listening

Growing up as the fourth of six boys in a family principally raised by our maternal grandparents, I did a lot of listening. I realized that my older siblings were not particularly interested in what I had to say, but were invested in externalizing their thoughts and needed a listening ear. That listener became me. I listened without interrupting (FYI: Nobody likes being interrupted, no matter what they say) and continued the practice well beyond adolescence. Much later, that helped when I was being trained as a counselor, as presence was one skill I had honed very well. I have included active listening in this workbook because the quality of your relationships often depends on your being a good listener and seeking to understand others as much as you desire to have others understand you.

Because this is a workbook to help readers manage and heal trauma, or anxiety, and stress, listening here is more friend-to-friend type as opposed to counselor-therapist training. I have trained many peer helpers in becoming effective, compassionate listeners, and I will offer tips in this section of the chapter.

Tip 1: Don't Hijack a Conversation

I have long suggested in my professional training courses that if you wish to be a good friend, work on being a good listener. For example, when a friend says, "I just went to a great concert!" Instead of replying with, "Great! Let me tell you about when I heard Adele in concert!" While such is common, you have just hijacked the conversation. Your friend likely wanted to share their experience with you, but you took that opportunity off board. Again, this example is very typical of Western conversation, where we both desire to be heard over being understood. Consider the following conversation between two friends at a conference:

Jane: "Wow, I just went to this amazing training on wellbeing!" (She's excited and wants to share the message)

Jim: "Really? I always get bored in those. Our training was on AI, and let me tell you about it..."

Jim has just hijacked the conversation, and Jane likely feels devalued. It would be fine if Jim listened to Jane and then, at the opportune time, mentioned the training he attended. This way, both parties have an opportunity for a two-way conversation. Consider the two-way conversation below:

Jane: "I just went to this amazing well-being training!"

Jim: "Wow, tell me about it." (Notice Jim keeps the focus on Jane's story)

Jane: "Well, we worked on Box Breathing, vagus nerve resets to manage anxiety, and..." (and Jane talks for several minutes while Jim listens with interest). After a few minutes, Jim mentions his session.

Jim: "Glad you enjoyed it. Our session was on AI in the workplace, and wow, was it a mindbender! I'm not entirely sure that any of us will have a job soon!" (Jane listens with interest)

Tip 2: Be Present in the Relationship

Probably nobody I have studied has exemplified presence like psychologist Carl Rogers and Buddhist monk Thich Nhat Hanh. These two very different people both taught millions of people how to be more present. Rogers' best-selling, *On Becoming a Person* (1961), and his *Client-Centered Therapy* (1965) remain staples in counselor training programs. Rogers theorized that effective helping required therapeutic presence, and presence was demonstrated through what he called the necessary conditions for therapy, which he opined as the counselor being genuine (or authentic), empathetic (seeking to understand), and exhibiting unconditional positive regard (1965). Thich Nhat Hanh focused on mindfulness (1999) as the source of genuine presence. He viewed mindfulness as keeping one's consciousness alive to the present reality. Hanh explained mindfulness as keeping one's consciousness alive to the present reality by being aware of the present moment with your mind and body together (1999).

Rogers recounts a story in *On Becoming a Person* of how he completely missed a good friend's distress because he was plagued by some deadline or other responsibility. However, his hypocrisy gnawed at him, realizing he had not been fully present to his friend's need. He called the friend, apologized, and inquired with genuine interest about his friend's well-being. He reports that his friend unpacked a significant concern. Rogers goes on to write that while he (Rogers) did not fix anything, his presence as a listener was what was called for. I have found this to be true myself. Most of the time, my spouse, close friends, and colleagues want me to be present as they unburden their concerns, as opposed to my taking action based on preconceived beliefs.

Thich Nhat Hanh had a story on this himself. Once, a close friend and fellow monk came to visit him at Plum Village, France. Hanh had made dinner, so his friend volunteered to wash the dishes, and thereafter the two friends would drink tea together. Hanh noticed, however, that his friend was rushing through the dishwashing in his desire to get to tea and their conversation. He chided his friend gently by asking, "Brother, are you washing the dishes to wash the dishes, or rushing to get to tea?" Essentially, he was expressing the need to be fully present with whatever one is involved in. Counseling work falls into a similar venue. Namely, that one must be fully present to the immediate moment. To borrow from John Kabat-Zinn, counseling, like mindfulness, requires paying attention, on purpose, in the present moment, and with wisdom (Kabat-Zinn, 2024). Healing from trauma, managing anxiety, daily stress, grief, and the like holds the same type of requirements. Active listening requires the same type of immediacy, setting aside other distractions, noticing and releasing any mind wandering, focusing on your breath, and remaining as present as possible while listening to a friend unburdening themselves before you. (Note: In my experience, presence is the most difficult of all therapeutic interventions to teach.)

Tip 3: Set Healthy Limits

Yes, we covered this area previously in Chapter 6. So, I'd suggest that you review the previous chapter and practice setting healthy limits with family, friends, and colleagues. Like getting physically and emotionally fit, there is no finish line, as it requires lifelong work. For readers wounded by trauma inflicted by close family members, setting healthy boundaries will take much work, ongoing practice, and possibly coaching from a therapist, as they have been conditioned that others will violate their boundaries. Setting and maintaining healthy boundaries is a must for healing; otherwise, you will find yourself feeling disrespected and violated.

My Responsibility to Heal

The following exercise is one I was taught during my graduate student years. I found it very helpful and have often assigned it to my clients. As always, I recommend you record this exercise in your Trauma Recovery Journal.

1 Many readers who were traumatized during childhood have become overly responsible and blame themselves for the trauma they have suffered. As in

a previous chapter, processing the story helps you lose your fear of the trauma. Consider the details of the traumatic event(s) you experienced, at least as best as you can recall. Make sure you use "I" statements and refrain from speaking in the third person.

____

____

____

2 Now, on a scale from 1 to 10, with 1 representing "I blame myself entirely for my trauma," and 10 representing "I blame the perpetrator completely," what number would you assign? My score = __/10
3 Now, consider the score you gave yourself in the previous question. If a close friend had suffered your level of abuse and trauma and gave themselves the same score as you assigned on item 2 above, how might you counsel them? Would you suggest they keep the same score, lower, or raise their score? Please explain.

____

____

4 Now that you have addressed a friend's score while using your own traumatic experience(s), in what ways do you continue to feel responsible for your pain?

____

____

5 Self-compassion has been mentioned several times in this workbook. Part of self-compassion involved forgiveness, most especially self-forgiveness. Perhaps you were traumatized as a child or adolescent and then found yourself attracted to abusers, who hurt you further, adding to your self-blame. Take the space in your Trauma Recovery Journal to write about how you will begin or continue the process of self-forgiveness. Be specific regarding the ways you can habituate the daily practice of self-forgiveness.

____

____

6 The Miracle Question: Okay, in this case, you have created the miraculous and have been practicing self-compassion and self-forgiveness for several months. What do you notice being different about yourself and your life? What do family members and close friends notice that is different about you?

____

____

7 Consider the previous six questions and ask yourself, "What have I learned about my responsibility to heal my trauma? What was *not* part of my responsibility?"

___

___

8 Shoulding all over myself: Catching, Challenging, and Changing the *Shoulds* and *Oughts* we tell ourselves. Albert Ellis (2011) was the master of instructing clients to address their absolutist self-talk, especially the should and ought statements. Imagine yet another empty chair conversation. This time, place Should in the empty chair, and using "I" statements, explain to her/him how you feel when she/he's occupying some space in your thoughts. Tell her/him what she or he has taught you. Then, switch chairs and let Should speak with you, and see what she/he has to say. Hold the same conversation with Ought.

9 What personal qualities do you truly love about yourself? Now, this is not a narcissism exercise, but a time to embrace a type of healthy, healing self-love. If you cannot think of anything, then ask a friend whom you trust what qualities they admire in you. Then, reflect on those qualities and record them in your Trauma Recovery Journal

___

___

10 This may have been a particularly difficult exercise to complete. Because traumatized people are frequently self-critical (van der Kolk, 2014), this is a brief space to praise yourself for completing the exercise and for facing your fears and leaning into the healing process. So, praise yourself in your journal.

___

___

My Short Essay on How I Began to Heal My Trauma (or Manage My Anxiety or Stress)

This exercise can be as brief or as expansive as you decide to make it. Some readers relate very well to narrative exercises, while others are less inclined toward writing. With this understanding, in your Trauma Recovery Journal, write an essay describing how you discovered the courage, determination, and grit to start and continue the healing process. As is the usual practice, use "I" statements in your essay. The essay can be as short as a few sentences or as long as several pages. Remember, you are the primary author of your healing.

Lessons Learned from This Chapter

Use your Trauma Recovery Journal to answer the following questions.

1. What is the most important lesson I learned from the exercises in this chapter?
2. How will I put the lessons I learned from this chapter into regular practice?
3. What is the most difficult part of healing your trauma/managing anxiety/stress?
4. What is the most rewarding part of healing your trauma/managing anxiety/stress?
5. During your trauma healing process, who have been your primary supports? (Name 3–4 people)

8 Calming the Lizard Brain for Home Life, Improved Work Relations, and Quality Sleep

Trauma, anxiety, and stress all overstimulate your autonomic nervous system, releasing cortisol and activating the fight, flight, or freeze impulse. Because your body has prepared you for activity, you are having difficulty sleeping. When you cannot relax and sleep, your physical and emotional health is going to suffer. This hyper-aroused state often leads to snapping at loved ones and colleagues, constant fatigue, difficulty concentrating, and being easily startled, causing you to hover in a state where you are one trigger away from blowing up at someone verbally or physically.

Once, I recall a college basketball coach expressing that he would tell his players, "Look, your body is like a very specialized car. You must put premium food in your body, like raw fruits and vegetables, get adequate sleep, and keep your attitude positive." He went on to emphasize that the hidden factor in performance was proper sleep. "I want my athletes to get eight hours," I recall him saying. Regardless of who we are, our personal situation, occupation, and so forth, everything will go better when we sleep and relax well. Trauma survivors and those with very stressful occupations and life circumstances are likely to struggle to relax and sleep. This chapter will target relaxation, offering examples of how you can begin to calm your anxious mind and relax and sleep. Now, if you are under the care of a physician, make sure that person understands your symptoms. I have my own doctor, and I follow his sound medical advice.

Creating More Restful Sleep

Many people need no assistance in falling asleep and remaining asleep. I once had a college roommate who could sleep through any noise. He slept a solid eight hours a night and always reported sleeping soundly and restfully. It's not that he always adhered to a healthy diet, refrained from excessive caffeine, or eschewed alcohol. In fact, he drank copious amounts of stout and black coffee, ate processed foods, including desserts, and was fond of a few beers on the weekends. He did little formal exercise, except that he was a firm believer in walking any distance less than 30 minutes. Long before counting steps was popular, he would easily have garnered 10 thousand plus daily, given walking

DOI: 10.4324/9781003689232-8

to campus (10 minutes), then across to where his classes were (another 10 minutes), walking around campus to the student center and library, back home, and sometimes to his favorite café 15 minutes from our residence. Now, he was fortunate, seemingly had never been traumatized, and suffered from no excessive anxiety (save occasional test anxiety), and was a high honor graduate. Likely, all readers of this workbook have known someone in their life like my former roommate.

Having treated people with sleep problems, my training led me to help clients prepare for bed in a variety of ways, which I shall briefly explain before moving on to relaxation exercises.

Trauma Survivors

I can recall one training session long ago where the trainer offered the less-than-sage advice that a key method of PTSD sufferers preparing for bed was to refrain from thinking about the abuse in the hour before bed. I found this advice stunning, as if trauma survivors, particularly sexual abuse survivors who were traumatized in bed, ***could somehow not think of their past abuse, especially around bedtime!*** My experience was that they were triggered by the time of day and preparation for bed, suffered significant anxiety at bedtime, and many had nightmares regarding their abuse. My long experience treating trauma survivors has taught me that they will indeed be triggered, disturbing memories will return, their sympathetic nervous system will go into overdrive, nightmares will occasionally or often occur, and their sleep will be of poor quality. Anyone who suffers from poor sleep will experience a myriad of health problems.

For Trauma Survivors, Consider the Following to Prepare for Sleep

1 First off, are you currently in treatment for trauma with a therapist specifically trained in treating trauma? (Or have you completed treatment?)
2 Were you physically active for at least 20 minutes during the day? (e.g., walking, yoga, jogging, swimming) Body movement is important in managing trauma and stress (McGonigal, 2017).
3 Mindfulness activity: Meditation is helpful for most trauma survivors. Now, roughly 5% of survivors are triggered by meditation (van der Kolk, 2014). So, if meditation is traumatic for you, instead of meditation, use the 5 senses approach (5 I can see, 4 I can hear, 3 I can smell, 2 I can feel, 1 I can taste).

Use aromatherapy with soothing scents, and slowly drink a warm, non-caffeinated beverage, focusing on the taste and temperature, how it feels sliding down your throat, and any warm, comforting sensation in your stomach.

Physical grounding is another approach: try squeezing a rubber ball, rolling it in your hands, knitting, or doing a self-hug with your arms (or hugging someone you trust), using the EFT tapping points, or the 5 senses exercise (above), Voo exhale, etc.

Body awareness: Perform simple exercises like the body scan (start at the soles of your feet and imagine a warm sensation slowly moving up your legs, midsection, chest, neck, and head), clench and unclench your fists, tense and release leg or other muscles, and then feel the release of tension and subsequent warmth.

Journaling: Use your Trauma Recovery Journal to explore your thoughts, feelings, and insights; identify triggers, and note any progress you have made in treatment. Create a narrative of how you are healing your trauma through therapy, support groups, body movement/exercise, breath work, journaling, art, spiritual life, and social support.

Calming the Lizard Mind: Now, when addressing intrusive memories, ironically, I always suggest the trauma survivor begin with the vagus nerve activities and music, breathing, focusing, etc. Focusing on thought replacement usually makes the thoughts more frequent and unmanageable. To quiet those intrusive, abusive memories, I suggest exercises like the following:

Try the EFT Tapping exercise from an earlier chapter (it's available online as well) and touch the 7 or 11 points three times each (I use the 11 points and tap three rounds for 33 taps total). Next, I use the Voo exhale: tilt your head slowly back, breathe deeply and naturally for 3–4 seconds, and exhale out your mouth for several seconds, making a Voo sound with pursed lips. Then, allow your lungs to fill naturally and repeat several times. I do 10 Voo exhales each morning right after my EFT tapping.

Another somatic exercise is taking a rock, ball, or other object, rolling it in your hand and focusing on the texture (smooth? rough?), temperature (does it feel cold or slightly warm?), and shape (is it round, jagged, or another shape?). What name might you give it?

Gratitude Acknowledgment: Each morning, I verbally acknowledge three people, things, etc. I am grateful for. First, I am grateful for my health, as it is not something to take for granted; second, I am grateful for my supportive spouse, as she's been a real blessing, and third, I am grateful that I found a fulfilling career as a counselor and professor, as I can recall being an undergraduate student struggling about and wondering if I'd ever amount to anything. So dear reader, what are your three gratitudes? You may acknowledge the same gratitudes daily, or different ones, whatever you wish.

Empty Chair Conversation (Brief Version): I explained the Empty Chair conversation in an early chapter and mentioned it several times since. When those unwelcome traumatic memories come knocking in the evening, try the previous somatic exercises to stimulate the vagus nerve. To top it off, speak to your traumatic memories. Explain that while you understand that they are actually saying to you, "Heal Me," you are working to heal yourself. Ask your traumatic memories if they might be quieter and gentler, as for you to heal, you need restful sleep. Then, switch chairs and channel the traumatic memories into one voice and let them advise you on how best to quiet them. Keep this conversation before bed brief (say, 10 minutes maximum, as you need sleep).

When in bed: Okay, you have gone through your vagus nerve work, relaxation exercises, meditation or other exercise, gratitudes, etc. Now, in bed, do not try and push any unpleasant thoughts away. Instead, focus on your ceiling, walls, or anything you might see, however dark the room may be. When I was younger and struggling with trauma recovery, I would imagine my bedroom ceiling as a giant world atlas; the small cracks and uneven parts of the rough ceiling represented mountains, canyons, deserts, and the ocean, and I would imagine traveling to these far-off locations and how amazing these experiences would be. Eventually, I would drift off to sleep during this imaginary geographic trek.

Another intervention to try is the Safe Place visualization that I have mentioned before. One trauma survivor's safe place was her van. She and her dog would drive to the coast, an hour away, and then park for the night. She'd crack the windows slightly and fall asleep to the rhythmic sound of the waves coming in and going out, the ever-present wind, and the occasional rain tapping on the metal roof of her van, all the while being safe locked in her van with her dog. The key is that your Safe Place is only for you, unless you choose to invite another person in (someone who has earned your trust, a pet, or a stuffed animal).

Other Pre-bedtime Wind Down Activities for Sleep

This is not an exhaustive list, but here are some suggestions that you may find helpful:

1. Listen to calm, relaxing music.
2. Meditate, pray, or do something else you find meaningful.
3. Read a relaxing book.
4. Practice regularity in going to bed at roughly the same time each night and rising at the same time each morning.
5. If you have difficulty sleeping, avoid all caffeine after the morning hours.
6. Sleep in the same bed each night (travelers will need to make adaptations).
7. Take a walk in the early evening to tire your body.
8. If you worry at night, spend time imagining those worries floating past as if on a river. Many people meditate in this manner. Also, use your box breathing (breathe in for 4 seconds, hold for 4 seconds, then exhale for 4 seconds, then hold for 4 seconds, and then repeat for 1–2 minutes).
9. Take a warm bath or shower before going to bed. As your body cools, you may find it easier to fall asleep (I do this most nights).
10. If you have a favorite stuffed animal, special blanket, pillow, etc., keep it close to your body.
11. Use your imagination by focusing on images you find relaxing. My image is that of sleeping in my old van on a cool, rainy night, rain lightly tapping on the roof. Another variation on this intervention is imagining your favorite relaxing activity. One client had taken a two-week camping trip

in the South Island of New Zealand and imagined himself on a 10-hour hike through the Otago Peninsula. He would fall asleep while imagining tramping through this beautiful scenery.

12 Do not try and force sleep. If you feel restless after, say, 30 minutes, get out of bed and do a quiet activity in dim light until you feel tired. (Refrain from using the internet surfing, reading news, etc.)

My Relaxation before Bedtime Routine

In your Trauma Recovery Journal, list your bedtime relaxation plan. You can make it as long or brief as needed. Some people may need only one helpful intervention, while others may require several interventions, so experiment and find what works for you. Consider the vagus nerve interventions (EFT tapping, Voo exhaling, etc.), visualizations (safe place, meditations, relaxing memories, etc.), breath work (box breathing, meditation, Voo exhaling), light physical activity (e.g., walking, gentle yoga), etc.

1 ____

2 ____

3 ____

4 ____

5 ____

I will stop at five, as that's quite a number. Try your routine for two weeks and see how it works regarding sleep improvement. Which of the interventions seemed to work particularly well? Which worked less well? You will need to tailor your list. After, say, one month, you may drop some interventions that seem to have no effect and try new ones.

What about Those Nights When I Cannot Sleep?

While I have healed my trauma and learned to sleep well, I have those occasional nights when I cannot seem to fall asleep. There are numerous variations in what people have found helps with insomnia. One therapist I worked with recommended getting out of bed and spending 30–45 minutes on an unpleasant cleaning chore. One sleep workshop I attended suggested reading a boring novel or listening to soothing music. I previously tried these latter approaches and found they did not work for me. What has worked for me is my Safe Place visualization, where I focus on the sounds of rain, waves, and wind, the cozy feel of my body under the quilt, locked away safely inside my old van. Soon, within this safe place visualization, I find myself drifting off to sleep. Now, you list as many of these strategies as you can. Record this list in your Trauma Recovery Journal.

Strategies to Relax on Those Nights When I Have Insomnia

1 ____________________

2 ____________________

3 ____________________

4 ____________________

5 ____________________

Start with these five above and see how well they work. Feel free to experiment, as that's how most of us find what works.

Cognitive Reframing of Upsetting, Unpleasant, and Traumatic Thoughts: Healing the Second Arrow of Pain

In Buddhism, being wounded by abuse (e.g., physical, verbal, or sexual), neglect, grief, or anything unpleasant represents the First Arrow's pain. The Second Arrow is our anger response and any additional pain we inflict upon ourselves through our overreactions, negative thoughts, and unhealthy activities like self-medication through alcohol or other drugs (Hahn, 1999). Trauma survivors often weaponize the second arrow and then inflict abuse on those closest to themselves, especially spouses or partners, children, co-workers, etc.

There are other types of suffering caused by reacting to the First Arrow. Remember, our unhealthy reaction becomes the Second Arrow. Common Second Arrow examples can include:

1 Negative self-talk: "I'm such a loser for failing to achieve the promotion!"
2 Catastrophizing: When we imagine the worst-case scenarios. Example: "My fiancée broke up with me, and nobody will ever want me!"
3 Awfulizing Narrative: Convincing ourselves that we will never get over that breakup or be accepted to our top college, means we'll never succeed; being fired means I'll never get another job, etc.
4 The second arrow can come in the form of self-abusive behaviors (SIBS), through cutting, burning, scratching, etc. I would express that self-medication through abusing chemical substances (e.g., alcohol & other drugs), engaging in unhealthy sexuality, and entering and remaining in abusive relationships are also examples of that second arrow.

Essentially, you can think of the Second Arrow as the one you shoot yourself with and sometimes other people. That Second Arrow is a significant reason for self-medication, losing family members, friends, being fired, etc. I had initially considered using the Second Arrow as part of this book's title. However, others have used it, and I wanted something particular to this book.

Refraining from Loading the Second Arrow (e.g., Disappointment, Rejection, Trauma)

Interestingly, I have found Second Arrow advice from Buddhist teachers like Thich Nhat Hanh to be very similar to Albert Ellis' shame-attacking approach (1999), albeit with far less profanity. As the Buddha explained, "In life, we cannot always control the First Arrow. However, the Second Arrow is our reaction to the First. The Second Arrow is optional." Basic steps to avoiding the Second Arrow might be:

1 **Be honest with yourself:** Lying to yourself only compounds the pain (Ex.: "Getting divorced was no big deal…"). Honestly acknowledge the pain you have experienced: Ex.: "Wow, this divorce really hurts!"
2 **Stimulus and Response:** As Viktor Frankl (2006) suggested, create a pause space between the stimulus (i.e., the First Arrow) and your response to it (the Second Arrow). This may involve counting to 10, box breathing, or briefly removing yourself from the stimulus (e.g., family member, co-worker, rude person on the train). A healthy pause may save you from making a difficult situation far worse. (I speak from painful experience on this!)
3 **Mentally observe your reaction and make a note:** Ex.: "I am noticing that I am feeling very hurt and angry at my former spouse." (Habituate this practice.) Vocalizing how you are feeling without any judgment towards self or others is a healthy practice to develop.
4 **Remember, you have choices:** Choose wisely. Many people in this world never consider that they have a choice when it comes to pain and disappointment (Corey, Corey, & Muratori, 2017). So, use breathwork (e.g., meditation, box breathing, Voo exhaling), vagus nerve work (e.g., EFT tapping, 5 senses), mental observation ("I am noticing that I am…"), and by cognitive revising of the negative story we are telling ourselves. (From "I am a complete loser!" to "I am human and do make mistakes at times").
5 **Practice acceptance**: I have written practice, as this is mostly what healing any mental, emotional, and physical pain involves. Athletes, actors, musicians, and many others practice long hours before performing, and this is a lesson for healing as well. This workbook is all about practicing so that we will *choose not to load* that Second Arrow into our bow. Practicing acceptance involves acknowledging reality ("Emotional rejection really hurts!"), observing our reaction without judgment (Self-compassion: "Okay, I am hurt and angry over being rejected."), releasing control over others ("I cannot change his/her mind. I can only work on my grief and anger"), understanding our resistance to emotional pain ("Hurt and anger are part of my human make-up"), and then taking appropriate action. (Going for grief counseling, joining a support group, daily meditation and prayer, acknowledging pain, being open to its lessons, etc.).
6 **Get emotional support**: One of the reasons cited for the continued success of 12-step recovery programs is the social support they offer. I recall conversing with a former professor of mine who had achieved sobriety

through AA. He reported that the most helpful aspect of AA was the personal support and accountability AA offered. He always had a sponsor to call when he felt ready to relapse. When he went on the road, he always checked to see where and when the AA chapter met. Some have advocated the development of a 12-step approach to PTSD recovery (March, 2020), something I believe is certainly worthwhile.

7. **Creative Visualization**: When you find yourself ruminating with anger, take a mental stroll through somewhere you find relaxing. That could be a beautiful beach, forest, desert, or any other location you find comforting. As you engage in this visualization, remember to use meditative breathing, slowly inhaling through your nose and slowly exhaling out your mouth. I like to spend at least 10 minutes on creative visualization.
8. **Use of Art:** Many people, especially those skilled in visual arts, find drawing, painting, or another related outlet an effective method of releasing anger, anxiety, and stress. For example, you might consider drawing what anger looks like. Then, make a second drawing of what peace or mindfulness looks like. Then compare the two drawings side by side. Which of these drawings would you wish to put your energy into? Do not judge yourself for feeling anger, as it's a natural human emotion. The important part is not to weaponize your anger but instead to transform it into a creative force. A third drawing could represent how to move from anger to peacefulness/mindfulness.
9. **Movement:** Movement is very helpful in managing anxiety and stress (McGonigal, 2017). Sometimes, taking a walk when upset can help to calm oneself and prevent the loading and shooting of that Second Arrow. Therapeutic movement is the most underrated component of mental and emotional well-being.
10. **Ask yourself**: "What do I want?" and "Will my expression of anger help me get what I want?" Now, you will need to practice radical honesty here, as it's easy to convince ourselves of what we desire to hear. (I know this all too well!) This is where an objective friend is very valuable for our well-being. If you have only friends who tell you what you desire to hear, you need new friends.

Recognizing My Anger Signals: Keeping the Second Arrow Unloaded

Once again, anger is a natural human emotion, much like joy, albeit not as enjoyable (Ellis, 2011; Matsakis, 2002). Trauma survivors, in particular, fear anger due to emotional dysregulation. Many people feel anger in their bodies more than anywhere else, due to the vagus nerve system. Some feel it in their stomach, others in their shoulders, lower back, etc. Many notice that their self-talk becomes angry, and thus the story they are telling themselves is harsh and full of blame for themselves and others. Sometimes, people who get angry lash out verbally or physically at others; some self-abuse by cutting or burning themselves, punching the wall, or using substances like alcohol or other drugs to ease the pain. In this exercise, record in your Trauma Recovery Journal answers to the following:

What are your signals of anger, and where in your body are these signals located?

____

____

Instead of lashing out in anger toward others, self-abuse, or self-medication (e.g., alcohol and drugs), I could use healthier outlets like:

1 ____

2 ____

3 ____

4 ____

5 ____

What do your answers suggest about you and the way you choose to express your anger?

____

____

What changes would you like to make in the ways that you express your anger?

____

____

Consider three people you know who are skilled at managing their anger. Write their names down and then ask them for tips on anger management. (Note: Three people skilled at managing their anger, not stuffing their anger)

1 ____

2 ____

3 ____

My Approach to Anger Management

While previous strategies for managing anger have been mentioned, this exercise provides specific responses for anger management. Remember, you will become angry at times, as such is part of the human set of emotions. This approach is to assist you in managing that anger. Record your answers in your Trauma Recovery Journal.

1 What are your most common anger triggers?

____

____

2 How might mindfulness-based breathwork help you manage your anger? (e.g., box breathing, Voo exhaling, meditation)

____

____

3 How might creative visualization assist in managing your anger? (e.g., Safe Place, Creative Visualization)

____

____

4 What's a special object you might hold that could help you manage your anger? (e.g., sacred object, special stone, important book)

____

____

5 When we are triggered and become angry, the story we are telling ourselves tends to be full of anger and blame of oneself and others (Brown, 2015; Ellis, 2011). How might you begin to revise your weaponized anger toward yourself or someone else?

____

____

6 What's a self-soothing technique or intervention that tends to help you reduce your anger? (e.g., EFT/Meridian tapping points, Voo exhaling, box breathing)

____

____

7 If you were to advise a loved one having trouble with anger management, what helpful suggestions might you make? (say 2–3)

____

____

8 Even people who have struggled with their anger also successfully manage it at other times. What's different about the times you practice successful anger management?

____

____

9 Consider someone in your network who you notice manages their anger well. Consider asking that person for suggestions on anger management.

____

____

10 What's a small reward you can give yourself for the times you successfully manage your anger? (e.g., coffee break, snack treat, short talk with a friend)

____

____

Situations That Cause Me to Become Angry

Keep in mind that anger is a common experience and emotion in everyone's life. Use your self-awareness from the exercises offered in this workbook and from others you may have learned previously. Use your Trauma Recovery Journal to answer the following questions regarding a situation that upsets you.

The situation that most upsets and triggers my anger is

____

My response in this situation usually is:

____

What I am thinking in this situation is:

____

My needs in this situation are:

____

My fears in this situation are:

____

My regrets in this situation are:

____

One way I could be more successful in managing my anger during this situation is:

____

What resources do I already possess that might help me manage my anger during this situation?

____

Healthy, alternative ways to manage my anger in this situation could involve:

____

My Forgiveness Routine

A significant part of stored-up anger involved old wounds. These wounds are commonly suffered in childhood and adolescence, although they may be experienced at any age, given domestic violence, workplace bullying, sexual assault, etc. (Briere & Scott, 2015). Forgiveness was discussed in the previous chapter, and a simple approach is utilized. Remember, forgiveness does not mean negating the wound, excusing the perpetrator, or minimizing the trauma. Forgiveness is simply a way of acknowledging the need to release the burden of long-held, self-destructive anger. There is an adage that "hurt people hurt people." As a therapist, I have found this universally true. I would also add that people previously hurt by others also tend to hurt themselves. Thus, I like to have the client begin with self-forgiveness.

The Verbal Approach to Forgiveness

1 **Forgiving yourself:** Stand before a mirror and look kindly at your reflection and say, "I forgive you for the mistakes you have made. You are only human, and I love you."

   As in 12-step programs, self-acknowledgment of a problem is the first and most important step. I encourage you to express genuine self-forgiveness and compassionate love. So, repeat this exercise for several days, or as long as needed until you believe what you are saying.

2 **Forgiving others:** As I noted in the previous chapter, you must be emotionally ready to forgive the perpetrator. Do not force this exercise on yourself. For example, *I do not recommend you try this* if the experience(s) was extremely traumatic (i.e., sexual assault) unless you have been in treatment for that trauma. If you have been in treatment and are ready, then use the empty chair conversation and say to the abuser, "I forgive you. I forgive you even though you did not ask for my forgiveness. I forgive you so that I may be free of you and the oppressive hold you have held over me. I forgive you, and now I shall be free of you." (This exercise may require periodic self-reminding.) In most cases, *I do not recommend the traditional empty chair exercise where the other party (i.e., perpetrator) speaks back to the abused person.*

The Narrative Approach to Forgiveness

1. **Forgiving yourself:** Write a forgiveness letter to yourself explaining that you are forgiving yourself for being imperfect, for making mistakes, using harsh self-judgment, relapses, etc. Use the I-statements approach. When finished, address and sign it. Keep the letter as proof of forgiveness when you are tempted to engage in self-blame.
2. **Forgiving others:** Write a forgiveness letter/email message to whomever you wish to forgive. Express why you are forgiving them, while acknowledging the hurt they have caused you. Use I-statements and refrain from taking on self-blame. (You may need to write several of these letters). Now, you do not necessarily need to send these letters/emails to the person you have forgiven, as that might not be appropriate. Writing them, especially when writing by hand, tends to make a stronger impact on the person writing the message (Pennebaker, 2004; Van der Weel & Van der Weel, 2024). Thus, I encourage you to write the letters the old-fashioned way by pen, preferably, but write them by whatever means necessary that increases your likelihood of writing them.

The Creative Approach to Forgiveness

1. **Forgiving yourself:** The important part to remember here is that one need not be a great visual artist, writer, poet, musician, etc., to use creativity. Using whatever medium you prefer, write a paragraph on forgiving yourself, a self-forgiveness poem, a short story on self-forgiveness, write a self-forgiveness song, paint or draw a self-forgiveness painting or drawing, create a self-forgiveness collage, etc. Expressing self-forgiveness is an important part of the exercise, while the medium and quality of expression are up to you.
2. Forgiving others: Review the self-forgiveness portion above and use the creative outlet you prefer. Again, make sure you have the emotional bandwidth to engage in the act of forgiving another person(s). Once again, do not force the act of forgiveness, as that can be emotionally damaging to oneself.

The Forgiveness Meditation

1. **Forgiving yourself:** You can do this in either a sitting or walking meditation, use the mantra of "I forgive you" (or something like this phrase), or simply do a silent meditation where you send thoughts of loving kindness towards yourself. For example, "May I be well, may I be kind, may I be happy, may I be healthy," or any other four-part self-compassionate set of statements.
2. **Forgiving others:** You can use the instructions above for forgiving others. The same disclaimer regarding readiness to forgive others applies here: Are you emotionally ready? Did you do your healing work in therapy/a 12-step program/something similar?

The Forgiveness Activity

1. **Forgiving yourself:** Many readers may find this exercise odd. However, I have found it very helpful personally, and some others have as well. This routine involves focusing on forgiving yourself while engaging in physical activity (e.g., yoga, walking, cycling, jogging). I have spent hours walking and jogging while simultaneously practicing self-forgiveness (AKA self-compassion). Use your favorite type of physical activity while focusing on the simple mantra of, "I forgive you."
2. **Forgiving others:** Use the same format as above, with the same caution on your readiness to forgive others. I usually find that when engaged in physical exertion, I am more compassionate toward myself and others.

Note to Readers

Forgiveness, whether regarding yourself or others, often involves ongoing practice (Lama & Cutler, 2009). So, be prepared that even when you have healed your wounds and practiced ongoing forgiveness and self-compassion, you will occasionally relapse to old, unhealthy thoughts, at least temporarily. When this occurs, remember your forgiveness mantras (above). The difficulty in being human is that we relapse back at moments to old, unhealthy ways (if not longer), and the reward in being human is that we are presented opportunities to practice what we already know in our hearts to be true, that is, love and forgiveness.

Furthermore, my experience as a longtime therapist, international trainer, friend, and family member is that articulating the words "I forgive you" (towards self or others) may be the three most difficult words in any language. I had always thought "I love you" was the most difficult phrase for many, but in my professional and personal experiences, it's "I forgive you."

Personal Boundaries: Setting Limits with Others

No one will be able to achieve or maintain good emotional health without setting appropriate boundaries with people in their lives. Boundaries protect us from being taken advantage of by others and keep us from developing resentment when we over-extend beyond reasonable limits. Consider how often you may have said "yes" when you wanted to say "no." People in trauma recovery, in my experience, often over-extend and have real difficulty in setting limits due to repeatedly having their boundaries violated by abusers. As one former client said to me, "My dad was so violent and disrespectful to my mom and siblings that our boundaries just didn't exist." In many regards, teaching survivors of long-term abuse often struggle to set and maintain healthy boundaries since they are so novel to them. In fact, beyond the usual abuse, boundary violation is a key dynamic of an abuser.

Setting boundaries is a critical form of self-care and one that all people must learn to master, even if others occasionally become angry with us. Setting boundaries is part of all theoretical approaches to counseling. Setting and maintaining boundaries, however, can be challenging for many people. Sometimes, it's helpful to have a framework for creating boundaries. The 4C's of Boundary Setting (Burnett, 2023) may be instructive. The 4 C's are:

1 **Clarity:** Be specific about your needs, comfort level, and where the limits are located. Vague boundaries will confuse others and be ineffective.
2 **Communication:** Clearly express your boundaries to others respectfully, openly, and firmly.
3 **Consistency:** Enforce your boundaries consistently. A healthy boundary is an ongoing practice, and practice habituates the desired trait.
4 **Consequences:** When your boundaries are crossed, clearly communicate what will happen. Consistent follow-through is critical so that others understand your boundaries are solid. One consequence is to inform the other party that they are acting inappropriately. If said party continues violating your boundaries, then you have choices depending on the relationship (e.g., spouse/partner, boss, colleague). In some cases, you may need to make very difficult choices, such as divorce, firing a boss, or filing a complaint with Human Resources or another such office.

   Note: Although it's not a word beginning with the letter c, I'd add practice as a fifth step in setting healthy boundaries. So, take the remainder of your life and practice setting limits with others.

Saying No: Practicing One of the Hardest, But Most Necessary Expressions

Regarding boundaries, you will need to develop a comfort level with saying "no" to others in your life; otherwise, the 4 C's of boundaries will be meaningless. Given that many struggle to say the word, my experience is that practice helps with confidence. Record your answers to the questions below in your Trauma Recovery Journal.

1 When I say "no," I usually feel guilty. True ___ False ___

2 If you checked "True" to the previous question, please explain your reasons for feeling guilty.

   ____

   ____

3 What is the most difficult part of saying "no" to others?

   ____

   ____

4 When you want to say "no" but say "yes" instead, how do you feel?

___

___

5 How could you begin to start saying "no" when you want to do so?

___

___

6 Stand before the mirror and, while looking yourself in the eye, say the word "No" for one minute. When you say "No," ask yourself, "Do I sound believable?" If you did not sound believable, what could you do to sound believable?

___

___

7 Set out two chairs facing one another. Take a seat and play the role of a colleague who asks you to do a task you do not wish to take on. In fact, speaking as that colleague, make the request out loud. Then, you will practice answering "No, I'm sorry, but I have too many tasks to add another at present." Practice this scenario for a full minute. An alternative scenario is to practice this with a close friend.

8 Regarding the previous situation, on a scale of 1–10, with 10 being you felt confident saying "no", what was your score? Now, how could you increase your confidence score by 1 point?

___

___

9 Regarding saying "no," practice saying "No," to a colleague twice a week for one month. Then, after a month of practice, check to see if your confidence score has increased. How much of an increase occurred over four weeks?

___

___

10 When you are consistently saying "No," how will your life be improved? What will others notice that is different about you?

___

___

Practical Boundary Practice: Finding and Maintaining Your Safe Space

This workbook is about habituating a practice of challenging and changing unhealthy thoughts and behaviors in practical and innovative ways. Consider the following exercises and record in your Trauma Recovery Journal:

1 What amount of personal space do you need to feel comfortable or safe? (i.e., 3 feet? 5 feet?) _____feet/or metric

2 How do you communicate that boundary to others when they approach you?

____

____

3 How do you maintain that safe/comfortable space?

____

____

4 How do you communicate your safe space boundary when others get too close to your physical space?

____

____

5 When someone violates your safe space, how do you feel in your body? (i.e., queasy, increased blood pressure, heart rate, and respiration)

____

____

6 Select a friend whom you trust and ask that person to walk towards you until you say the word "Stop." When you say "Stop," that space between you is your safe space. What is that safe space distance in feet? (or meters if not in the U.S.) Safe Space = ____ feet. Remember this distance in relationships with colleagues and enforce it consistently.

7 Now, with that same trusted friend, ask them to move into your safe zone. This is a boundary violation. Then, tell that friend to step back until they are outside your safe zone. Practice this exercise with that friend and ask several times so that you feel more confident in setting your limits.

8 Stand before the mirror and once a day, every day for four weeks, tell your reflection, "Stop! Now, step back ___ feet." (whatever distance your safe space requires)

9 As you practice your safe space before the mirror, grade your confidence in asserting your right to that safe space on a 1–10 scale, with 10 being fully confident. Do this daily for one month of practice. At the end of 30 days, what is your score?

10 The most important lesson regarding boundaries is to remember to keep your safe space and distance consistent with colleagues and others in your life. So, how will you maintain consistency in keeping your safe space with others?

____

____

Respect My Boundaries Assertiveness Worksheet

People will occasionally invade our boundaries for a variety of reasons. Some people will cross our boundaries accidentally, others because they are angry, and some because they are abusers. The following exercise is one where you can develop a script to gently, but firmly, inform boundary invaders that they have violated your space and dignity. After you fill this out (using your Trauma Recovery Journal), I suggest you practice by looking in the mirror and reading the statement.

By speaking rudely to me in front of others or individually, I feel __________ ________________________ (e.g., embarrassed, judged, humiliated, violated). I expect you to treat me with the respect you treat others. Should you continue to be ____________________________________ (be rude to me, disrespect me, try and humiliate me, etc.), I will __________ ____ (end the relationship, speak with your supervisor, file a harassment complaint, etc.).

Now, a few tips: if you do use this exercise with a supervisor or colleague, be prepared, you may not always get the results you desire. Generally, asserting your rights leads to being treated with respect—but not always. There are habitual abusers in the workplace, in government, in schools, in universities, in politics, in houses of worship, etc. Unfortunately, there are spineless supervisors, weak HR departments, and abusers in these positions who chronically fail to protect workplace rights. Remember, you will need to fire an employer should that workplace make you sick, if it tolerates abusive behavior, and traumatizes you.

Likewise, it must also be said that should you find yourself in a personal relationship (e.g., family, spouse or romantic partner, friend) with someone who disrespects and abuses you, you will need to get out of that relationship. Naturally, you will need emotional support from caring family, friends, and perhaps a counselor.

Remember, bullies do not disappear from our lives when we finish high school. They unfortunately present throughout the lifespan. One summer, I worked as an orderly in a residential nursing center. There were a few elderly bullies there as well, and they were on the lookout for victims.

My Healthy Boundaries Checklist

Review the following list and put a check mark beside statements that are true for you.

My personal boundaries are healthy because:

1 __ I have healthy boundaries in the following areas of my life (e.g., home, workplace, at school/college)

____

2 __ I take time to get to know a person better before trusting them with intimate details of my life.
3 __ I inform others of only what I am comfortable disclosing.
4 __ I do not change my values or behavior just to please others.
5 __ With a new romantic partner, I refrain from an intimate, sexual relationship until the relationship matures.
6 __ I do not accept being touched by others when I do not want it.
7 __ If someone violates my safe space/personal space, I inform that person that I am uncomfortable and step back.
8 __ Regarding the previous statement, if someone (e.g., co-worker, boyfriend, girlfriend, family member) continually violates my boundaries, I speak with a supervisor, HR official, or break up with that person (whatever applies).
9 __ I do not expect other people to know my needs unless I inform them.
10 __ I practice self-compassion (e.g., forgiving myself, refraining from self-judgment) regularly.
11 __ I respect my mental, emotional, and physical well-being by regular physical exercise, socializing with friends and family, getting regular sleep, refraining from drug use, and drinking alcohol responsibly if I drink.
12 __ When a potential romantic partner or someone I desire to be friends with rejects me, I acknowledge the disappointment and remain open to other friends and romantic partners.
13 __ When I receive disappointments (e.g., don't get the job offer, promotion, romantic partner) I acknowledge the disappointment, seek support from a trusted family member or friend, and do not self-medicate with alcohol or drugs.
14 __ When I find myself in a relationship (romantic relationship, family, friend, etc.) that is disrespectful and abusive, I end the relationship (and get support from therapy, friends, family, etc.)
15 __ I do not seek to please others just to earn a romantic partner or friend.

Now, how many of these did you check? The more you check, the healthier you likely are in establishing and maintaining healthy boundaries. For those statements you left blank, review the following exercise (in your Trauma Recovery Journal) and explore the beliefs behind why you left them unchecked. Remember, be honest but practice self-compassion in your answers.

The statements I left blank include:

1 ____________________

2 ____________________

3 ____________________

The beliefs that caused me to refrain from checking all statements are:

1 ____________________

2 ____________________

3 ____________________

I am willing to work on changing those beliefs by doing:

1 ____________________

2 ____________________

3 ____________________

Remember the work you have done to establish healthy boundaries. Now, be consistent in maintaining those healthy boundaries with family, friends, romantic partners, and co-workers. This will take ongoing work as you will be challenged and tempted to revert to old, unhealthy behavior patterns.

Writing Your Personal Short Story on Healing

If you were to write a brief short story (whatever length you are comfortable with) on your personal healing from trauma story, what would you write? Here's a suggestion: write a brief short story with you as the main character. Briefly describe your healing journey, who has been important in that healing (cite yourself and others), and how it has improved your life (e.g., emotional health, with family and friends, career). Include the life lessons that you have learned along your healing journey, and how you will continue to work on developing healthy relationships in the future (intimate, family, friends, co-workers).

Drawing Your Healing

Long ago, a client came into counseling with me for sobriety maintenance and trauma healing. She informed me she did not like talk therapy and stated her coping mechanism was drawing. She brought along her sketch pad and showed me several of her drawings. She was very skilled, especially in illustrating her life struggles in pictures. Having learned not to argue with clients, I asked her to draw her life, whereupon she sketched a very dark picture. She explained her drawing, recounting childhood trauma that continued into adulthood and accompanying self-medication. I explained that drawing would be the focus of our therapy. I then requested she draw a picture of what her healed self might look like. Whereupon she commenced with more enthusiasm. Her second sketch was full of light, bright colors, and joyful people. I explained this is our treatment goal and that we would need to get there in steps.

Each week, her homework assignment was to draw her life and any improvements or challenges. I would then ask clarifying questions and offer my insights and suggestions. She drew sketches of her 12-step meeting, relationship with her two young children, with her mother, her struggle with sobriety, her dreams for the future, and her healing journey. Throughout her therapy, her drawings became more upbeat, transforming from dark imagery to vivid colors, and eventually, earning her a one-year AA coin. Her final drawing involved graduating from therapy, wearing a cap and gown, a bright smile on her face, and the pathway towards a better future for her and her children.

So, if you are so inclined, draw how your life looks at the present, including any healing work you have done with trauma, stress management, and depression management. In fact, draw anything that seems relevant to your recovery. Then, when you finish that drawing, draw a second picture of how you want your life to look in six months. Then, draw what you would want your life to resemble in, say, 5 years (e.g., home, family, career). Your final sketch may be drawing how you will create the life you desire in 5 years (or whatever timeframe).

Lessons Learned

As usual, record in your Trauma Recovery Journal.

What was the most important lesson you learned from this chapter?

____

____

How will this lesson you have learned help in your continued healing journey?

____

____

During this chapter, a significant focus was placed on setting and maintaining healthy boundaries. What is the most challenging part of creating and maintaining healthy boundaries for you?

____

____

One Percent Better

On a scale of 1–10, with 10 being high, what's your current trauma healing score? Okay, what's one activity, or action, or change, you could make to improve your score by one point?

____

____

Tough Decisions

If you had to divorce an abuser, or fire an abusive boss, or file a complaint against an abusive boss with HR, or your state's Labor Commission, how would you find the courage to take this action?

____

____

____

Courage

Where does your courage to continue in the face of adversity come from?

____

____

How are you able to sustain your courage?

____

____

9 Managing Stress

EFT Tapping, Breathwork, Meditation, and Movement

Everyone, regardless of culture, age, gender, or other factors, experiences stress. Stress can be defined as a state of anxiety caused by a difficult or challenging situation (WHO, n.d.). Stress is a natural human response that prompts us to address challenges and threats in our lives. So, everyone gets stressed at times, and that is unavoidable. However, stress can be moderated through reframing our thoughts (Beck, 2019; Ellis, 2011), sustained body movement (McGonigal, 2017), meditation (Levine, 2011), and emotional support (Bentley et al., 2021). When we perceive a stressful situation, our bodies release stress hormones. These hormones (e.g., cortisol, adrenaline) evolved through evolution to help primitive humans escape large predators. When the threat passes, stress abates, and the formerly stressed person feels relieved. Now, imagine the person who had the misfortune of growing up in a violent or chaotic home or living in a war zone or a violent neighborhood. Many people who survived such traumatic experiences become traumatized (i.e., PTSD) and carry that trauma even when they are removed from that dangerous environment. Such people are described as emotionally dysregulated (van der Kolk, 2015), meaning they are always hypervigilant about danger. That hypervigilance leads to hypertension, emotional lability, and a fight, flight, or freeze mode when facing perceived threats (Briere & Scott, 2015).

Having treated trauma survivors for 25 years, self-medication with alcohol and drugs is a common coping mechanism, and addiction treatment programs are full of traumatized people. In fact, I cannot recall a single addict I counseled who was not traumatized. Perhaps the most memorable such client was a homeless, former combat veteran who had eight different DSM diagnoses! This intelligent, well-read ex-serviceman opined that his struggles were all about his trauma. His PTSD had led to numerous health issues, complicated by his self-medication. He went on to say that stress was one of his major triggers and that it tended to inflate like a balloon until it popped. The popping meant his explosive trigger was engaged, and as an ex-soldier, he fought, causing himself and his former spouse much additional trauma and legal problems.

DOI: 10.4324/9781003689232-9

Basic Facts Regarding Chronic Stress

For trauma survivors, stress engages in the fight-flight-freeze response through the amygdala and hippocampus, which release stress hormones. Because people with PTSD are always on the edge of panic, cortisol is constantly being released, resulting in hypervigilance and heart concerns, and may result in damaged adrenal glands. Chronic stress can also cause chronic fatigue, stomach problems, headaches, and a weakened immune system, among other maladies (Cleveland Clinic, n.d.). As has been mentioned previously, trauma and stress become stored in the body, and then we must utilize a multi-pronged approach to heal the mind, body, breath, and spirit of that trauma and stress. The following interventions represent different methods of releasing trauma and stress from our bodies. Most of them have been covered in previous chapters, but repetition is a part of any practice and improvement.

Breathwork

Breathwork regarding stress is two-fold, as it depends on how stress is manifesting in the body. As one who has taught meditation, it is often a common method of managing and reducing stress. However, if you experience a panic attack, box breathing will be more effective. In box breathing, you may sit comfortably in a chair or lie down on your back. Some therapists will ask you to place one hand on your chest and another on your stomach to help regulate the process (although I have not found the hand aspect necessary).

Box Breathing

1. Step 1: Breathe in normally through your nose, counting to four slowly, feeling the air fill your lungs.
2. Then, hold your breath for 4 seconds.
3. Then, slowly exhale out of your mouth for 4 seconds.
4. Then, hold your breath for another 4 seconds before breathing in via your nose and repeating the process. You may need to complete 2–3 cycles of box breathing.

If needed, repeat. Box breathing helps interrupt panic attacks by focusing on the breath count by shifting attention away from trigger stressors. Box breathing can be used to help with insomnia and help you refocus when having a difficult day (Felson, n.d.).

The second type of breathing recommended for stress management is the more popular type known as meditation. While most of us think of meditation as sitting silently on a cushion, several practices fall under the large tent of meditation (Hanh, 1999). Some of the more common types of meditation involve being aware of your thoughts as they pass through your mind (mindfulness meditation), focused meditation (counting breaths or using a mantra such as "May I be compassionate"), and moving meditation (e.g., Tai Chi, walking meditation, walking in a labyrinth, dancing meditation). My own approach to meditation is a variation on mindfulness meditation, whereby you cultivate an awareness of your thoughts, allowing them to float past as if on a river.

Mindful Meditation

1 Sit on a cushion, bench, or chair, whatever is most comfortable.
2 First, breathe in slowly through your nose for, say, 3–4 seconds.
3 Then, slowly exhale through your mouth for 3–4 seconds.
4 Repeat the process for several minutes. (For starters, I recommend 5 minutes.)
5 When your mind wanders—as it will—simply focus on your breath.

You may wish to experiment with a variety of meditation approaches, including using an app for guided meditation. Whatever works best for you is the approach to take.

Walking Meditation

1 Select a location you find calming (e.g., forest, park, beach, labyrinth) and where you have at least 15 minutes or more to walk.
2 Focus on your posture and the feel of your feet as you walk across the earth, sand, or sidewalk.
3 Pay attention to the process of each step: lifting, moving, contact with the ground, and lifting your feet, etc.
4 Breathe naturally and comfortably as you walk.
5 Engage your 5 senses: Be aware of what you see, smell, hear, feel, and taste.
6 When your mind wanders, gently bring your attention back to the sensation of your feet grounding on the earth or your 5 senses.

Again, some readers may find they prefer to listen to a guided walking meditation app while walking. If guided meditation feels more helpful for you, then I encourage you to use that style. I also encourage readers to experiment with meditation styles, as there are several meditation variations. The "best" one is the one that seems most natural for you.

Vagus Nerve Breathwork

One of my daily go-to breathwork practices is the Voo Exhale. Like many of the breath and body interventions, this one is likely 2000 years old (Levine, 2011). In fact, it was only very recently that the mental health field began to incorporate ancient body and breath intervention into Western-style psychotherapy. The first time someone tried to get me to use the Voo Exhale, I was very resistant, given my faith in Western approaches to counseling. However, a colleague finally convinced me to give it a try, and I found the intervention worked very well! The sustained Voo sound stimulates the vagus nerve, which assists in activating the parasympathetic nervous system, the body's reset system. This grounding technique seems to shift the body from the sympathetic nervous system to the parasympathetic nervous system. This shift often results in the individual moving from feeling overwhelmed or stressed to a state of calm (Levine, 2011).

Voo Exhale (Also Called the Voo Breath)

1. Sit or lie down in a comfortable position.
2. Inhale deeply through your nose, allowing your stomach and lungs to expand.
3. Exhale, making a low "Voo" sound that originates from your stomach and chest.
4. Notice the vibration this sound creates in your body, particularly in your stomach.
5. Repeat the process for several minutes. In my own practice, I do 10 Voo Exhale cycles each morning.

Meridian Tapping Points

As was mentioned in an earlier chapter, EFT/meridian tapping points are specific locations on the face and upper body where you can gently tap or simply touch with your fingertips to tap into the vagus nerve system to reduce stress and even chronic pain for temporary relief. While some variations in EFT/meridian tapping exist, common tapping points are the karate chop (side of the hand), eyebrow, side of the eye, under the eye, under the nose, chin, collarbone, under the arm, side of the ribs, top of the head, and the gamut spot between the ring and small finger.

You will find these tapping points located along traditional Chinese acupuncture meridians:

1. Karate Chop: The fleshy outer edge of your hand, below the little finger.
2. Top of Head: The crown of your head.
3. Eyebrow Point: At the beginning of the eyebrow, nearest the bridge of the nose.
4. Side of the Eye: On the bone at the outside edge of the eye. (tap both sides of the eye).
5. Under Eye: On the bone directly under the pupil.
6. Under Nose: The area directly between the nose and the upper lip.
7. Chin Point: In the indentation between the lower lip and chin.
8. Collarbone: On the collarbone, about an inch from the center notch, on either side.
9. Under Arm: On your side, about 4 inches below the armpit.
10. In the gamut between the ring finger and the little finger.

I recommend three rounds of tapping the above points (11 taps, counting both sides of the Eyebrow Point), for 33 tap points. I usually feel a warm feeling in my ankles, and then it moves upward. Some former clients have informed me that their chronic pain is temporarily lessened (one dropped from 9 to 1 on the pain scale!), and PTSD clients have generally volunteered that the tapping points helped them self-soothe.

Additional Information on Tapping

Some clinicians teach the client to make statements such as "I don't like feeling stressed." I take a different approach, making positive statements like, "I am managing my stress," or "My grief will slowly lift," and "I am grateful for..." My approach is to always focus on promoting a more positive approach to the issue, even if it's an incremental positive (e.g., "Small progress is progress"). I would also mention that many clients and people attending my workshops are skeptical regarding Meridian Tapping and Voo exhaling until they actually try them. So, give these ancient healing methods an honest effort, as you may be pleasantly surprised, as many of my former clients have been.

Healing Movements

Researchers have found that even moderate levels of exercise can help mitigate the risk of depression, anxiety, and stress and promote better quality sleep (Dishman et al., 2021; McGonigal, 2017). I define regular exercise as four times a week for 20 minutes per workout. My former clients would often ask, "What is the most important exercise to do?" My answer is, "The one you most enjoy and will continue with." For those who desire more information regarding the benefits of exercise, I recommend Kelly McGonigal's *The Joy of Movement: How Exercise Helps Us Find Happiness, Hope, Connection, and Courage* (2017). McGonigal points out that sustained movement for 20 minutes or longer stimulates the release of what she calls hope molecules into your brain, thus reducing depression and anxiety. I had noticed during my late teenage years, when struggling with both anxiety and depression, that my morning jogging routine always left me feeling very upbeat for 2–3 hours after my run was completed.

The difficult part of fitness, be it emotional or physical, is that there is no stopping point. Readers of this workbook are strongly encouraged to habituate a lifelong practice of physical activity for managing anxiety and depression, and reducing the risk of developing dementia (Wanigatunga et al., 2025). The important part here is that the researchers emphasize moderate exercise, meaning walking, dancing, cycling, etc. at a comfortable pace for the participant. Back in the late 1970s, cardiologist, marathoner, author, and running devotee Dr. George Sheehan recommended that the average marathoner should run at a pace where they could comfortably talk (Sheehan, 2018). Simply walking

20 or more minutes, four times per week, at a pace where you can carry on a conversation with an exercise partner helps manage anxiety and stress, and potentially prevent, or at least delay, dementia. Readers who have completed treatment for PTSD and those in treatment for PTSD, regular physical activity, as discussed here, will be very important in your recovery from and management of severe anxiety symptoms.

Trauma Release Exercises

Trauma release exercises (TRE) are intentional movements that induce muscle tremors to release tension, trauma, and stress held in the body. TREs involve gentle stretching to tire muscles, which then begin to shake, mimicking an animal's response to trauma and resetting their nervous system. TREs are a somatic approach method to address physical and emotional tension stored in the body and nervous system. TREs are a safe, self-help approach for managing daily stress, anxiety, and physical tension and may be adapted for most people.

Those who experience physical and emotional trauma feel trauma's impact on their body and breath, as well as their mind. While CBT, for example, is an efficacious approach to address faulty cognitions, it does little to address tension stored in the muscles (van der Kolk, 2015). A significant component of TREs is stretching. Stretching is deliberately lengthening a specific part of your body for improved flexibility, relaxation, and mobility. Yoga is one of the more popular approaches to deliberate stretching. Stretching promotes increased circulation to your muscles, which aids in relaxation and health. A regular stretching routine and deep breathing routine can help reduce the severity of PTSD symptoms (Kim et al., 2013). Remember, humans evolved as moving creatures (Harari, 2015; McGonigal, 2017), and movement is critical to healing trauma (van der Kolk, 2014)

While stretching is not a substitute for trauma-centered counseling, it can serve as a significant support for those in therapy for PTSD (Kim et al., 2013). The TRE approach focuses on a strong mind-body-breath connection to help facilitate the release of emotional trauma. TRE is designed to safely trigger the body's natural reflex to bring the body back to homeostasis (Levine, 2011). Like all other exercises in this workbook, the positive effect will vary depending on the person and their need. As one who performs some of the following exercises daily (and does additional stretching), I find my physical flexibility closely related to my emotional stability, something born out in research (Kim et al., 2013; Lynning et al., 2021). With this in mind, let's examine some examples of TRE stretching.

1 **Seated Side Bending**: You may perform this exercise sitting in a chair or on the floor. Elevate your hips, then reach your right arm toward the right while stretching the left arm up and over the head toward the right. Then, reverse sides. The physical benefit is creating more space in the spine and

increasing your range of motion. The emotional benefit lies in releasing tension from the muscles and spine region.

2 **Neck Rolls**: While sitting on the floor, in a chair, or standing, allow your chin to drop to your sternum to lengthen the back of your neck. Gently tilt the right ear toward the right shoulder to lengthen the left side of the neck. Then, switch sides. (Note: This is one of my go-to exercises.) The physical benefit is that it relaxes and stretches the neck muscles and alleviates tension and stiffness. The emotional benefit is that it can help relieve anxiety through subtle sensations in the body.
3 **Child's Pose:** Kneel and sit on your knees. Lean forward, keeping your buttocks on your heels, and fold your upper body forward. Rest your forehead on a towel to allow your neck to relax. Move your arms next to your legs, palms upward. The physical benefit is that it stretches your lower back and hips (I use this stretch each morning before my run and swear by it!). The emotional benefit is to help with grounding yourself for emotional stability. In fact, imagine yourself being connected to the solid floor, stabilizing your body and soul.
4 **Standing Forward Bend:** Stand with your feet hip-width apart and your upper body hanging over your lower body. Anchor through your feet and slightly bend your knees, leaving your arms free and dangling, or take hold of your opposite elbows. Hold this pose for 30 seconds before gently rolling back up to a standing position. The physical benefit involves stretching and lengthening the legs and hips, releasing tension from the spine to create more space. The emotional benefit involves calming the mind.
5 **Cat-Cow Pose**: Get on your hands and knees so that your wrists are directly underneath your shoulders and your knees are underneath your hips. Inhale and arch your spine into a small back bend, reaching the chest forward and up. On exhale, round the spine, moving your chin toward your chest, and drop your head. Repeat the sequence three times. The physical benefit is in stretching the wrists, hips, legs, and spine and strengthening the lower abdomen. The emotional benefit is that it grounds and syncs your breath to movement, increasing the mind-body-breath awareness.
6 **Reclined Knee to Chest Pose**: Lie on your back, drawing both knees into your chest, and then straighten one leg out in front. Keep the other leg hugged against your chest for 30 seconds. Then, switch legs. (This is one stretch that a former student who was a gymnast recommended to me 30 years ago. I use it each night at bedtime.) The physical benefit is that it lengthens the spine while stretching the lower back. The emotional benefit lies in increasing feelings of calm.
7 **Reclined Pigeon/Figure Four Pose:** Begin by lying on your back with your knees bent, feet on the floor, close to the hips. Lift your right knee and bring it close to your chest. Cross the right ankle over the left thigh and flex the right foot. For a deeper stretch, pull the thigh toward your torso and relax your shoulders to the ground. The physical benefit lies in stretching the glutes and hips to reduce lower-body tension. The emotional benefit is that it unlocks the emotional center and alleviates anxiety.

8 Another of my favorite stretches, and one I use each morning, is the Cat-Cow pose. Start on your hands and knees, then alternate between slowly arching your back (Cat) and slowly letting your belly drop while looking up (Cow). I do 30 seconds of the Cat and then the Cow pose.

These are just a few examples of TRE-type stretching that yoga professionals use in their training. I have two nieces and a sister-in-law who are yoga teachers (one of these nieces is also a physical therapist or physio), and they have strongly influenced me in incorporating yoga-type stretching into my daily routine. I have discovered I have a lot of tension that gets stored up, particularly in my lower back and neck. Simple exercises like the Child's Pose and Neck Rolls have made a significant difference in my body's flexibility and my mood. For example, when my neck is stiff and I have trouble turning it, I become very uncomfortable, and the same applies to my back. So, as this workbook is about holistic health, "get into your body," as the dance and movement therapists say.

Many people in this world have mobility problems, either due to age, injuries, or neuro-muscular conditions. An older sibling of mine has had Parkinson's disease for nearly 20 years. He was once a very fit and strong athlete who could complete 100 push-ups and then run for an hour. While challenged by his disease, he works out daily with light weights, takes walks, and does push-ups. So, while his routine has been curtailed—he cannot run nor cycle any longer—he meets each day with the determination that he will be as active as he can, and he maintains that the physicality involved with lifting light weights and walking has helped him manage his disease and his anxiety.

Therapeutic Massage

Massage might seem an unusual fit in this chapter, but as we are examining yoga and stretching, massage is an example of healing bodywork often recommended for clients in trauma recovery, those dealing with severe stress and anxiety. Therapeutic massage involves using various hands-on soft tissue manipulation techniques to stimulate blood flow and promote healing, restoring normal function, and alleviating pain by reducing somatic tension and injury. Because many clients in trauma recovery treatment have somatic problems for a variety of reasons, massage is strongly recommended as part of a holistic care routine.

Common Somatic Concerns in Trauma Recovery

1 Muscular pain throughout the body
2 Chronic lower back pain and fibromyalgia
3 Stiffness and restricted movement (e.g., back, neck, hips)
4 Headaches
5 Numbness throughout the body

Benefits of Therapeutic Massage

1 Improves blood circulation: Enhances blood flow, aiding in the body's natural healing process.
2 Reduced muscle tension: Helps release tight muscles and improves flexibility.
3 Increased mobility: helps restore the normal range of movement by relieving tight muscles.
4 Injury recovery: Facilitates healing through improved circulation.
5 Skilled massage also stimulates the vagus nerve system, resulting in relaxing the body, thus reducing anxiety (strongly recommended for those healing from PTSD).
6 Reduces stress: Better physical health is strongly correlated to overall emotional wellness (Levine, 2011).

I have made numerous referrals for clients in trauma recovery, those struggling with chronic stress, and anyone in chronic pain. While the level of help varied, all my clients reported some physical and emotional improvement. Deep tissue massage treatments are validated in assisting clients recovering from PTSD symptoms, stress, and anxiety, possibly due to regulating the parasympathetic nervous system (McGreevy & Boland, 2022).

Acupuncture for Trauma Reduction and Healing

Acupuncture can be an effective treatment for people recovering from PTSD and trauma-related symptoms by addressing mental and physical aspects of treatment (van der Kolk, 2015). Acupuncture helps reduce PTSD symptoms, likely by stimulating the polyvagal system of nerves, thus releasing stored tension in the body (Levine, 2011). Acupuncture can also help reduce physical symptoms linked to trauma, such as pain and muscle tension (McGreevy & Boland, 2022). Acupuncture has also been used in addiction treatment for over 30 years, as it has proven efficacy in the reduction of alcohol and drug cravings (Lee et al., 2021). Given that self-medication with alcohol and drugs is so prevalent for clients in trauma recovery, those treated for chronic stress and anxiety, I strongly recommend acupuncture.

Chair Yoga

Many years ago, my spouse and I visited my mother-in-law in a Detroit-area senior center where she had moved after retirement. One day, while strolling through the ground floor on my way to the library section of the large complex, I noticed a room full of seniors sitting in chairs, stretching, waving, moving their necks and heads, etc. Intrigued, I inquired what was happening, and the activity coordinator informed me it was a chair yoga class. She went on to say it was one of the most popular activities. I counted over 50 seniors participating and was impressed. Later, I noticed one of the residents who had been in the chair yoga class was in the library. I inquired about chair yoga, and she offered that she could now move her arms and head in ways she had not done in many years. Furthermore, she stated that the daily activity had lifted her depression and grief (her longtime spouse had died a few months prior). She had even recently begun swimming again and credited chair yoga with providing her with the range of motion and confidence to return to the pool. As the class was popular, it was a good social outlet, and she had made a couple of close friends through the chair yoga class. (Note: Taking a workout class or working out at a gym carries the added benefit of social support and encouragement, something that is also significant in any recovery.)

To Start Chair Yoga

1 Get a sturdy chair, preferably without arms, as you will need to move your arms freely.
2 Wear comfortable clothes that stretch and do not restrict body movement.
3 Sit upright, with your feet planted firmly on the floor, using pillows to adjust your height as needed. (Note: Some amputees are also involved in chair yoga and thus do not have their feet on the floor.)
4 Focus on your breath. Pay attention to your breathing throughout the session to promote fitness and calmness. When you begin, you may find chair yoga challenging, as you may not yet be in shape for this exercise. Still, the late marathoner Dr. George Sheehan's (2018) advice regarding exertion while still comfortable to talk is sound advice.
5 Research resources. *Yoga Journal*, *WebMD*, and chair yoga videos on YouTube are all worthwhile resources.

Recommendation: As a health psychologist and Stanford University researcher, Kelly McGonigal (2017) recommends doing 20 minutes of physical activity (chair yoga in this case), four times a week. Some people can start and maintain regular workout routines on their own (like me), while others need the encouragement of an instructor and class (like my spouse). One of the residents in our Brisbane high-rise downloads a floor routine and uses her phone to watch a video with an instructor. Find the method that works best for you.

Tai Chi

Tai Chi is a traditional Chinese practice that combines slow, gentle, and graceful movements, regulated breathing, and focused intention to promote a holistic sense of well-being. It was originally a martial arts practice, yet it has now broadened into a series of mind-body-spirit movements. Tai Chi is rooted in ancient Chinese philosophy with the concept of "Qi" or life energy and involves a balance of the yin and yang forces (Song, 2022). Millions of people worldwide practice Tai Chi for stress reduction, pain management, and flexibility. Tai Chi movements are continuous, circular movements that emphasize a straight spine, abdominal breathing, and meditation (Song, 2022).

Qigong

Qigong is a system of coordinated body posture and movement, breathing, and meditation practiced for flexibility, exercise, meditation, and overall well-being. Like Tai Chi, Qigong has roots in Chinese medicine, philosophy, and martial arts. Qigong is traditionally viewed by Chinese practitioners as a practice to cultivate and balance the qi or life force (Hooper, 2022). Qigong practice involves moving slowly, with deep rhythmic breathing, and focusing on a calm, meditative state of mind. Traditionalists will emphasize that Qigong is as much a moving meditation as it is a form of exercise (Hooper, 2022).

I am far more familiar with Tai Chi Qigong, although I have a friend and colleague who is a dedicated Qigong practitioner. Although the two ancient martial arts practices are similar, differences exist. Tai Chi is a more comprehensive martial art form with strict, flowing sequences and complex movements, while Qigong is a broader category of exercises that includes single, repeated movements and meditation (Just Breathe, n.d.). It may be easier to find a Tai Chi center and teachers than Qigong, unless you live in an urban area. Given the internet era, however, you can join an online class, and videos of both Tai Chi and Qigong are posted on the web. Any type of meditative, purposeful, gentle movement for the recommended time of 20+ minutes four times a week (or more) is likely to prove beneficial for your health.

Movement Meditation

I profiled walking meditation previously, but given that we are exploring mindful movements, I do not want to ignore it here. The great part of walking is that it requires no great economic output, save a decent pair of shoes. (Weather and location are issues, of course, but accommodations can be made.) Now, many meditation teachers likely will have you start with a sitting or standing meditation prior to starting a mindful walk. As a meditation teacher, I have taught this approach myself. I would express, however, that while any stationery meditation before a movement meditation is helpful, it is not necessary. To start walking mindfully, slowly lift one foot and take a step forward, bringing your attention to the movement. Pay close attention to the sensation of each step: the lifting of each foot, the contact it makes with the ground, and your breathing. Unlike power walking, where speed and exertion are the goals, mindful walking is all about paying attention, with purpose, in the present moment, to your body's movement, contact with the ground, and your meditative breathing. When your mind wanders, return the focus to your breath, as you would in a sitting or standing meditation. Remember, in meditation, it's always about the eternal present.

No question, it's always nice when one can take a long, meditative walk in a beautiful park, on a well-marked path through a forest, or along a long stretch of scenic coastline. Naturally, we cannot always access such locations nor the ideal weather to accompany bucolic settings. I recall once, when thousands of miles from home (in fact, I was in remote Australia), feeling lonely and unable to contact my spouse due to the time change, I did a mindful movement by walking back and forth across the modular unit I was staying in for two hours. I also know of someone who was wheelchair-bound. She did mindful travel in her wheelchair, focusing on the rhythm of her arms, hands on the wheels, the feel of the vibrations from the wheels' contact with the bike lane, the smell of the air, sounds in nature, things she saw, the tactile sensation of her gloved hands on the wheels, and the taste in her mouth. Thus, make whatever adaptations you need for mindful movement.

Getting Started

I cannot overemphasize the importance of a regular fitness well-being routine for recovery from trauma, in managing anxiety and stress, and in the close relationship that mind-body-and breath have in overall health. In fact, I will venture as far as saying that it's going to be very, very difficult to recover from trauma and manage anxiety and stress absent a regular fitness routine. There are two significant challenges to bodily fitness: getting started and, even more importantly, continuing with your fitness program. Like emotional well-being, there is no stopping point with fitness. As my master at the monastery counseled regarding daily gratitude practice, you must do it every day for the rest of your life. Like my spiritual master also opined, the habituation of the practice (in this case, working out) is even more important than the practice itself. My experience of a regular workout routine after 52 years is that my daily workout is indeed a type of mindful activity, much like meditation.

Some Tips for Getting Started

Because readers of this book vary from those who are uber fit (perhaps college athletes, marathon runners, professional dancers, etc.), who already have an established fitness plan, to readers who have not worked out in a long period of time, I am going to offer a plan that focuses on this latter group (and many in between who work out for a few months and then stop for a few months).

1 **Question 1:** What are your goals? I strongly suggest that a key goal is recovery from trauma and managing anxiety and stress. You may have others, like losing weight, a healthier cardiovascular system, and lower blood pressure. Whatever your goals, write them down. I recommend the **SMART** acronym:

   Specific: I want to manage stress and attain a healthy weight for myself by becoming physically fit. (**Note:** Be mindful here. Too many people, especially young women, become obsessed with thinness and develop an eating disorder.)

Measurable: Measure by setting your workouts at 20 minutes a day, for 4 days a week, for 1 month. Then, assess if you wish to increase your activity to 30 minutes, five times a week. Assess stress reduction with the SUDS 1–10 scale, with 10 being highly stressed and 1 being unstressed. Assess your stress level before and after your workout, and hopefully it goes down at least a little (mine always does). You can easily assess weight reduction with a scale. Remember, healthy weight loss, and not overly thin.

Attainable: Set realistic goals. So, start with slow jogging for 4 days a week. If in 1 month you are ready to increase to 5 days a week at a slightly faster pace, go ahead. The real issue here is the sustainability of your workout. If you like the workout or like what it does for you (e.g., reduction of stress, healthy target weight, a clearer mind), you are more likely to continue the workout. Remember, habituation of the workout is the goal, meaning working out when you do not feel like it.

Relevant: Your goals must be related to your likes/dislikes and abilities. If you hate running, for example, don't select that as your primary workout. If walking, cycling, swimming, etc., are more enjoyable, select one of them or a combination of them. Example: Walking workout on Monday, Wednesday, and Friday. Swim workout on Tuesdays and Thursdays. Be creative!

Timely: Your goals need a timeline for completion. For example, if your goal is to walk 4 times a week for 20 minutes at a time for 1 month, that's a timely goal. Again, once you have completed 1 month of your set workout cycle, you can evaluate for increased time or remain with the same time frame.

2 **Question 2:** How much time can you devote to exercise? Many readers can set aside an hour a day. However, a working adult with kids may not be able to do that. Remember, too, you can break the workout into different parts. One former coworker of mine rose at 5:00 AM each morning, jogged on the treadmill for 20 minutes, and then cleaned up and fed her kids' breakfast. Thereafter, she drove to work, where on her lunch break, she walked up 5 flights of stairs for 20 minutes, then cleaned up, ate a quick snack, and was back at her desk. After dinner and putting her kids to bed, she would put on her headphones and walk for 20 minutes on her treadmill. She did this five days a week.

3 **Question 3:** Where do you plan to work out? At a gym? At home? In a park or by the seashore? My best advice here is, where is the best location for you to work out? Many people like working out with others and join a fitness center where they do aerobics, yoga, spinning class, weight training, etc., with others for structure, peer support, and to fit a social need. Others, like me, prefer the solitary aspect of working out and have no problem doing it alone. What approach is most likely to help you continue your workout? Habituating a healthy fitness routine is the prime directive.

4 **Question 4**: How will you keep yourself motivated to continue with your workout routine? This is the most important question of all. Many people use workout buddies. One colleague had a friend he would run with during his lunch hour. Usually, he'd eat a PB&J sandwich at his desk around 11:00 AM, then run with his workout buddy at noon, and eat another snack at his desk when he returned to the office. If you do not have a friend or colleague you see as a viable workout buddy, websites and apps like Gym Buddy and Airtasker connect people with similar fitness goals.

I can think of additional examples of workout buddies for support. Many years ago, I had a colleague who was an addictions counselor and a member of AA. He and his longtime sponsor would hold each other accountable for exercising five days a week by meeting at the fitness club in the early morning before work. Each month, they would reward themselves by having dinner together at their favorite restaurant. Essentially, find a method to keep yourself engaged with the activity you choose, such as running, swimming, cycling, yoga, Tai Chi, or walking.

Self-Reflection Questions Regarding Your Activity/Fitness Plan

As Per Usual, Record in Your Trauma Recovery Journal or Other Journal

1 What is the fitness plan/activity you are committing to for the next 30/60/90 days?

____

____

2 How many days a week do you plan to engage in this activity? __________days/week

3 What is the average length of time you will spend on your activity? (For example, walking 25 minutes each workout.) ___________/minutes or hours

4 How realistic is the plan you have selected? Briefly explain why it's realistic below.

____

____

5 What are the barriers or difficulties to starting and following through on your fitness/activity plan? (Be realistic, as that will help you manage challenges.)

____

____

6 How will you ensure continuing with your workout plan and fitness activity?

____

____

7 On a scale of 1–10, with 10 representing "Completely Committed," what number would you select? _____/10. Why have you selected this number?

____

____

8 On a scale of 1–10, with 10 representing "Completely Confident," what number would you select? _____/10. Why have you selected this number?

____

____

9 On the days you do not feel motivated to work your activity plan, how will you create that motivation? (e.g., put on workout clothes, contact workout buddy, listen to an inspirational message, music)

____

____

10 Behavioral plans work because of rewards. What rewards have you built into your workout/activity plan to ensure that you continue with it? Rewards are the primary reasons behavioral plans work.

____

____

11 Starting a new workout routine will take much discipline, flexibility, patience, and self-compassion. My experience is that people often become frustrated and quit their fitness routine and then punish themselves with harsh internal statements. As important as a regular fitness routine is, self-compassion is even more important. Remember to encourage yourself without criticizing yourself. Explain how you will encourage yourself while silencing your inner critic (practicing self-compassion):

____

____

Lessons Learned

Use your Trauma Recovery Journal or another journal to reply to the following questions:

1 What is the most important insight you learned through reading and reflecting on this chapter?

____

____

2 Which of the breathing interventions are you most likely to use (e.g., box breathing, meditation, Voo exhaling)?

____

____

3 Thus far, during your counseling work and in reading and working the exercises in this workbook, what intervention has been most helpful, and why has that intervention the most helpful? (Note: You may feel that it's two to three interventions that were most helpful. If so, write about those.)

____

____

4 Self-compassion has been mentioned several times in this workbook. At this point, describe what active self-compassion means to you and how you are practicing it daily.

____

____

5 The importance of movement in healing trauma and managing anxiety and stress has been mentioned in this chapter and throughout this workbook. What is your favorite body movement exercise/activity? What makes that exercise/body movement your favorite?

____

____

10 Helping First Responders

First responders, such as members of the armed services, paramedics, EMTs, Emergency Room medical professionals, firefighters, police officers, Park Rangers, and game wardens, among others, are regularly exposed to traumatic situations involving repeated automobile and industrial accidents, fires, shootings, combat, and other trauma resulting in serious injury and death (Arena et al., 2025). Common symptoms can include guilt, emotional numbing, explosive rage, anxiety, depression, and self-medication with alcohol and drugs, compassion fatigue, burnout, and vulnerability to suicidality (van der Kolk, 2015).

Any first responder will tell you their work involves repeated exposure to traumatic incidents such as severe injuries and death, and the cumulative stress of repeated exposure to trauma can lead to a gradual buildup of symptoms and increased distress over time. My brother was a paramedic for 40 years. When I inquired how his training prepared him to deal with ongoing trauma such as violent injuries, bodily dismemberment, and death, he laughed and replied, "We relaxed in our off hours by drinking beer." He now teaches in a paramedic program, and the training focuses on debriefing with superiors, peer support groups, and counseling is encouraged. He admits, however, that an unfortunate stigma remains regarding seeking mental health care, something born out in research (Arena et al., 2025). Naturally, the level of trauma first responders experience, coupled with self-medication and reluctance to seek treatment, is a very toxic and potentially deadly mix.

In *Chapter 3 Addressing Your Trauma*, the focus is on healing, addressing flashbacks, writing your healing story, etc. I suggest reviewing that chapter, in addition to focusing on the material and exercises in this chapter. No doubt, as first responders, flashbacks, nightmares, feeling hypervigilant, and being easily triggered are very common. This chapter builds off previous chapters in this workbook, and of course, there will be some repetition. When training first responders on addressing and managing trauma, I encourage them to work on breaking down stereotypical beliefs that seeking treatment is a weakness. As one former ER physician, and longtime AA member, opined to me, "You gotta be strong enough to ask for help."

DOI: 10.4324/9781003689232-10

One of the positive attributes of the internet era is the existence of helpful websites like Black Dog.com and Firstresponder-Wellness.com. Interestingly, I have had many first responders refer family, friends, and patients to me for counseling. Yet, ironically, many of these same first responder professionals providing the referral would not seek counseling themselves due to the stigma counseling carries. A further complication for first responders is that, as they are the helpers, they ***should not*** be the ones seeking help. This is a very destructive type of thinking, and it is all too common among our uniformed service professionals (and sadly among mental health professionals). For first responders reading this workbook, here are some tips regarding asking for help.

Asking for Help: It Takes Strength and Courage

1 **Are you strong enough to ask for help?** Ironically, asking for help takes far more strength than holding grief and guilt inside and self-medicating the pain with alcohol and drugs.
2 **Who do you feel most comfortable reaching out to?** People, especially those in uniform, will only seek counsel from those they trust. Likely, a first responder will initially reach out to a colleague they know and trust.
3 **Give yourself time.** Ask a trusted colleague for time to talk when you think they would have time (not at a peak busy time).
4 **Don't apologize for asking for time.** It's common for people to feel they are burdening others by asking for time to discuss a concern. Many begin by expressing, "I hate to bother you, but..." However, it is essential that anyone, especially first responders, seek help when needed. Apologizing can make it seem like you are doing something wrong by asking, which is not the case. During my years as a clinic director, I wanted my staff to seek me out. As a professor, I want my colleagues to seek me out. As a loved one, I want my family and friends to seek me out. Being a concerned, present listener is part of our personal and professional responsibility.
5 **Expect them to ask questions.** The person you seek out for help may ask clarifying questions to understand your concern. Most likely, they are simply coming from a place of concern. The best listeners are those colleagues and friends who are very present, allowing you to express yourself completely with minimal interruption and without hijacking the conversation (e.g., "You know, that happened to me. Let me tell you...")
6 **It's possible you may not get the response you hoped for**. If you reach out to a colleague and are met with, "Oh, you're going to be okay, so don't worry about it," or something like this, you will likely feel discouraged. If they do not understand, a strong suggestion is to speak with another colleague. Most first responder organizations employ chaplains trained in basic counseling and can maintain confidentiality, absent the exception of danger to self and others.
7 **You will likely feel a sense of relief**. After opening up and sharing your concern with a trusted friend or colleague, it can feel like a weight has been

lifted off you. Possibly, you will feel less isolated knowing someone out there is supportive.

8 **Seeking counseling for secondary trauma is a strength**. Secondary trauma (AKA vicarious trauma) and burnout are real concerns. My strong recommendation is for first responders to seek counseling when needed. My further recommendation is for first responder supervisors to encourage counseling and for supervisors to seek counseling when needed, as this helps break down the fear of punishment for seeking help.

Adapted from First Responder Wellness (n.d.)

Tips for Being a Good Listening Friend or Colleague

Now, as readers, you may be the person a colleague reaches out to for help with a concern. Having trained many peer helpers over the decades, I wish to emphasize that the best service you can offer a family member, colleague, or friend is your presence. You do not need to solve the problem, nor are there any magic words to soothe another's pain. The best service you can offer a friend or colleague is to be fully present to their pain. Here are some tips on being present:

1 **Listen patiently and without judgment**: When a colleague or friend asks for time to talk, listen actively. Offer nonverbal support by keeping steady eye contact and nodding your head to illustrate that you are listening. Do not interrupt unless the other person is being repetitive or seems in crisis (i.e., making threats). Regardless of what the person says, display outward calm, patience, and a nonjudgmental attitude.

2 **Allow silence to fill the gap**: Western societies tend to have brief pause times. I'd encourage you to pause for, say, 3 seconds when your colleague or friend stops talking. This ensures you don't talk over them. Thank them for being brave enough to seek your support: "Sue, I'm glad you came to talk, as that takes courage."

3 **Watch their nonverbal behavior**: Sometimes, people will tell us they are okay, yet their body language suggests otherwise. If a colleague expresses, "I'm doing just fine," but their nonverbal behavior suggests anxiety (e.g., hand wringing, constantly shifting their body, pacing, flat affect), point this out and encourage them to seek professional help. Respect their decision while letting them know you are concerned for their well-being. Example: "You know, Jack, I'm concerned about you and hope you change your mind about counseling. I can be there when you make the call if you need."

4 **Paraphrase and summarize what you hear to ensure you understand them**: **Paraphrasing:** "Henry, it sounds like you are feeling stressed, right?"

   Summarizing: "Henry, it sounds like you are dealing with a lot of demands that are taking a toll, like work stress and marital issues. These seem to be taking a toll on you."

5 **Ask their opinion**: "Karen, what do you believe would be helpful for you right now?" Be aware; they may not know, but you thought to ask as opposed to jumping into solving a problem they may not want you to fix.
6 **Let them know they are not alone**. "Sean, we all need support at times, especially helpers, given the stress we're under. It takes courage to come forward."
7 **Recognize your limits and maintain boundaries**: Unless you are a professional therapist providing services in a clinical setting, don't try to be one. Again, encourage your colleague or friend to seek out counseling. If you have benefited from counseling, consider letting your colleague know, as such knowledge can help break stigma barriers.
8 **Refrain from offering advice:** Do not give in to the temptation of problem-solving advice, as tempting as it may seem, as this almost always derails the situation by becoming more about the advice-giver than the person seeking support. Your nonjudgmental presence and time are your gifts. Again, if your colleague or friend seems to need ongoing help, recommend professional counseling.
9 **Debriefing:** Helpers like yourself will need others to provide time for you. Do you have a trustworthy friend or colleague who can give you quality presence for debriefing? (**Note**: I formerly trained people in listening partnerships. These were training courses for non-therapists to become more present, nonjudgmental listeners. I would encourage businesses and non-profit organizations to develop such listening partnerships programs.)

Self-Reflection on Seeking Help

In your Trauma Recovery Journal, answer the following questions:

1 I know I need to seek help when ______________________________

____

2 What stops me from asking for help is __________________________

____

3 To ask for help, I would need to ______________________________

____

4 If a close colleague or friend sought help, my opinion of them would

____

____

5 Many people fear being a burden. If someone seeks your help, how do you feel about them?

___

___

6 Have you ever asked anyone for help? If so, how did you feel afterwards?

___

___

7 Is your reluctance to ask for help a response due to previous trauma? Yes ___ No ___

8 If you answered yes on the previous question, how might you work through your fear and mistrust and ask someone you trust for help?

___

___

9 Regarding the previous question, consider someone you have a high degree of trust in. What qualities does that person possess that have earned your trust?

___

___

10 What's the worst and best thing that could happen if you ask for help? What's the worst thing that could happen if you do not seek help?

___

___

11 I will ask this person I trust for time to talk by: Date: __/___/___

The Empty Chair Exercise Practice in Asking for Help

In this workbook, I have frequently suggested numerous variations on the empty chair intervention. Typically, you set out two chairs facing one another and then sit on one of them. Pretend you are asking a friend or colleague you trust for help. Remember, this is practice, and practice always helps us prepare for the experience, and the reason athletic teams, musicians, dancers, actors, etc. practice. Imagine your colleague/friend in that empty chair, and then ask for help, no matter how difficult it may be. Then, switch chairs and play the role of your friend/colleague and speak as you believe that person would reply. (remember, there's a reason you trust her or him) Okay, then, repeat the process as many times as needed to feel comfortable with the conversation. Practicing this exercise makes it more likely you will be strong enough to ask for help. (Yes, asking for help suggests real strength.)

Addressing Compassion Fatigue and Burnout

No question, compassion fatigue is a significant predictor of burnout, especially for first responders and therapists, or anyone working with high-needs populations (Stamm, 2009). The Professional Quality of Life Scale (ProQuol; https://proqol.org/proqol-measure) is a free, online, validated scale for assessing three key components in predicting burnout. The first component is Compassion Satisfaction (CS). We want our Compassion Satisfaction score to be high, as a high score suggests we enjoy our job and are feeling healthy and vibrant in that job. The second component measured is secondary traumatic stress (STS), and we want that score to be low. High scores on the STS component suggest we are becoming weary of the heavy responsibilities that being a first responder carries with the job. High scores do not mean we are burned out but suggest burnout is a risk. The third and most concerning component is burnout (BO). High burnout scores suggest we are impinging on our emotional and physical health and likely need a break. I would encourage anyone who works in a stressful work environment to take the ProQuol every 6 months (or sooner if you feel overly stressed for extended periods) to assess your well-being.

I would suggest that readers of the workbook may be experiencing a lot of stress. Stress and trauma are significant reasons that we need to develop an ongoing well-being or self-care practice. Thus far in this workbook, we have explored healthy practices like cognitive reframing, breathwork (box breathing, Voo exhaling, and meditation), physical exercise, practicing self-compassion, etc. My regular well-being routine goes like this:

a Rise early and have a light snack, coffee, and then start with my gratitude acknowledgment (acknowledge 3)
b Then, after 45 minutes or so, go for my run (Tuesday-Friday, and my long run is Saturday.)
c After cleaning up and breakfast, do my EFT/Meridian Tapping (11 points), then the Voo exhaling.
d Then, catch the train and meditate on the 40–45-minute trip to my campus.

You may have a very different well-being routine. Whatever that routine may be, make it regular practice and give that practice as high a priority as your job, as our emotional and physical health is paramount, as otherwise you will not be as productive an employee and may even suffer burnout. Habituating a well-being-mindfulness routine is even more important than the routine itself, as the routine then becomes as natural as eating a meal.

Developing Presence to Help Others

Mindfulness practice is good preparation for developing presence as a good listener. A daily meditation practice, for example, helps clear the mind of distractions so that we can be more focused (or present) with family, colleagues, and friends. Previously, I mentioned using engaged body posture, eye contact, paraphrasing, summarizing, open-ended questions, etc. Try to understand the speaker's perspective without judgment, which can be challenging at times. Nevertheless, work to show a nonjudgmental face and encouraging body posture (e.g., lean forward, be open, appropriate eye contact)

A Minimize Distractions to Stay Present

1 **Remove distractions**: Put your phone out of sight, turn off the TV, and shut the door to eliminate distractions.
2 **Still your mind**: Psychiatrist Mark Epstein (2013) recommends a 1-minute meditation when switching between patients. I followed this recommendation and found it helpful. So, when you are busy transitioning between appointments, people, projects, etc., I also recommend the 1-minute meditation to focus the mind.
3 **Mind wandering**: When your mind wanders (and it will), focus on your breath, just as in meditation.
4 **Maintain eye contact**: Use a steady gaze and adjust for cultural norms.
5 **Body posture language:** Lean slightly toward your speaker, nod your head at appropriate times (as encouragement), use open body posture (avoid rigid posture, tightly crossed arms, frowns, etc.), and consider what conveys interest to your speaker, as that is an invitation to speak freely.
6 **Maintain a calm facial expression:** A soft gaze and calm expression convey respect and understanding.

B Active Listening Suggestions

1 **Seek first to understand:** Work to understand the speaker's concern and perspective and seek assistance from that person for clarification. Ex.: "Juan, what I understand you saying is that you are very stressed right now. Is that correct?"
2 **Ask open-ended questions and clarifying questions:** Open-ended questions facilitate the speaker to expand on their message and usually begin with "How and What": "How did you feel when…?" Or "What was going on for you when you said…?"
3 **Paraphrase and summarize:** Briefly rephrase the important part of the speaker's message.

Paraphrase: "So, you are feeling stressed."
Summarization: "Kay, it seems you have mentioned having a lot going on right now. Your son has been diagnosed with leukemia, your elderly mother has moved in with you, and this promotion has compounded your life stress."

4 **Use minimal encouragers:** "I see," or "Uh-huh," "Okay," etc.
5 **Use silence:** Make use of pregnant pauses. Silence often signals that you are listening actively, and it facilitates the speaker to elaborate further.
6 **Don't interrupt:** Avoid interrupting and allow the speaker to elaborate. Wait for a natural pause before speaking. On the rare occasions when interrupting is required (i.e., the speaker is rambling, making threats), do so firmly, but as gently as possible.
7 **Use encouraging language:** "Steve, it takes real guts to ask for help. I appreciate you taking this step. Now, how can I help?"

C Demonstrate Compassion and Refrain from Judgment

1 **Bracket judgment:** Remember, being helpful is not about agreement but more about the speaker feeling understood.
2 **Validate the speaker's perspective: For example,** "I can see this is a challenging time for you." Or "It sounds like you have been struggling with this decision/issue/situation/etc. for some time."
3 **Don't hijack the conversation:** Keep your attention on the speaker and their issue as opposed to your own.

Do: "Sun-Ae, could you say more about...?"
Don't: "You know, Sun-Ae, the same thing happened to me. Let me tell you..."
In the former example, the listener keeps the focus on the speaker, while in the latter, it's about the listener, and the speaker likely wonders, "What happened to my concern?"

4 **Setting healthy boundaries:** You will need to set some basic parameters as an active listener.
5 **If you are actively involved in something and cannot give focused time, seek a delay and reschedule:** "I can't talk now as I have a meeting in 5 minutes. How about in one hour when I am free?"
6 **Set a time limit and stay with it:** "I have 30 minutes." Time limits are good for both the listener and talker.
7 **Referrals:** If the person keeps seeking your help, it's likely time for a referral to a counselor. Example: "Steve, it seems that you have been under stress for a while. I think you should talk with a professional therapist."

When I ran clinics, I occasionally provided listening time to the staff. However, I did not counsel them, as that would not have been appropriate. On occasion, I encouraged them to make an appointment with an off-site provider. Remember, it takes real strength to seek help.

Narrative Responses for Adjusting to Past Trauma

Clearly, combat can severely harm a soldier's mental and emotional health (Anxious Minds, n.d.). Constant danger lurking about, watching friends killed and severely wounded, and always remaining hypervigilant often leads to PTSD and various other mental health problems. Addressing combat stress and providing trauma-informed care to support veterans as they adjust to civilian life is crucial. The Veterans Administration medical centers offer a wide range of services, including counseling and treatment for PTSD. The following are some general guidelines for fellow first responders to consider when offering assistance. Now, all first responders, beyond armed service veterans, are also exposed to trauma as a routine part of the job (e.g., police, firefighters, paramedics and EMTs, ER medical professionals, trauma therapists)

First Responder Re-entry Questions for Exploration

Using your Trauma Recovery Journal, write brief responses to the following questions. (Note: If you are a combat veteran and have not received trauma-informed counseling, you may wish to refrain from answering these questions.)

1 Given that you encounter traumatic situations daily, how often are you plagued by stress, anxiety, sleep disturbance, and nightmares? (e.g., nightly, weekly, monthly)

____

____

2 Have you found it difficult to relax while off duty? For example, do you find yourself feeling a rush of adrenaline during even minor conflicts at home or work? Do those minor conflicts sometimes escalate verbally or physically? Have those conflicts been increasing?

____

____

3 How much trust do you have in your family? In friends? Work colleagues?

____

____

4 Regarding the previous question, who is/are the person/people you trust most? Why do you trust them?

____

____

5 Emotional expression is a basic part of human experience. How comfortable are you in expressing happiness, sadness, and anger? How might you become more comfortable with emotional expression?

____

____

6 Regarding the above question, how could you begin to feel safer in expressing positive and negative emotions?

____

____

7 Have you found anyone that you can talk to about your traumatic experiences? (e.g., VA therapist, chaplain, colleague, friend)

____

____

8 If you have found someone you feel safe talking with about job-related trauma, what has been helpful about those conversations?

____

____

9 What is one thing you can do differently to help you manage the stress you have been experiencing? That one thing may be something small, but that's a start.

____

____

10 If you were to provide advice to a young first responder just starting in the profession, what advice might you offer regarding managing on-the-job trauma and stress?

____

____

Addressing Survivor Guilt

Survivors' guilt is a difficult emotion to navigate through, particularly for first responders, as they are more inclined than the general population to encounter traumatic situations. As someone with first responder family members, traumatic situations are simply part of the job description. As we have seen in the media over the years, anyone working in a school, house of worship, business, government office, etc., may become a victim of violence. However, armed service members, police, firefighters, paramedics, and others regularly encounter traumatic situations that are simply part of the job.

While first responders expect to deal with trauma, they, too, are human and prone to the same emotional vulnerabilities as anyone else. Encountering so much tragedy and death can naturally take a heavy toll on first responders.

I remember a former student who, as a police officer, continued to have feelings of guilt two decades after his partner's suicide. I recall him saying, "I keep asking myself, 'What could I have done differently?'" This type of question can inevitably take a heavy toll on the person who feels they could (or should) have done something to prevent the tragedy.

Becoming Aware of Survivor Guilt Signs

People struggling with survivor's guilt sometimes express their inner guilt in narrative ways. The following statements represent common thoughts regarding survivor's guilt:

"I should have been able to have done more to prevent it."

1 "I can't help but think that I could have prevented it."
2 "I think that if only I had…"
3 "I will always blame myself for…"
4 "Why me? Why did I survive?"
5 "It should have been me who died."
6 "If I could undo the situation, I would…"
7 "If only…"

Steps to Addressing Survivor's Guilt

Experiencing survivors' guilt is a basic human response. However, if the survivor continues to weaponize their survival as a type of emotional self-injury, depression, and potential suicide are possible outcomes. The following are suggestions on managing survivors' guilt.

1 **What you are feeling is normal.** Tell yourself, "I am having a normal response to an abnormal experience" (Linehan, 2015). Your survivor's guilt is a combination of ongoing trauma and grief. Your emotional response is normal, but the trauma you experienced is not. (Note: First responders' normal is not like other people's normal. However, the first responder "normal" is not normal for a human and thus the difficulty.)
2 **Coping techniques:**
   a Move your body through yoga, dance, running, swimming, strength training, etc. Movement promotes hope molecules that help in managing depression and anxiety (McGonigal, 2017).
   b Peer support: Who is one friend you can talk with about your concerns? Better yet, consider joining a support group for first responders (some are online, if not in your community).
   c Go for counseling yourself to address survivors' guilt. Then, encourage colleagues to do the same. Role-modeling is transformational and can help save careers, relationships, and lives.

- d Breathwork: As in previous chapters, box breathing for panic (breathe in deeply through your nose for 4 seconds, hold for 4 seconds, then exhale slowly through your mouth for 4 seconds, then hold your breath for 4 seconds). Repeat as many times as necessary; mindfulness meditation for relaxation: Breathe slowly in through your nose and then exhale slowly out through your mouth. Continue for, say, 5 minutes (or longer). When your mind wanders, focus on your breath; Voo exhaling: take a deep breath in, then purse your lips, and exhale slowly out your mouth, making a Voo sound (the exhale usually takes 6–9 seconds). Relax, and then repeat. Do 5–10 of these Voo exhales. The Voo exhale stimulates the vagus nerve system and helps calm anxiety (Levine, 2011).
- e Spiritual support: If you are a spiritual/religious person, seek out spiritual support that helps you cope with external demands (e.g., house of worship, 12-step meetings, reading sacred texts, mantra meditation, prayer). If you are not a spiritual person, then use those meaningful activities that are helpful for you. One non-spiritual client found reading meaningful books like *The Meditations of Marcus Aurelius* or another such text or meaningful activity. A different client found playing chess relaxing. Find what works for you.

3 **Pay-it-forward behavior:**

- a Do volunteer work that is meaningful to you (e.g., food bank, animal shelter, aged care volunteer at nursing homes or hospital, Big Sister-Big Brother programs, local library).
- b Take part in annual fundraisers related to preventing first responder suicide.
- c Become part of a peer group offering ongoing support to first responders.
- d Offer encouragement to first responder colleagues.

4 **Reflective questions to address survivor's guilt.** (Use your Trauma Recovery Journal to answer these questions in writing.)

- a Consider the guilty feelings you are harboring and ask yourself, "Who is benefiting from my guilt?" Or challenge that guilt by asking, "Is this guilt proportional to the situation, or based on unrealistic expectations?"
- b Practice self-compassion: Self-compassion is setting aside guilt and treating yourself as you would treat a loved one, close friend, or colleague.
- c Many people struggling with survivors' guilt are experiencing grief. If you were to express your grief in a healthy manner (that is, helpful to you, your loved ones, and other first responders), what would you be doing?
- d Ask yourself, what helpful lesson is this guilt trying to teach me? (Hint: *It isn't about guilt.*)
- e If a friend or close colleague were suffering from guilt and sought your counsel, what helpful advice might you give that person?

f If you were to take one helpful action to address your guilt and grief, what would you do? (Remember, focus on just 10% improvement for starters…)
g Consider a future time when you have addressed your grief and guilt. For example, while you remain sad about your late colleague, you no longer are plagued by guilt and grief. What would you notice as being better about your life? What would your family, friends, and colleagues notice being different about you?
h Regarding the previous question, how can you begin to create this healing future?

Writing and PTSD: A Cathartic Approach

There are several benefits to writing about one's PTSD (or any other mental health issue). A recent study (Sloan et al., 2023) highlights the benefits of writing about PTSD as a means of managing trauma symptoms, gaining new insights on healing, decreasing anxiety, and exploring healthy coping strategies. The study was conducted using military veterans utilizing writing exposure therapy (WET), essentially a form of CBT-Cognitive Processing Therapy. Naturally, first responders of any type can benefit from writing about their trauma and how they are healing from that trauma. In the next series of exercises, readers will explore different narrative methods of writing about their trauma recovery and healing process.

The Narrative: Telling My Story

Michael White, co-founder of Narrative Therapy, believed that giving voice to our joys and fears in a narrative manner (story-like) could provide just enough personal distance to be therapeutic for the speaker or writer (White, 2007). Part of his hypothesis is that trauma, grief, stress, etc., is as much about the story we tell ourselves about that trauma as it is about the actual trauma, grief, stress, etc. A narrative is a written testimony to help the person organize their thoughts in a meaningful way. For combat veterans, police, paramedics, and other first responders, it provides a space for putting painful experiences, thoughts, and emotions into words and developing a different perspective. Writing out a narrative carries the added benefit of being able to edit one's experiences and as Pennebaker (2004) notes, makes a deeper impression. Michael White further posits the narrative in a summarized manner below:

1 The primary focus of the narrative is the expression of personal life experiences. (in this case, first responder experiences).
2 The individual's experiences are interpreted by the same individual.
3 Interpretations provide experiences with meaning.

4 The meaning gleaned from writing a narrative is likely to change over time.
5 The narrative process of writing one's story requires re-reading, revising, re-processing, and re-conceptualizing your experiences.
6 The process of writing a narrative provides a framework that allows one to retell difficult experiences while reframing the meaning learned. For example, from "I am permanently wounded" to "Yes, I have my scars but am healing and have learned valuable lessons."
7 Narrative writing provides you with the opportunity to link your stories to others who have had similar experiences.

For narrative writing, consider including many of the following elements:

8 Describing yourself as a heroine or hero or as the main character in your narrative.
9 Including a symbol to describe an event or person that injured you physically and/or psychologically. For example, a flower might symbolize hope, a butterfly may symbolize transformation, and so forth.
10 Include objects that symbolize resilience and healing (examples: the Lotus Flower, Phoenix, Tree of Life, Kintsugi-Japanese art of repairing broken pottery with gold to symbolize strength comes from brokenness), or whatever language is meaningful to you.

Telling My Story

In this exercise, you will write a brief self-story about your resilience and healing through assisting others in traumatic and painful situations. Give yourself free rein to write freely and without self-judgment. I would suggest writing in first person (I statements), but if third person feels more comfortable, then use that (he, she, his, her, or they). You will write as a practitioner of self-compassion, displaying the same kindness you would show to a loved one or close friend. While writing your story, remember the Japanese art of kintsugi, repairing fragility or brokenness with words of gold. Set aside your inner editor or critic and write the story you want to write. You may continue writing ongoing stories in your Trauma Healing Journal. Your story can include the pain, difficulty, stress, doubt, and so forth that you experienced, as such experiences are human. However, you are encouraged to write about how you found strength, support, encouragement, and empowerment to continue moving forward on your life journey. Write also about your well-being or self-care plan, including physical activity, hobbies, peer support, and spiritual support. Write as briefly or lengthily as you feel led to write. Remember, you are the main author, main character, and editor. Finally, do not worry about grammar rules, how creative the story might or might not be, and emancipate your story from any such restrictions or inhibitions. Remember, this is your story, and yours to tell.

Reflections on Telling My Story

In this exercise, consider what you have learned from the Telling My Story exercise. Feel free to write just one narrative story or to write ongoing stories regularly.

1 What were the major challenges for you in the Telling My Story exercise?

____

____

2 What did you find cathartic or healing about writing a story based on your occupational experiences?

____

____

3 What did you learn about yourself from the Telling My Story exercise?

____

____

4 Based on your story, what are your greatest strengths?

____

____

5 What's one area of your life that you might want to change, even if only a small change?

____

____

6 Regarding the previous question, how might you make that healthy change?

____

____

7 Who is the person you most admire? What admirable qualities does that person possess? (list a few of these key qualities)

____

____

8 What admirable qualities do you possess? If you are feeling stuck, consider asking someone you trust about your admirable qualities. List those qualities.

____

____

9 What is a positive change you have made due to your occupation as a first responder? (e.g., more compassionate, sense of justice)

____

____

10 If you were to write a brief story about how you would want your colleagues to remember you, what would you write? (Consider writing a second short story or just a sentence or two.)

____

____

My Trauma Recovery Journal

Throughout this workbook, I have advocated completing the exercises in a Trauma Recovery Journal. As a realist, I recognize most readers will complete some of the exercises in this workbook in journal form while completing others verbally or silently. Now, in the event you have focused solely on this chapter (if so, you likely are, or were, a first responder), I will provide suggestions on writing a journal. While there are no exact rules, after all, this is for your personal development and healing and not for a grade in school. The following represent some basic considerations for journal writing:

A Creating a Safe, Comfortable Space for Writing

1 Your writing space can be a desk, table, bed, or a picnic table in nature. Write wherever you feel most comfortable.
2 All you need is your laptop, or if you prefer, a pen and a spiral-bound notebook.
3 You may wish to bring a box of tissues for emotional periods.
4 Given the nature of the issues involved, my suggestion is to do your journal writing in a private space (e.g., home office or another place where you will not be recognized, and thus there are no inquiries about what you are writing).

B Establish a Writing Routine

1 As a writer, I suggest setting a regular schedule, as that helps to habituate an ongoing journaling practice.
2 Start with small goals, say writing a paragraph a day as a manageable practice that lasts.
3 Provide yourself with small, weekly rewards for meeting weekly writing goals.

4 Decide how long you will continue your journal writing. In some cases, it may be for as long as you are in treatment, or as an aftercare practice (for say, 3–6 months), or as an ongoing practice.

C Be Honest

1 The journal is a private space to write about your healing from trauma. Express your thoughts and experience without judgment or self-censorship.
2 Let go of perfection. Neither grammar, spelling, nor literary quality is the goal here, but rather your healing and well-being.

D Facilitating Your Journal Writing

1 Write about the trauma and how you felt emotionally, physically, and spiritually.
2 Write about how the trauma continues to impact you. Write also about how you have taken steps to heal the trauma through counseling, support groups, and a 12-step program (as self-medication is common).
3 Be self-reflective, asking "How am I feeling about my trauma and my healing?" and "What have my trauma history and my healing process taught me?" Another influential question to consider is, "When I am fully healed, how will I be different in thoughts, feelings, my actions, and in my relationships with others?"
4 Gratitude acknowledgment: Consider starting (or ending) your journal entry with something you are grateful for.

E Practice Ongoing Self-Care

1 Physical exercise is strongly recommended, as well as breathwork (e.g., box breathing, meditation, Voo exhaling), Meridian tapping points.
2 Stop writing anytime you feel overwhelmed. You might consider a 1–10 scale of anxiety. If your score rises to the 7–10 red line of the SUDS scale, take a break.
3 Self-compassion: Remember, you will not write about self-blame or criticism or shame yourself. Your Trauma Recovery Journal is about healing and well-being and is your safe space.
4 While journaling is an efficacious method of addressing trauma and your healing journey, you can still become triggered. If you are in therapy, speak with your therapist, a trusted family member, a close friend, a spiritual guide, etc.

F Remember the Self-fulfilling Prophecy

1 Believe you will heal: If you believe you will heal, then you will heal. This is born out in research, and I have witnessed the power of belief, followed by work, firsthand. I have worked with many survivors of long-term trauma who believed they could heal, then worked on their treatment plan, and healed. If you do not believe you can heal, then it's unlikely you will do the work to facilitate healing.

2 As you write in your journal, never forget that the most important construct in healing is one's attitude about their ability to heal.
3 After cultivating a healing attitude, the second most important construct is doing healing work, represented by counseling, working through a workbook like this one, and building in peer support for encouragement.
4 Remember, 12-step programs work because they foster a belief in healing, build in peer support, posit a spiritual or meaningful approach, and provide the structure and encouragement for healing. Remember these important components.

Lessons Learned

Use your Trauma Recovery Journal to answer the questions below.

1 What was the most important lesson or intervention you learned in this chapter?

____

____

2 Why was this the most important lesson/intervention?

____

____

3 On a scale of 1–10, with 10 being "I'm managing secondary traumatic stress very well, what score would you assign yourself? ___/10"

4 How could you raise your score by 1 point?

____

____

5 What's the story you are telling yourself regarding your ability to heal your trauma?

____

____

6 Remembering the power of self-fulfilling prophecy, how might you strengthen your belief in your ability to heal from trauma?

____

____

11 Creating a Meaningful Life

Practical Exercises

Psychiatrist Viktor Frankl was the first therapist to develop an approach based on the concept of meaning in life (Frankl, 1986). Frankl survived the Nazi Holocaust, perhaps the most tragic and depraved example of human cruelty. His entire family was murdered along with several million others simply because of Hitler's antisemitism. Ironically, out of this horrible, ultra-traumatic experience, Frankl somehow emerged and re-entered society with a renewed belief in humanity's goodness. Frankl described two types of concentration camp prisoners: those who lost all faith and hope in humanity, and those who exhibited small acts of kindness toward their fellow prisoners as a means of keeping hope alive in a hopeless place (Frankl, 2006). His experience was that the former category of prisoners was more likely to persevere and possibly survive, whereas the latter often gave up and died. Frankl posited that for him, finding small doses of meaning each day helped him survive a hellish existence. Frankl explained that the will to meaning is the primary motivation for living—and acting:

> Man's search for meaning is the primary motivation in his life and not a 'secondary rationalization' of instinctual drives. This meaning is unique and specific in that it must and can be fulfilled by him alone; only then does it achieve a significance which will satisfy his own will to meaning.
>
> (Frankl, 2006, p. 99)

So, just to understand what we are exploring, here's Frankl's definition of meaning in life:

"Meaning is a concrete response to a hidden potential that brings something of value to the doer and/or to the world" (Frankl, n.d.).

My own experiences as a counselor providing therapy for PTSD, depression, anxiety, and chronic mental illness, among other concerns, are that every client who entered my various offices throughout this world came because they had lost some degree of meaning in their life. That includes the 6-year-old whose parents were divorcing, thus breaking up his family, up to the 90-year-old WWII veteran traumatized during the war and who wanted to feel better before he died and all others in between these two extremes in age and life circumstance. Now, I still needed to help people heal from and/or manage their

DOI: 10.4324/9781003689232-11

trauma, depression, chronic mental illness, etc. However, the pressing issue underneath these various maladies seemed to be the loss of meaning and purpose in the clients' lives. Although this chapter specifically addresses meaning in life, this entire workbook is reclaiming the joy that a meaningful life brings. The meaning of healing, then, can be viewed as transcending suffering, much as Viktor Frankl described in his writings (Egnew, 2005).

Years ago, while directing a small university counseling service, a young woman came to see me for counseling, as many students did. The campus enrollment was around 2,000 students, and there was little social distancing between students, faculty, and staff, as everyone was required to serve on a committee or task force. I shall refer to this student as Carol (pseudonym). Carol had been a campus leader, a high Honors student, involved in numerous campus activities, and was one of the friendliest and most social students I had met. The woman before me, however, was a facsimile of the Carol I knew. This Carol was sobbing, and her language was very distraught. When she finally took a pause, I inquired what had happened. She then tearfully recounted having attended an off-campus party the past Saturday evening, where she had been sexually assaulted. In just one evening, she had gone from being a confident, self-assured young woman, an academic and social star, to a traumatized survivor. She mentioned "feeling dirty" and wondered if she would ever feel her former confident self again. After assessing her for suicidality, we made an appointment for the next day. (She was adamant in not wanting to pursue legal charges, given the trauma of the process.) Thereafter, she spent the remainder of the term in therapy with me, making slow yet steady progress.

Through MCBT interventions and homework, plus good family and peer support, she began to heal. One of the litmus tests of her healing was my weekly Meaning Scale, as she had initially mentioned that she felt life "no longer held any meaning" for her. Through her willingness to engage with the interventions (breathwork, meridian tapping, cognitive restructuring, reviewing the trauma, empty-chair conversations with past and future self, etc.), her meaning in life score rose from 1 on a 1–10 scale (10 being high) and finished at a 9 by graduation. Carol went through a very difficult, protracted healing process, complete with numerous challenging points, emotional pain, and copious tears, before she transitioned into post-traumatic growth with a strong sense of meaning and purpose. When I inquired what had helped most in her healing, she replied that when her sense of meaning rose, everything else improved. So, let's spend this chapter addressing your sense of meaning in life.

Meaning in Life

The Meaning in Life Questionnaire (MLQ) was developed by Steger et al. (2006). The 10-item questionnaire has two subscales that represent two dimensions of meaning in life: (1) Presence of Meaning: how much respondents feel their lives have meaning, and (2) Search for Meaning: how much respondents strive to find meaning and understanding in their lives. I encourage all readers to go online and complete the MIL.

MIL Specifics

1 10 items: 5 on the presence of meaning; 5 on the search for meaning.
2 Response scale ranges from 1 (absolutely untrue) to 7 (absolutely true).
3 Self-report, paper and pencil, or online.
4 Negatively worded items are reverse-scored.
5 To access the MIL: http://www.michaelfsteger.com/?page_id=13

Some Questions Regarding Meaning in Life

As per usual, answer the following reflective questions in your Trauma Recovery Journal.

1 In what ways is meaning present in your life?

____

____

2 How has your sense of personal meaning in your life changed since you began working to heal your trauma? (or manage your stress, anxiety, other issues, etc.)

____

____

3 On a scale of 1–10, with 10 high, what score would you assign to your personal sense of meaning in life? ___/10. Now, how might you raise your score by 1 point?

____

____

4 How was your life different when you had a strong sense of personal meaning?

____

____

5 If you were to have an empty-chair conversation with your younger self about creating a meaningful life, what advice would you give?

____

____

6 If you were to have an empty-chair conversation with your future self about creating a meaningful life, what advice would you give?"

____

____

7 What is your life asking of you? (If stumped by this question, consider an empty-chair conversation with your life.)

____

____

8 What is the primary passion (or goal) in your life?

____

____

9 The Harvard Study of Adult Development suggests that our physical and emotional health is strongly correlated with the quality of our relationships (Waldinger & Schulz, 2023). Briefly describe your happiness level with key relationships (e.g., spouse, children, close friends).

____

____

10 Regarding the previous question, if you are not particularly happy with the quality of your key relationships, briefly describe how you might go about improving those relationships.

____

____

Writing a Meaning in Life Journal

With all the reminders regarding completing the assessments in your Trauma Recovery Journal, you likely may groan at the mention of keeping another journal. The good news is that you can make the meaning journal a section of the Trauma Recovery Journal. I am also realistic that many readers will not complete all exercises, and many will not even keep a journal. Regardless, engaging with the exercises even verbally can be an asset to recovery. I further expect that some readers will keep a journal to reflect on the meaning in their lives.

Many theologians and philosophers have written about the role meaning plays in our lives, and some have written on the absence of meaning, or existential nihilism. Roman Emperor Marcus Aurelius grappled with his own existential questions in his famous private journal, later published as *The Meditations of Marcus Aurelius* (2006), a book I strongly recommend for readers interested in meaning and stoicism. As there is no one way to write about meaning in life, I will suggest a journal focused on critical life questions. Those salient questions may be guided by my suggestions below. Later, however, and more importantly, exploring personal meaning through your own questions and experiences is likely to be even more helpful. I have been guided by exploring the meaning and purpose in my own life, and a few years ago, I published a book titled *Creating a Meaningful Life: A Practical Guide for Counselors, Therapists, and Other Helping Professionals* (2023). Those other helping professionals could be people from any occupation. Regardless, here are some focus questions for keeping a Meaning in My Life Journal (or in your Trauma Recovery Journal):

1 **Consider focus questions: "What is the meaning of my life?"** Now, it is okay not to know the answer to this question. Perhaps a more fruitful question to consider and then reflect on in your journal is, *"What is the meaning in my life?"* You may well discover, as I did, that meaning often emanated from my writing on the subject.
2 **Meaning is self-defined:** Numerous psychologists/psychiatrists (e.g., Abraham Maslow, Carl Rogers, Viktor Frankl), spiritual teachers (e.g., Buddha, Jesus, Muhammad), philosophers (Socrates, Kierkegaard, Sartre, de Beauvoir, etc.), and everyday people have spent many years teaching and writing about the meaning in life (or the lack thereof, depending on perspective). Considering the multiple perspectives, the meaning in your life then is yours to create. So, a second question to journal on could be, "How can I go about creating a meaningful like?"
3 **Journaling:** Another possibility is to write about one meaningful experience you had during the day: "Today I had a meaningful encounter with meaning in the form of…" Your journal writing does not have to be voluminous in length, as even a simple paragraph may be enough. Remember to tailor the length to your specifications.
4 **Discomfort as teacher:** As readers are working through past trauma, major stress, anxiety, etc., a key question for consideration could be, "What is my trauma/anxiety/stress/unemployment/incarceration/etc. trying to teach me about the meaning in my life?" Again, much of that meaning likely lies within the exploration of the question rather than the question itself.
5 **Early Life Recollections**: Alfred Adler, who founded Individual Psychology (AKA Adlerian Psychology), posited that early life recollections (ER) are critical for exploration in therapy. For example, a friend of mine who was an Adlerian therapist would ask clients, "What is the most significant early recollection you can recall?" Then, he would ask his clients about significant recollections from childhood and adolescence. These early recollections can be joyful or painful. The question: "What is a significant early recollection you have from childhood?" could be a good beginning on this theme. Remember, early recollections are simply a window into your past and how you view and make sense of the world. Another variation on ER could be to identify 3 ERs, 1 from early childhood (up to age 8), 1 from middle years (age 9–14), and then 1 from adolescence (age 15–18). What did you learn from these early recollections? How do you view those ERs now? (i.e., the same, different?)
6 **As if Meaningful:** Let's say your thinking is somewhat along the lines of "My life is meaningless." Perhaps then you begin a long process of exploring

the question of, "If my life were meaningful, it might look like..." Or "If I were to create a meaningful life, I would create it in the following way..." Then, as you begin completing these sentence stems, the meaning is likely found in the process of exploration. Perhaps a more relevant question for consideration then is, "Do I view meaning in life as a process or an end goal, or both?

7 **Love's impact:** I recommend journaling on these types of questions as well: "What has the love for my spouse/partner, children, parents, siblings, close friends, etc., taught me about the meaning in my life?" As love is the most powerful human emotion we possess, it teaches us many lessons, some rewarding, others painful, but all of them very instructive.
8 **Grief:** What has grief taught me about the meaning in my life? Grief is another powerful emotion and, as a one-time pastoral counselor, one that many of my former clients preferred to avoid. As avoiding is counter-therapeutic, consider the question: "What has my grief taught me about the meaning in my life?" Grief commonly comes from the death of a loved one but also through divorce, estrangement, dementia, etc. Author and grief therapist Francis Weller posits grief recovery as being sacred work involving meaningful rituals that teach us about life and death (2015).
9 **Routines:** As a long-distance runner for over 50 years, many of my meaningful meditations have come from my daily jogging. I find a strong sense of meaning and purpose in moving my body, my feet touching the ground, through my 5 senses coming alive, whether in nature or even in a city; my rhythmic breathing; and simply letting go of any thought focus, allowing any thoughts to float past as if on a river. You might explore in your journal topics like the joy I felt in my weekly dance class, the fulfillment my morning Pilates class brings me, how I feel connected to nature during my weekly hikes through the woods/along the beach/strolling through the park, etc.
10 **Simple conversations:** Some of the most enjoyable moments in my life have come from a long conversation over coffee. Think of simple times when you discover a deep sense of connection over a long conversation with a close friend.

Suggestions for Writing Your Meaning in My Life Journal (or whatever title you choose)

1 Begin by selecting a time and place for writing. I had a roommate who set aside 30 minutes before bedtime to write in his journal. Each evening, he would sit at the kitchen table and scribe, a thoughtful expression on his face.
2 Your journal is just that; yours! So, write it in any manner you find meaningful. I have offered several suggestions, but consider what is meaningful to you and write from that perspective.

3 Consider chronological order or journal about what meaningful occurrences happened on that particular day.
4 Anytime you feel you need a break from daily or weekly journaling, take it. Furthermore, if you have been in treatment for past trauma and find your journal writing is triggering you, either stop journaling or change the focus to writing about the simple joys in your life. Naturally, if you feel in crisis (self-harm, especially suicidal), then contact your therapist, return to therapy, or call the national crisis line at 988 (in the U.S.).
5 I would also suggest that after 1 year of journaling, write on the following question: "What has this past year of journaling on the meaning in my life taught me about meaning? What are the lessons I have learned from writing this journal on meaning in my life?"

Drawing: Another Creative Outlet

In an earlier chapter, I recounted an adult client who informed me that standard talk therapy had not been helpful for her. She stated that drawing was what helped her cope with her trauma and asked if she could draw as a means of conducting therapy. I agreed to try and then suggested she draw her life as it was at present. She drew a dark picture of a fractured life, with an abusive father, and images of her self-medicating the pain. She drew her two children living with her mother, as she had lost custody due to addiction and irresponsible parenting behavior. Then, using a variation of de Shazer's miracle question (2010), I suggested she draw what she would like her life to resemble. She then drew a picture full of color and light, with her and her children in the same home, her with a fulfilling career, and a life of healed trauma and free of addiction. My message to her was that we start a series of drawings to help her create that second picture. She became an enthusiastic patient, and, over several weeks, she drew pictures of increasing brightness, albeit with some setbacks along the way. She continued with her 12-step group and gradually was allowed to live with her mother and have co-parenting rights with her mother. She completed counseling and began achieving occupational goals, such as her promotion to assistant manager of the convenience store and maintaining sobriety.

One year later, before moving across the country to another rural community, I encountered her somewhere in town. I initially failed to recognize her as she looked healthy, happy, and completely transformed from the depressed, chemically dependent woman who first entered my clinic office. She was working on an associate's degree in business at the local community college and planning to transfer to a 4-year college next fall to complete her bachelor's degree. I asked what made the difference in her turning her life around, and she reported that it was her therapeutic drawing. She further volunteered that drawing was her version of an ongoing journal, "just entries in sketches," I recall her saying. I encouraged her to continue her drawing. She smiled and replied that she could not imagine her life without her drawings.

Some Suggestions

Likely, all readers have some familiarity with art therapy. While I am a strong advocate for art therapy (and all the creative arts approaches), meaningful drawing is therapeutic, but it is not the same as art therapy. Art therapy involves a highly skilled art therapist working from a particular theoretical approach, utilizing art in the therapy session. Meaningful drawing, as I am presenting it here, is a variation on the Meaning Journal. Like my former client, previously mentioned, this exercise is for those people healing from trauma, coping with stress and anxiety, addiction, or all of these.

Drawing, like writing with a pen or pencil, seems to stimulate multiple sites in the brain in a way that typing or keyboarding does not (Van der Weel & Van der Meer, 2024). More importantly, it seems to improve memory and promote learning new material (Van der Weel & Van der Meer, 2024). Thus, I strongly encourage the use of drawing, along with journaling, as a means of assisting in healing from trauma and managing other challenging stressors. Interested people can purchase therapeutic drawing books or, like my former client, may prefer to use more of a free drawing on art paper or a standard journal table. You may use pens, pencils, crayons, or markers to express yourself. Another variation for many is to make a collage and use it the same way as in the sample drawing exercises below.

Sample Drawing Therapy Exercises

1 **Gratitude drawing**: Draw what you are most grateful for to remind yourself of your blessings.
2 **Draw your healing process**: Most particularly, draw your healing progress, even if it's incremental, because slight healing is still healing. Remember, drawing helps you remember your progress and helps you build on that progress.
3 **Emotion drawing**: Sketch what you are feeling in the present. Include the range of feelings you are experiencing, both the positive ones (bright colors) and the negative ones (shades of gray and black). Remember, all emotions, including negative ones, are part of being human.
4 **Self-compassion drawing:** What does treating yourself in a self-compassionate manner look like?
5 **Drawing meditation**: Another former client used drawing as a meditation. He used breathwork and drew both real-life and abstract images during his 1–2-hour meditations. (His drawings were fascinating!)
6 **Drawing your life journey**: This is a common exercise using a lifeline. However, feel free to draw your life journey any way you feel led to draw it.
7 **Miracle drawing**: This is a variation on de Shazer's miracle question (de Shazer, 2010). In this case, make two drawings: In the first, draw what you would like your life to look like; then, in the second, draw how you can go about creating the life you want. Include pertinent people, personal accomplishments, a sense of fulfillment, peace, etc.

8 **Free drawing with no plan**: In this case, draw with no plan in mind and see what emerges. This could prove to be the most interesting drawing of all.
9 **Meaning in life drawing:** Viktor Frankl posited meaning as the primary motivating force in life (1986). In this drawing, draw what you believe a meaningful life would look like.

Reflective Questions on Your Drawing (or Collage) Journal

1 What has your drawing/collage journal taught you about healing from trauma, managing stress, anxiety, and maintaining sobriety?
2 Regarding your drawings/collages, what did you find most helpful about the process?
3 What have your drawings/collages taught you about yourself? Your life?
4 How might these same drawings/collages look if you were to draw them one year later?

Lessons Learned

This may have been the most unusual chapter thus far. Here are two basic questions to record in your Trauma Recovery Journal:

1 What was the most important lesson you learned from reading and working on the exercises in this chapter?
2 Self-compassion has been a theme throughout this workbook. What have you learned about the importance of self-compassion in your healing journey?
3 Regarding meaning in life, how are you doing in creating a strong sense of meaning in your life?
4 The Harvard Study of Adult Development has suggested that the quality of our relationships is what brings us the most joy and fulfillment in life. How fulfilling are your significant relationships? If they are not as fulfilling as you would like, what could you do to enhance your fulfillment?

12 Lessons Learned through Healing

Post-traumatic Growth's Rewards

No doubt, healing from trauma, managing anxiety or stress, and getting and maintaining sobriety—all of which trauma healing requires—is a difficult journey. Perhaps the most rewarding part of healing, other than feeling healthier and pain-free, is the lessons one learns through the journey of healing from pain. Post-traumatic growth (PTG) has become a common phrase in mental health circles and reflects a recognition that healing from trauma requires emotional growth. Many of my former clients have remarked that while they were not happy to have been traumatized, the necessary work to heal, unpleasant as it was, brought about a sense of satisfaction at accomplishing something significant. As one former client, a survivor of decades of intimate partner violence, remarked, "Of course, I would have never chosen to be physically and psychologically abused to grow." No, absolutely no one ever has said they wished to be traumatized to experience significant personal growth. That same client also remarked, however, "Healing from trauma was my best choice. I already knew self-medication wasn't working."

Tedeschi et al. (2018) defined PTG as a "positive psychological changes experienced as a result of the struggle with trauma or highly challenging situations" (p. 3). No doubt, anyone who has experienced significant trauma, either a single episode (e.g., auto accident, sexual assault, robbery victim) or ongoing trauma (e.g., childhood sexual abuse, combat duty, domestic violence, long-term bullying at school or work) will readily agree that their trauma certainly was highly challenging. After a long career treating PTSD, providing workshops on treating trauma and preventing vicarious trauma, I cannot recall a single person ever remarking that their healing came easily, nor can I remember anyone articulating a desire for more growth-producing trauma. No question, growth through trauma is not the type of challenge anyone would ever select for personal transcendence. Sadly, of course, far too many people are forced to confront the aftermath of being damaged, leaving the rough road to healing as their best option.

DOI: 10.4324/9781003689232-12

Healing from trauma, much like that of grief, is a very personal process (in fact, grief and trauma tend to elicit the same types of human behavior, such as denial, anger, depression, etc.). The self-reflective questions below are designed to have you consider your PTG and how it has helped you grow.

Significant Reflections on Your Healing

I suggest you write answers to the following questions in your Trauma Recovery Journal.

1 What is the most important lesson your healing journey has taught you?

____

____

2 Self-compassion has been mentioned several times in this workbook. How has self-compassion assisted you in your healing journey?

____

____

3 We explored reframing negative self-statements. Ex.: "I deserved my pain," to "Unfortunately, I was traumatized, but now I have healed and am a stronger, more resilient person. Consider a negative self-statement you may have thought or articulated. Now, reframe that same statement into something more positive and realistic."

____

____

4 Throughout this workbook, readers have been encouraged to keep a Trauma Recovery Journal. Describe how journaling has aided you in:

a Processing your traumatic experiences:
b Helping you identify trauma triggers:
c Charting your progress:

____

____

5 Developing and maintaining healthy boundaries is a key ingredient in healing. How has setting healthy boundaries with family, friends, co-workers, etc., helped you on your healing journey?

6 You have made a significant amount of progress during your healing journey. What part of your progress are you most proud of? (Don't be afraid to brag about yourself)

7 If you were to have a conversation with your younger self on trauma recovery and healing, what might you say? What advice might you offer your younger self?

8 If you were to have a conversation with your future self, what would you wish to say?

9 A significant part of any healing involves the understanding that no one completes the healing journey alone. Healing trauma involves a skilled therapist, support group (12-step or otherwise), family, supportive friends, etc. Briefly describe your process in learning to ask for help.

10 If a loved one were to seek advice on healing their trauma, what advice would you offer them?

Charting Your Healing Journey

Charting a healing journey involves several methods, such as journaling (Trauma Recovery Journal for reflections on healing, joys, fears, doubts, hopes, successes, setbacks, etc.), visual timelines, scaling questions on healing, healing drawings, paintings, collages, setting new goals (e.g., running a marathon, walking the Camino or other meaningful quest, beginning a new career, permitting yourself to ask for help), prioritizing self-care and self-compassion, etc.

Start at the Beginning

Use your Trauma Recovery Journal to record your answers to the following questions:

1 When you have healed, what will you notice being different regarding your mood, thoughts, behaviors, family, and collegial relationships?

____

____

2 What will others likely notice about your healed self?

____

____

3 You have made a lot of progress to have reached this milestone in the healing process.
Regarding your healing process, what are you most proud of?

____

____

4 You have likely learned many lessons along the healing journey. What are the top three lessons you have learned during your healing?

a ____

b ____

c ____

5 When we are on a healing journey, some people support us during that arduous process. List some notable people who will be key supporters in your staying healthy. (These are people you can ask for help from when needed.)

____

____

6 You are starting a new phase in your life. What new goals have you set? What new goals would you like to set?

____

____

1 Your healing journey has involved changes in your thinking, behavior, breathwork, and spirit. What regular and ongoing practices have you committed to continuing in your life regarding:

Mind (e.g., Healthy Mantras, Cognitive Reframing-the story you are telling yourself):

____

____

Behavior (e.g., asking for help, healthy work-life balance, healthy diet, refraining from tobacco, alcohol free or very limited consumption)

____

____

Body (e.g., yoga, Pilates, swimming, walking, jogging)

____

____

Breath (e.g., meditation, box breathing, vagus nerve Voo exhaling)

____

____

Spirit (e.g., meaning/purpose in life): Basically, what brings meaning to your life? Family, spiritual practice, meaningful routines, etc.

____

____

2 It is helpful and realistic to pinpoint challenges and setbacks to progress. What do you see as three challenges to your continued healing?

a ____

b ____

c ____

3 In the previous chapter, Nietzsche's statement that the person with a *why* can endure almost any *how* was addressed. What is your *why* that continues to guide you through your ongoing life journey?

____

____

4 The important issue of setting boundaries was part of a previous chapter. Maintaining firm, though flexible boundaries, will help you continue a healthy pathway. This will mean saying "No" when necessary. Briefly outline your success in establishing and maintaining healthy boundaries by saying "No."

____

____

Charting Your Healing from Trauma

There are several approaches to charting healing from trauma. I will recommend a comprehensive yet simple set of activities taught to me long ago. Note: If you are not currently in treatment with a therapist, you may wish to postpone this intervention. If you have completed treatment yet feel triggered beyond your management level, please discontinue the activity and contact your therapist.

A Create a trauma timeline

1 Draw a line on a blank page (I suggest using poster-size paper). Use a pen, pencil, magic marker, or crayon.
2 Next, starting with your birth at the beginning of the line, add significant traumatic events in chronological order. Add the date and a brief description of what occurred.
3 For each event, briefly list the emotions, self-belief, and physical symptoms you experienced.
4 Record any coping mechanisms you used in response to that traumatic event.
5 Record new lessons learned through your trauma healing work and management. Remember, it's all about growth through the healing work.
6 The trauma timeline provides a visual history of your traumatic experiences and how those experiences have impacted your development, relationships, and self-belief. The trauma timeline can provide valuable information for your therapist as well as for you to understand your own experiences and resilience.
7 Take your trauma timeline up to the present time.

B Write a trauma narrative

1 After completing the trauma timeline, select a specific traumatic incident and write a comprehensive narrative about it.
2 Begin with the basic facts: who, what, where, when, and how.
3 As best as you can, describe the behaviors, thoughts, and feelings resulting from your traumatic experience.
4 Then, returning to the present, what have you learned from surviving that/those traumatic experience(s), and how have you grown from the healing work required in response to the trauma? (This is a significant part of PTG.)

C Creating a daily or weekly healing chart

1 Tracking physical sensations: As van der Kolk writes about the body keeping the score (2015), you will focus on somatic sensations. For example, if your trauma caused headaches, you would record headaches. If you feel numbness related to the trauma anywhere in your body, record that.

Notice when your heart is racing, any hyperventilation, high blood pressure, etc.

2 Monitor self-care and well-being: Chart your regular self-care interventions. For example, acknowledging gratitude practice; meditation (sitting, walking, silent, with mantra, etc.), box breathing, vagus nerve interventions such as EFT tapping, Voo exhaling, and any bodywork (e.g., yoga, Pilates, massage), regular workouts (e.g., swimming, dancing, walking), and anything else.

3 Record triggers: Keep track of what triggers your symptoms and how you respond when triggered. Remember, be gentle with yourself, as everyone gets triggered. The goal is to learn to manage and reduce triggers.

4 Record cognitive reframing: Remember, as Brene Brown says,

What's the story you are telling yourself (Brown, 2010)? Pick 3 times per day to notice when your inner or external voice is harsh, then reframe in a self-compassionate, growth-oriented manner.

Example: "I did not get that job I wanted. They think I'm a loser!"

Reframe: "Unfortunately, they hired someone else. However, I learned from this healthy risk and will be a stronger candidate next time."

Alternate reframe: "Okay, that's one rejection closer to success." (This is my favorite reframe!)

5 Celebrate small successes: Record any progress, no matter how small, like going out grocery shopping when feeling afraid, or noticing when you successfully managed a conflict with a family member, friend, or co-worker. Remember, big success often is constructed of numerous small successes.

6 Lessons learned: As always, how have you grown through your recovery from the trauma?

D Further journaling for continued growth and self-exploration in your Trauma Recovery Journal

1 Write an account of what you are learning (or have learned) from trauma charting: Describe the process of charting your healing from trauma. What did you learn regarding your emotional, physical, sexual, spiritual, etc., growth? Remember, healing involves personal growth, creating a more resilient you.

2 Miracle question: Consider a future when you have healed your trauma and are solidly in PTG (e.g., have reduced triggers; are successfully managing your triggers; are regularly reframing negative self-stories; and are practicing daily self-care activities) (e.g., gratitudes, vagus nerve exercises (tapping, Voo exhaling), active routines (e.g., walking, yoga, swimming), and anything else. What will be different about you emotionally, socially, spiritually, sexually, occupationally, etc.? What will others close to you notice as being different?

E Daily Visual Encouragers

1 Post encouraging message reminders where you regularly see them: For example, a friend used to post encouraging messages on her refrigerator door, as she would be reminded several times a day. A former client wrote encouraging messages and inspirational messages on her bathroom mirror using erasable magic markers. Others I have known posted uplifting scenes in strategic places (like on their computer).
2 Post any successes, regardless of how small, in strategic locations: like above, on the refrigerator, mirror, your bedroom door, your office, etc.
3 Share your successes: Share your successes with people who will validate your successes: your close loved ones, friends, trusted colleagues, etc. Remember, we are social creatures, and as we honor others' success, allow some to honor yours.

F Personal Resilience Award:

1 Give yourself an award to recognize your post-traumatic growth and healing. Create a Personal Resilience Award acknowledging your strength and persistence in navigating the difficult emotional, social, and psychospiritual journey towards healing and wholeness.
2 Wording: "Awarded to ______________________ (your name), on this date __/__/ in recognition of your significant accomplishment in navigating the difficult journey towards healing. Your courage in facing difficult life experiences, discipline, and dedication to personal growth and well-being are hereby recognized and honored."
3 After creating the certificate: Depending on how you feel, post it on your refrigerator, in your home office, or somewhere you feel comfortable. Or place the completed certificate in your Trauma Recovery Journal.

G An Award Ceremony (optional):

You may wish to consider gathering trusted friends and loved ones for a ceremony. The ceremony could involve a reception, then brief words from a few people who have supported you through your healing journey (e.g., close family, trusted friends, a 12-step sponsor, a spiritual mentor, or anyone you feel you want in attendance). Choose someone to be the master or mistress of the ceremony (MC), and that person can call on others to speak briefly regarding your significant accomplishment. Afterwards, you are awarded the Personal Resilience Award in front of the gathering, and everyone claps.

Remind Yourself You've Earned the Award: Take this award ceremony suggestion seriously. It may be the hardest and most important work you've ever done. Make sure you acknowledge it and silence the critics inside your mind using cognitive reframing, meditation, positive self-talk, etc., that this workbook has focused on.

Healing Meditations

There are numerous helpful apps one can download and listen to guided meditations. I typically use 2–3 apps and prefer guided meditations of 5–10 minutes. At other times, I will use music as a type of meditation, usually instrumental music such as classical piano, violin, or another soothing instrumental arrangement. Some nights, I listen to smooth jazz for relaxation, occasionally becoming so relaxed that I fall asleep in the chair. The important thing is to make use of what works for you. In this section, I will offer examples of meditations you can utilize to assist you in your healing journey. Naturally, feel free to create your own meditations.

Some Tips to Remember If You Are New to Meditation

1. Remember, just be natural and remember that your breath is the most important part of meditation. So long as you are using slow inhales through your nose and slow rhythmic exhaling out of your mouth, you will derive some benefit from the guided meditation.
2. Using a self-guided meditation may feel odd for a while, but with practice, it will become more natural.
3. When using a self-guided meditation, either in your voice or on a recording, speak slowly and naturally.
4. Whether a guided meditation or a silent one, take your time. Make sure it's a time of day or evening when you can get at least 10 minutes to make a sustained guided, somatic meditation. Rushing through this exercise will negate any potential benefits. Healing, whether physical, psychological, emotional, spiritual, etc., takes time and discipline.
5. Do not force yourself to sit and meditate for long periods of time. Start slowly, with brief meditations of 5–10 minutes. Sit in a comfortable chair or even lie on the couch or in your bed. The important part is getting unstressed by regulating your breathing through deep meditation breaths.
6. Practice self-compassion by noticing and releasing mind wandering thoughts as if they are simply floating past on a river. Mind wandering is very natural.
7. If holding a special (or sacred) object helps your concentration, then use it.
8. If possible, schedule your brief meditation at the same time each day. For example, I meditate on my 40-minute train ride to campus.
9. Remember to be yourself. Meditation is about releasing inner tension so that we may become our kinder, gentler selves. Many people, especially monks, meditate on the mantra of loving kindness: "May I be loving, may I be kind," or other such mantras.
10. As our body is the temple of our being, pay attention to any tension or stiffness in your physical being. Meditate on releasing that tension and perhaps incorporate the EFT/meridian tapping into your meditation practice.

Self-Guided Healing Meditation

Step 1: Preparing Your Mind and Body

Start by getting yourself into a comfortable position, either by sitting in a relaxed posture or lying down. Depending on your comfort level, close your eyes, soften your gaze, or stare at a fixed point or object, whatever feels most natural. Take a few deep breaths through your nose and exhale through your mouth.

For around 5% of trauma survivors, meditation can trigger panic. Therefore, if you feel a guided meditation is triggering you, please stop, and use a self-soothing activity (e.g., meridian tapping, Voo exhaling, box breathing, body movement). Regarding how much time to take, I suggest that you experiment. I meditate for an hour daily, but you may prefer a shorter timeframe. Even 10 minutes of meditation can assist with anxiety management, emotional regulation, and memory (Bass et al., 2019).

Step 2: Connecting to the Ground/Earth/Floor/Seat/Whatever You Are Sitting or Lying On

Acknowledging the support of the earth or the surface you are resting upon. Allow your body to rest fully, feeling the support of that surface, using as little energy as possible to support your body. If you lie down, imagine your body fully supported by that surface.

Step 3: Pay Attention to Your Breath

Become attuned to the natural rhythm of your breath. Take long, slow, in-breaths through your nose, and then exhale slowly and naturally out your mouth. With each exhale, imagine your body becoming more relaxed. Feel the connection between your breath and the supporting surface, allowing each exhale to relax your body.

Step 4: Visualize a Healing Light

Imagine the space all around you is filled with a bright, comfortable light. This light is a healing light, generated by the loving kindness present in your life. While being held by this warm, healing light, consider someone or something that brings you peace and joy, whether it's a loved one, a pet, a favorite place, or an activity you love. As you reflect upon these thoughts, the healing light brightens and comforts you, comforting you in its healing embrace.

Step 5: Inhale the Healing Light

As you inhale, imagine breathing in the warm, soothing, healing light into your body through your nose, filling your lungs, seeping into your muscles, bones, organs, and bloodstream. With each exhale, imagine yourself releasing any tension, negative thoughts, or heaviness. Focus on the inhalation of the healing light and allow the exhalation to be long and relaxed.

Step 6: Direct the Healing Light toward the Needed Areas of Your Body

Next, focus on a part of your body that needs healing. Perhaps it's where you are experiencing pain, discomfort, or the effects of injury or illness. With each inhale, focus the healing light on this area, allowing it to soothe and repair what needs repairing, soothe what needs soothing, and realign what is misaligned. With each exhale, release any residue of pain or discomfort while imagining the light to heal what needs healing.

Step 7: Communicating with Your Body

Remember that your body is a close friend. Take a moment to ask aloud or silently what that ailing part of your body needs. Listen carefully to your body's answer. Perhaps it's trying to teach you a self-care lesson like "be gentler," or "remember I am part of your whole," or the answer may be healing silence, possibly the richest answer of all. Remain open to any answer that arises. Let your body know, "I hear you and want us to heal together."

Step 8: Move the Focus to another Area of Your Body

When you feel ready, shift your focus to another part of your body that needs healing. Repeat the previous process of inhaling the healing light, focusing it on the area of pain or discomfort, and imaging releasing what needs releasing with each exhale. Continue this process, moving to a third area if that feels right. Allow the healing light to fill you with warmth and loving kindness.

Step 9: Reflect on Your Experience

Take a long moment to cloak yourself in the healing light. Surrender yourself to this peaceful moment, supported by the light's gentle embrace. Imagine yourself resting in this peaceful state, unencumbered by any concern, as you slowly inhale through your nose and exhale through your mouth. When you are ready to conclude the healing meditation, slowly begin to release the light and feel your body returning to the present. Remember any promises you may have made to your body during the meditation and follow through on those promises that feel authentic and healing.

Step 10: In Finishing, Acknowledging Three Gratitudes before Fully Returning to the Active World

For example, they might be (1) I'm grateful for my healing; (2) I'm grateful for my spouse/partner/child/close friends; (3) I'm grateful for this new day/anything else.

For additional impact, consider journaling on the following questions:

1. What was the most valuable part of the guided meditation? Was it the breath, the healing light, the guided meditation (recorded, verbal, or imagined silently), or something else? What made that the most important component of the experience?
2. When imagining the healing light repairing a part of your body, what was that experience like?
3. When you were communicating with your body, did you gain any insights from that experience? (e.g., regarding healing or anything else)
4. Should you continue this type of guided healing meditation, how might regular practice change the relationship you have with your body?

Vagus Nerve Guided Meditation

The following example is simply one example of a vagus nerve meditation.

Step 1: Get Comfortable

Start by finding a comfortable position. You may be standing, sitting, or lying down, whichever seems more relaxing to you.

Step 2: Prepare by Doing a Pre-check, Noticing Areas of Tension

Close your eyes or soften your gaze or focus on a fixed point or object (whatever seems best to you). Feel your body being supported by the ground, floor, bed, and begin to experience the solid grounding of what surface supports you. Scan your body and notice any stress or tension you may be holding in your head, face, jaw, shoulders, back, or stomach. Simply observe these sensations without the need to do anything other than become aware of how your body feels at present.

Step 3: Position Your Hands Strategically

Place one hand on your stomach so that your palm is covering your navel. Place the other hand at your heart region. Allow your elbows to relax, and if you are lying down, prop your elbows up for support. Feel the warmth and connection between your hands and your body, preparing for the relaxing breathwork ahead.

Step 4: Begin with a Voo Exhale

As has been explained in previous chapters, breathe in slowly through your nose, pause for 1–2 seconds, and then purse your lips and slowly exhale through your mouth, making a Voo sound, exhale for 5–8 seconds. Then, repeat this sequence for 5 rounds. (10 rounds if you get serious) Remember, do this breathing gently and rhythmically, avoiding any strain on your body. Keep the inhale, and Voo exhale smoothly.

Step 5: Continue Breathing and Focusing on the Sensation

While you are breathing and exhaling, notice the sensations in your body. Feel your stomach swell, and your ribs rise as you inhale. When you Voo exhale, focus on the release of tension and the ensuing relaxation. Feel the vibration in your body when you engage the Voo exhaling. The vibrations can help calm your sympathetic nervous system.

Step 6: Engaging the Vagus Nerve and Calming Your Body

This practice involves relaxed breathing, and Voo exhaling stimulates the vagus nerve and is critical for creating a more relaxed state of being. With each breath, you are improving your body's oxygen intake and offloading carbon dioxide, bringing forth a deeper state of relaxation. As you continue this practice, you may also feel a sense of warmth moving throughout your body, further enhancing your sense of calm.

Step 7: Present Moment Return

After, say, 5–7 minutes of calming breath and vagus nerve stimulation, release your hands from your stomach and your heart area. Notice the effects of the exercise on your body (less tension) and on your thoughts (calmer and peaceful). Take a moment to reflect on the practice you have cultivated. Breathe in the calm and exhale out any remaining tension.

Step 8: Senses and Gratitude Acknowledgment

Acknowledge:

(1) one object you can see; (2) one sound you can hear; and (3) one object you can feel and describe the feeling. Then, acknowledge three gratitudes.

Reflecting on the Vagus Nerve Meditation

Spend some time reflecting on your meditation. Consider journaling on the following questions:

1 What somatic sensations did you notice during the Voo exhaling?
2 How did your breath influence your state of relaxation?
3 How did your thoughts change during the meditation?
4 How might daily vagus nerve exhaling improve your state of relaxation?

What Disappointment Is Trying to Teach Me

Western culture is particularly fond of financial success, occupational success, sports-related success, and always winning. However, no one is successful 100% of the time. Furthermore, lessons learned through the crucible of failure and disappointment can include increased resilience, self-awareness, and compassion and instill the importance of patience. Disappointment, or perhaps failure, may help in clarifying what one values, revising for more appropriate expectations, and navigating a new direction after a setback. A key ingredient in learning from and transforming disappointment is the cognitive tool of reframing. By reframing disappointment as a learning opportunity, you will likely feel more optimistic and able to transform painful experiences into stepping stones for personal growth and emotional resilience.

Some Potential Lessons from Disappointment

1. **Developing resilience**: Building emotional strength from disappointments for future success.
2. **Lessons learned**: What valuable lessons has failure taught you? How can those lessons help prepare you for future success?
3. **Increased self-reflection and awareness**: disappointment can highlight areas that need skill-building for future success.
4. **Developing self-compassion**: the wrong message in failure is self-flagellation. Instead, be gentle and encouraging in your self-talk. For example: "Okay, losing out on that promotion/job/award was a disappointment. However, I learned much through this process and will be a stronger candidate the next time." (Or my favorite self-statement: "I am disappointed, but stronger for it, and it's one disappointment closer to success.")
5. **Success may be a developmental process**: My own experience is that success, whether landing a job, getting a promotion, winning an award, etc., is often a series of steps as opposed to achievement on the first try. Again, be self-compassionate and resilient and reframe that failure/disappointment into building blocks to success. (see example in the previous bullet point)
6. **Failure may be a requirement for future success**: I recall a close friend being rejected for a position she believed was her dream job. She was crushed, and I spent a good deal of time being present to her disappointment. To replace the void of disappointment, she upskilled herself by enrolling in a training course in adventure-based therapy certification (for 1 year) and discovered this newfound occupation was her true love. She often joked that previous failure had been a gift in disguise. So, remember that disappointment might be the best medicine, even when it goes down hard.
7. **Focus on new challenges**: Take some time to process your disappointment, and then when ready, seek out new goals and challenges. As one former colleague was fond of expressing, "Never let a really tough disappointment go to waste!"

Working through Disappointment Exercises

The following are self-reflection exercises to transform disappointment into learning and future success. Use your Trauma Recovery Journal to address these questions in writing.

Think of a recent disappointment you may have experienced. Now, list five take-away lessons you have learned from disappointment:

Lesson 1: ____

Lesson 2: ____

Lesson 3: ____

Lesson 4: ____

Lesson 5: ____

Note: If you cannot think of five lessons, cite as many as you can, reflect on the matter, and see what emerges later.

Journaling: Select one of the lessons you cited having learned from disappointment and journal about that lesson. Be very honest regarding your disappointment, and then write about how you transformed that disappointment into constructive action (Example: My friend who retrained into a new career).

Drawing or Collage: First, make two drawings or collages. In the first, draw or collage disappointment. Then, when finished, draw or collage a second picture of achievement. Finally, construct a third drawing or collage of how you will transition from the disappointing picture into the achievement picture. Remember, success often is a developmental process and not a single-shot option.

Empty Chair Conversation: Readers having progressed this far through the chapters are now familiar with Moreno's Empty Chair conversations. In this case, I suggest holding two conversations with the empty chair. First, hold a conversation with Ms. or Mr. Disappointment. Take 10–15 minutes and discuss your frustration, anger, and pain in being disappointed. When the set time has elapsed, switch chairs and then allow Ms/Mr./They Disappointment to speak with you regarding how this disappointment occurred, and how disappointment is preparing you for future success. Let disappointment encourage you to reframe disappointment into something constructive. You may feel the need to hold ongoing conversations with Ms./Mr. Disappointment. Take note of how the conversations evolve if you continue a series of these conversations.

Seeking Support: Think of a trusted, honest friend, one who you know can be present to your frustration but also tell you the truth when you ask (and not just what you wish to hear). That is, a friend who won't hijack the conversation by "Let me tell you about my disappointment..." If you lack such a friend, I'd suggest talking with a therapist. Ask your friend if you can schedule one hour for this conversation. Also, when finished, ask your friend for any suggestions on managing the disappointment or improvements for the future.

Movement: Humans have evolved through movement, and recreational movement is part of emotional and physical healing (McGonigal, 2017). If you have a regular movement routine like Pilates, yoga, cycling, jogging, make sure you continue to engage in it 4 times per week for at least 20 minutes, as this regular activity helps in managing sadness (McGonigal, 2017). It is common to feel de-energized when hit with a major disappointment. I recommend you challenge that post-setback, low-energy phase with sustained movement. If, however, you cannot get yourself to engage in your regular workout, just spend 10 minutes walking back and forth across your living room. Then, take a 5-minute break and walk for 10 more minutes. Keep this low-key approach going each day until you are ready to resume your regular workout. I well understand, as I can recall struggling to continue my workouts in the aftermath of a major disappointment several years ago. However, even lowering my workout intensity helped me cope and move forward.

Mindfulness routine: This section will also be a repeat of what has been mentioned in previous chapters. Some helpful mindfulness activities:

a **Daily gratitude acknowledgment**: Begin each day by acknowledging three gratitudes.
b **Meridian tapping:** Tap/touch 11 points included in a previous chapter: karate chop, palm the top of the head, the left and the right side of the eye, then just below the eye, then the divot above the mouth, and then just below the center of the mouth, then the clavicle, then 4 inches under the armpit on the ribs, then the space between the small bones of the fourth and fifth finger, and finally place your hand on heart section of the chest. Do three rounds of these 11 points.
c **Meditation:** You do not need to spend long periods of time in meditation to achieve healthy benefits. Some former clients have volunteered that just 5 minutes helped them manage stress. You may sit in silence, make use of a mantra, download a guided meditation, use an app, do a walking meditation, etc.
d **Self-Acknowledgment**: Managing disappointment can be difficult. So, each day, acknowledge something you like about yourself. Stand before a mirror and, using your name, articulate that acknowledgment out loud: "Helene, I really admire the compassion you show to others." I suggest acknowledging something different each day. You may decide to make a list of your positive attributes before beginning this exercise.

Life Lessons, Trauma Healing, and Post-traumatic Growth Have Taught Me

Healing from trauma clearly requires lots of work, persistence, and resilience. As you move through the phases of trauma healing into PTG, you likely have learned many life lessons that can help you adapt to continued challenges, as life involves ongoing growth, along with the joys and sorrows that we encounter along life's journey. The following may represent some of the lessons you may have learned. Use your Trauma Recovery Journal to record your written responses to the lessons below.

1 **Prioritizing emotional well-being**: Good emotional health does not simply happen. Throughout this workbook, numerous examples of well-being have been offered. Create a daily well-being routine that works for you. Now, list four activities your daily wellness plan includes:

   a ______________________________

   b ______________________________

   c ______________________________

   d ______________________________

2 **Establishing healthy boundaries:** We addressed clear boundaries in a previous chapter. People who grew up in traumatic situations, or who have escaped domestic violence, for example, have routinely experienced boundary violations. Cite three strategies you will employ to set and maintain firm boundaries.

   a ______________________________

   b ______________________________

   c ______________________________

3 **Peer support:** Creating healthy friendships for a social life and healthy support. Humans evolved as social creatures, and we need healthy friendships to give and receive healthy support. In the spaces below, list three close friends you can trust and rely on for support. If you do not have three such friends, then cite three strategies to create these supportive friendships, as human support is crucial for well-being.

   a ______________________________

   b ______________________________

   c ______________________________

4 **Body liberation**: Focus on noticing and then releasing tension held in your body. Throughout this workbook, we have examined numerous methods of freeing somatic tension (e.g., meridian tapping, meditation, Voo exhaling, physical activity, massage). Cite three strategies to liberate your body from tension.

   a ______________________________

   b ______________________________

c ____

5 **Cognitive Reframing**: Because we are human and prone to backsliding into unhealthy thoughts and behavioral patterns, you will need to practice what some of us call the 3Cs: (1) Catch that negative self-statement (e.g., "I'm stupid!"); (2) Challenge that negative self-statement by examining the evidence (e.g., "Well, I am educated, have a good job, am well read"); Change it to something more realistic (Ex.: "Okay, I'm not an Einstein, but the evidence contradicts me being stupid. So, I am intelligent and capable, although not perfect"). My suggestion is that you practice the 3Cs daily so that your negative self-statements do not become beliefs that are acted on behaviorally.

a Catch it: ________________________________

b Challenge it: ____________________________

c Change it: _______________________________

6 **Accepting human fallibility**: As we are imperfect beings, we must understand that occasionally we will continue to make errors. Some readers recovering from trauma may have escaped abusive homes where mistakes were treated as serious transgressions, resulting in abuse. Freedom from abuse means you are free to live your life and make errors without being abused. Many of us who have healed from trauma have found it helpful to remind ourselves that making mistakes is both human and healthy. In your journal, write out three self-compassionate, verbal statements as gentle reminders. For example: "Okay, I goofed. That's human." Or "Alright, I could have said that better. I will make amends with my co-worker/spouse/friend and do better the next time."

a ____

b ____

c ____

7 **What's your why?** In the previous chapter, meaning in life was addressed. Readers were encouraged to find their *why* (meaning). To paraphrase Nietzsche's famous statement, those with a *why* can endure almost any *how*. Your why provides a means for transforming your pain, sorrow, and disappointment in a way that helps you move forward. In your journal, briefly answer the following questions:

a What is the why in your life?

____

____

b How has your why helped you in your healing process?

____

____

8 **Emotional regulation (ER):** ER was part of Chapter 1. Basically, how do you manage anger, sadness, frustration, grief, etc., when you are triggered? While it is important to acknowledge these human emotions, you must regulate them for your emotional health. We have addressed several strategies in this workbook to regulate emotions (e.g., noticing and managing your triggers, box breathing, meridian tapping, meditation, taking a short break, walking/exercise to calm). In your Trauma Recovery Journal, cite four strategies you will use to help regulate your emotions:

a ____

b ____

c ____

d ____

9 **Remember, everything is temporary**: Nothing in life lasts forever. Your joy, sadness, success, disappointment, etc., will end. These endings help you move forward through life and teach valuable lessons. In your Trauma Recovery Journal, cite four disappointments that taught you a valuable lesson.

a ____

b ____

c ____

d ____

10 **Reclaiming our selfhood**: Many people who have survived long-term trauma mention the loss of their own selfhood as a means of pleasing the abuser to survive. One of the common treatment components is assisting the trauma survivors in discovering their own selfhood. In your Trauma Recovery Journal, write a brief essay using the title below (*This is who I am essay*). This essay can be as brief or as lengthy as it seems natural. Do not concern yourself with whether it is grammatically correct, and let go of any need to make it a publishable story in a journal. Just use the essay to discuss who you are as a person. While trauma will impact us in ways, it does not have to rob us of our humanity or essential being.

This is who I am essay:

____

____

____

____

Conversations with Myself

Throughout this workbook, Moreno's empty-chair intervention has been used in several chapters. Many therapists have made extensive use of it in our counseling sessions with clients. In the next set of interventions, consider the following empty chair conversations.

An empty chair conversation with my younger self:

A **Part 1**: Set an empty chair facing you and hold an extended conversation with your younger self. Set a timer for, say, 15–20 minutes (or longer). You might consider addressing topics such as praising your younger self for surviving past trauma, not giving up on life, addressing the healthy decisions you made when younger, forgiving your younger self for past mistakes, and anything you wish to say to your younger self. Finally, be sure to tell your younger self, "I love you."

Part 2: Change seats and then speak as your younger self, using a timer and the same timeframe as the previous conversation. Consider telling your current self how proud you are for surviving; the courage to heal, to grow, and change; any successes; showing self-compassion for mistakes made along the healing journey; and anything else that seems appropriate. As above, tell your current self, "I love you."

An empty chair conversation with my future self

B **Part 1**: Now, using the same format as the previous empty-chair conversations, hold an empty-chair conversation with your future self. Tell your future self whatever seems appropriate, including perhaps how proud you are of them, their wisdom, growth, resilience, and work ethic. As above, tell your future self, "I love you."

Part 2: Change seats and then speak as your older self. Consider telling your current self how proud you are of all the hard work done, successes, working through setbacks and failures, and having the courage to learn newer, healthier lessons, and anything else that seems appropriate. Tell your current self, "I love you."

C **Important Lessons:** In your Trauma Recovery Journal, list five important lessons you learned from these empty-chair conversations with yourself:

Lesson 1: ____

Lesson 2: ____

Lesson 3: ____

Lesson 4: ____

Lesson 5: ____

D Learning into Action: An important component of learning lessons is how we incorporate those lessons into our daily lives. So, in your Trauma Recovery Journal, briefly write about how you will put these five lessons into action in your life. Consider the different phases of your life, such as the relationship with your family, friends, colleagues and superiors at work. How will these five lessons you have learned from the empty chair conversations impact these relationships?

Lessons Learned from This Chapter and Beyond

As this is the final chapter in this workbook, consider the following questions. Use your Trauma Recovery Journal to record your answers.

1. What was the most helpful exercise in this chapter?
2. Why did you find that exercise more important than others?
3. Beyond this chapter, or even this workbook, what is the most important lesson your failures have taught you?
4. Like the previous question, what is the most important lesson your successes have taught you?
5. What has been the most challenging part of healing your trauma?
6. Who has been the most important support person during your healing?
7. Of all the progress you have made in your healing journey, what are you the proudest of?
8. Healing can significantly transform one's life. What is the most rewarding change that healing has brought to your life?
9. Given all your hard work and subsequent growth, what are you looking most forward to in your life?
10. If you could offer one piece of advice to someone beginning their healing journey, what would that advice be?

Postscript

Congratulations, you have completed this workbook! As you move forward, here are some suggestions, some of which are similar to interventions in this workbook:

1. Create a certificate of accomplishment praising yourself for all your hard work.
2. Write a letter of congratulations to yourself, praising yourself for your hard work, accomplishments, resilience, and anything else you want to note. Tell yourself that you will be happy to serve as a reference for yourself anytime to anyone you deem deserving of your special gifts and talents. Make sure

you sign and date the letter. Then, occasionally, reread the letter to remind yourself that you are indeed a very special person to yourself and others.

3 Recommendation: Each time you achieve something important, whatever you deem important, celebrate that achievement. Take your spouse/partner out for a special dinner celebration. If you are single, ask a special friend to join you and let them know the occasion. While it might seem self-centered, send yourself an e-card (or get an old-fashioned one), and write a congratulatory note to yourself, just as you would do for your spouse or partner, daughter or son, close friend, etc. Remember, celebrate your successes.
4 From this time forward, remember to practice self-compassion, which is the type of loving kindness you would show a loved one or close friend.
5 Work on your daily well-being plan, starting with your daily gratitude acknowledgment.

Afterword

In the preface of this workbook, I compared healing trauma to a caterpillar's transformation into a beautiful butterfly through metamorphosis. You have put in a lot of transformative work and are now ready for the next stage of life. Just as a butterfly is no longer compelled to crawl about in its old self, you also are now free to take flight. So, dear reader, when you feel ready, put on your wings and fly!

References

American Psychiatric Association (2022). *Diagnostic and statistical manual of mental disorders, fifth edition-text revision*. Author. https://doi.org/10.1176/appi.books.9780890425787

Arena, A.F., Gregory, M., Collins, D.A.J., Vilus, B., Bryant, R., Harvey, S.B., & Deady, M. (2025). Global PTSD prevalence among first responders and trends over recent years: A systematic review and meta-analysis. *Clinical Psychology Review, 120*. https://doi.org/10.1016/j.cpr.2025.102622.

Aurelius, M. (2006). *The meditations of Marcus Aurelius*. Penguin Classic.

Bach, D., Groesbeck, G., Stapelton, P., Sims, R., Blickheuser, K., Dawson, C. (2019). Clinical EFT (Emotional Freedom Techniques) improves multiple physiological markers of health. *Journal of Evidence-Based Integrated Medicine, 19(24)*. https://doi.org/10.1177/2515690X18823691

Bass, J.C., McHale, A., Ende, V., Oberlin, D.J., & Suzuki, W.A. (2019). Brief, daily meditation enhances attention, memory, mood, and emotional regulation in non-experienced meditators. *Behavioural Brain Research, 356*, 208–220. https://doi.org/10.1016/j.bbr.2018.08.023

Beck, A.T. (2019). A 60-year evolution of cognitive theory and therapy. *Perspectives on Psychological Science, 14(1)*, 16–20.

Beck, J.S. (2021). *Cognitive therapy: Basics and beyond, third edition*. Guilford.

Bentley, K.H., Bernstein, E.E., Wallace, B., & Mischoulon (2021). Treatment for anxiety and comorbid depressive disorders: Transdiagnostic cognitive-behavioral strategies. *Psychiatric Annals, 51(5)*, 226–230. https://doi.org/10.3928/00485713-20210414-01.

Boyle, G. (2024). *Cherished belonging: The healing power of love in divided times*. Simon & Schuster.

Briere, J.N., & Scott, C. (2015). *Principles of trauma therapy: A guide to symptoms, evaluation, and treatment, second edition* (DSM Update). Sage Publications, Inc.

Brooks, A. C., & Winfrey, O. (2023). *Build the life you want*. Portfolio.

Brown, B. (2010). *The gifts of imperfection: Let go of who you think you're supposed to be and embrace who you are*. Hazelden Publishing.

Brown, B. (2013). *Daring greatly: How the courage to be vulnerable transforms the way we live, love, parent, and lead*. Penguin Life.

Brown, B. (2015). *Rising strong: This is a book about getting back up*. Vermilion-Mass Market.

Burnett, M. (2023, Feb. 23). ADHD and boundaries: The 4 c's of boundary setting. *Unconventional Organisation*. https://unconventionalorganisation.com

Cappachione, L. (2001). *Living with feeling: The art of emotional expression*. Penguin.

Cleveland Clinic (n.d.). *Symptoms and causes of stress*. https://www.my.clevelandclinic.org.

Corey, G., Corey, M.S., & Muratori, M. (2017). *I never knew I had a choice: Explorations in personal growth, eleventh edition*. Cengage.

Dickens, L.R. (2017). Using gratitude to promote positive change: A series of meta-analyses investigating the effectiveness of gratitude interventions. *Basic and Applied Psychology, 39(4)*, 193–208. https://doi.org/10.1080/01973533.2017.1323638

de Shazer, S. (2010). *Words were originally magic*. W.W. Norton & Co.

Dishman, R.K., McDowell, C.P., & Herring, M.P. (2021). Customary physical activity and Odds of depression: A systematic review and meta-analysis of 111 prospective cohort Studies. *British Journal of Sports Medicine, 55(16)*, 929–934. https://doi.org/10.1136/bjsports-2020-103140

Egnew, T.R. (2005). The meaning of healing: Transcending suffering. *Annals of Family Medicine, 3(3)*, 255–262. https://doi.org/10.1370/afm.313

Ellis, A.E. (1999). *How to make yourself happy and remarkably less disturbed*. Impact.

Ellis, A.E. (2011). *Rational emotive behavior therapy*. American Psychological Association.

Epstein, M. (2013). *Thoughts without a thinker: Psychotherapy from a Buddhist perspective, revised edition*. Basic Books.

Felson, S. (n.d.). What is box breathing? WebMD. https://www.webmd.com

Figley, C.R. (1995). *Compassion fatigue: Coping with secondary traumatic stress disorder in those who treat the traumatized*. Brunner Mazel.

Fincham, G.W., Epel, E., Colasanti, A., Strauss, C. & Cavanaugh, K. (2024). Effects of brief Remote ventilation breathwork with retention on mental health and wellbeing: A randomised, placebo-controlled trial. *Scientific Reports, 14(1)*. https://doi.org/10.1038/s41598-024-64254-7

First Responder Wellness (n.d.). *Tips on how to ask for help*. https://www.firstresponder-wellness.com

Foa, E.B., & McLean, C.P. (2016). The efficacy of exposure therapy for anxiety-related Disorders and its underlying mechanisms: The case of OCD and PTSD. *Annual Review of Clinical Psychology, 12(1)*, 1–28.

Frankl, V.E. (n.d.). Operational definition of meaning. *Viktor Frankl Institute of Logotherapy in Israel*. www.themeaningseeker.org.

Frankl, V.E. (1986). *The doctor and the soul: From therapy to logotherapy, third edition*. Vintage.

Frankl, V.E. (2006). *Man's search for meaning*. Beacon Press.

Friedman, M.J. (2000). *Posttraumatic stress disorder*. Compact Chemicals.

Germer, C., & Neff, K.D. (2019). Mindful Self-Compassion (MSC). In I.Itvzan (Ed.) *The handbook of mindfulness-based programs: Every established intervention, from medicine to education* (pp. 357–367). London: Routledge.

Glass, O., Dreusicke, M., Evans, J., Bechaed, E., & Wolver, R.O. (2019). Expressive writing to improve resilience to trauma: A feasibility trial. *Complementary Therapies in Clinical Practice, 34*, 240–246.

Hahn, T.N. (1999). *The miracle of mindfulness: An introduction to the practice of meditation*. Beacon Press.

Harari, Y.N. (2015). *Sapiens: A brief history of humankind*. Vintage.

Herman, J. (1992). *Trauma and recovery*. Basic Books.

Herman, J.L. (1994). *Trauma and recovery: The aftermath of violence- from domestic abuse Political terror*. Basic Books.

Hodges, S. (2023). *Creating a meaningful life: A practical guide for counsellors, therapists, and other helping professionals.* Routledge.

Hooper, J. (2022, May 22). The ancient art of Qi Gong is the answer to our modern daily ailments. *Body+Soul.* https://www.bodyandsoul.com.au

Hunt, D.F., Bailey, J., & Vincent, C. (2021). Enhancing psychological safety in mental health services. *International Journal of Mental Health Services, 15(33),* 1–18. https://doi.org/10.1186/s13033-021-00439-1

Just Breathe (n.d.). Tai Chi v Qigong: What's the difference? *Just Breathe.* https://www.justbreathetaichi.com

Kabit-Zinn, J. (2017). John Kabit-Zinn: Defining mindfulness. *Mindful: Healthy and unhealthy life.* www.mindful.org

Kabit-Zinn, J. (2024). *Wherever you go, there you are- 30th anniversary issue.* Piatkus.

Kim, S.H., Schneider, S.M., Bevans, M., Kravitz, L., Mermier, C., Qualla, C., & Burge, M.R. (2013). PTSD symptom reduction with mindfulness-based stretching and deep Breathing exercise: Randomized controlled clinical trials of efficacy. *The Journal of Clinical Endocrinology & Metabolism, 98(7),* 2984–2992. https://doi.org/10.1210/jc.2012-3742.

Kornfield, J. (2005). *Meditation for beginners.* Transworld Publishers.

Kumar, K., & Begum, J. (2025). Why do navy seals use box breathing? *MedicineNet.* www.medicinenet.com

Kumar, K., & Uttekar, P.S. (2011, November 11). Why do Navy Seals use box breathing? *Medicine Net.* https://www.medicinenet.com)

Lama, D., & Cutler, H.C. (2009). *The art of happiness: A handbook for living,* 10th *anniversary edition.* Riverhead Books.

Lee, M.Y., Lee, B.H., Kim, H.Y., & Yang, C.H. (2021). Bidirectional role of acupuncture in the treatment of drug addiction. *Neuroscience & Biobehavioral Reviews, 126,* 382–397. https://doi.org/10.1016/j.neubiorev.2021.04.004

Levine, P. (2011). *Waking the tiger: Healing trauma.* North Atlantic.

Linehan, M.M. (2015). *DBT skills manual, second edition.* Guilford Press.

Lynning, M., Savane, C., Westrgaard, K., Bergien, S.O., Gunnersen, S.R., & Skovgaard, L. (2021). Tension and trauma releasing exercises for people with multiple sclerosis- An exploratory pilot study. *Journal of Contemporary Medicine, 11(5),* 383–389. https://doi.org/10.1016/j.jtcme.2021.02.003

March, J. (2020). *Trauma and the 12 steps: An inclusive guide to enhancing recovery.* North Atlantic.

Maren, S., & Holmen, A. (2016). Stress and fear extinction. *Neuropsychopharmacology Reviews, 41,* 58–79. https://doi.org/10.1038/npp.2015.80

Matsakis, A. (1994). *Post-traumatic stress disorder: A complete treatment guide.* New Harbinger.

Matsakis, A. (2002). *I can't get over it: A handbook for trauma survivors, second edition.* New Harbinger Publications.

McGonigal, K. (2019). *The joy of movement: How exercise us find happiness, hope, connection, and courage.* Penguin.

Mayo Clinic (nd). Post-traumatic stress disorder (PTSD). https://www.mayoclinic.org.

Meichenbaum, D. (2003). *A clinical handbook/practical therapist manual for assessing and treating adults with post-traumatic stress disorder (PTSD).* The Melissa Institute.

Meichenbaum, D. (1994). *A clinical handbook/practical therapist manual for assessing and treating adults with post-traumatic stress disorder.* Institute Press.

Meichenbaum, D. (2014). Ways to bolster resilience in traumatized clients: Implications for psychotherapists. *Journal of Constructive Psychology, 27*, 329–336.
McGonigal, K. (2017). *The joy of movement: How exercise helps us find happiness, hope, connection, and courage*. Avery.
McGreevy, S., & Boland, R. (2022). Touch: An integrated review of a somatosensory approach to the treatment of adults with symptoms of post-traumatic stress disorder. *European Journal of Integrative Medicine, 54*. https://doi.org/10.1016/j.eujim.2022.102168
Moreno, J.L. (2020). *Psychodrama, Vol. I*. Psychodrama Press.
Muss, D.C. (1991). A new technique for treating post-traumatic stress disorder. *The British Journal of Clinical Psychology, 30(1)*, 91–92. https://doi.org/10.1111/j.2044-8260.1991.tb00924.x
National Center for PTSD. (2020). *How common is PTSD in veterans?* http://ptsd.va.gov
Navarro, T. (2019). *Kintsugi: The Japanese art of embracing the imperfect and loving your flaws*. Sounds True.
Neff, K. (2019). *Self-compassion: Stop beating yourself up and leave insecurity behind*. William Morrow & Company.
Neff, K.D. (2011). Self-compassion, self-esteem, and well-being. *Social and Personal Psychology Compass, 5(1)*, 1–12. https://doi.org/10.1111/j.1751-9004.2010.00330.x
Novotney, A. (2019). The risks of isolation. *APA Monitor, 50(5)*, 32.
Nugent, N.R., Sumner, J.A., & Amstadter, A.B. (2014). Resilience after trauma: From surviving to thriving. *European Journal of Psychotraumatology, 1(5)*. https://doi.org/10.3402/ejpt.v5.25339
O'Hanlon, B. (2013). *Do one thing different: Ten simple ways to change your life, 20th anniversary edition*. HarperCollins.
Pennebaker, J.D. (2004). *Writing to heal: A guided journal for recovery from trauma and emotional upheaval*. New Harbinger.
Pennebaker, J.D. (2017, October 17). *How to write expressively and heal yourself* (Video). YouTube. https://www.youtube.com/watch?v=zP2O-dE9E8
Prochaska, J.O., DiClemente, C.C., & Norcross, J.O. (1992). In search of how people change: Applications to addictive behaviors. *American Psychologist, 47*, 1102–1114. https://doi.org/10.1037/0003-066X.47.9.1102
Reisman, M. (2016). PTSD treatment for veterans: What's working, what's not, and what's next. *Pharmacy and Therapeutics, 41(10)*, 623–627.
Rogers, C.R. (1961). *On becoming a person*. Houghton-Mifflin.
Rogers, C.R. (1965). *Client-centered therapy*. Houghton-Mifflin.
Rosenbloom, D. & Williams, M.B. (2010). *Life after trauma, second edition: A workbook for healing*. Routledge-Taylor & Francis.
Rothschild, B. (2000). *The body remembers: The psychophysiology of trauma and trauma treatment*. W. W. Norton & Company.
Shapiro, F. (1996). Eye movement desensitization and reprocessing (EMDR): Evaluation of controlled PTSD research. *Journal of Behavior and Experiential Psychiatry, 27(3)*, 211–217. https://doi.org/10.1016/s0005-7916(96)00029-8.
Sheehan, G. (2018). *Running & being: The total experience*. Clarkson-Potter/10 Speed Press.
Singh, D., & Newberg, M. (2021). Spiritual fitness: A new dimension in Alzheimer's disease prevention. *Journal of Alzheimer's Disease, 80(2)*, 505–519. https://doi.org/10.3233/JAD-201433. PMD: 33554917; PMCID: PMC8075383

Sloan, D.M., Marx, B.P., Acierno, R., Messina, M., Muzzy, W., Gallagher, M.W., … & Sloan, C. (2023). Written exposure therapy vs. prolonged exposure therapy in the treatment of posttraumatic stress disorder: A randomized clinical trial. *JAMA Psychiatry, 80(11)*, 1093–1100. https://doi.org/10:1001/jamapsychiatry.2023.2810.

Song, C. (2022). *Internal tai chi for beginners-and intermediates: Powerful tai chi lessons and easy exercises for adults & seniors, improve your memory, mood, sleep & flexibility and find grounding and inner peace.* Dimensions.

Stamn, B.H. (2009). *Professional quality of life: Compassion satisfaction and fatigue version 5 (ProQuol).* https://proqol.org/.

Steger, M.F., Frazier, P., Oishi, S., & Kalen, M. (2006). The meaning in life questionnaire: Assessing the presence of and search for meaning in life. *Journal of Counseling Psychology, 53*, 80–93. https://doi.org.10.1037/0022-0167.53.1.80

Tedeschi, R.G., Shakespeare-Finch, J., Taku, K., & Calhoun, L.G. (2018). *Posttraumatic growth: Theory, research, and applications.* Routledge.

Van der Kolk, B. (2014). *The body keeps the score: Brain, mind, and body in the healing of trauma.* Penguin Books.

Van der Kolk, B. (2015). *The body keeps the score: Brain, mind, and body in the healing of trauma.* Penguin.

Van der Weel, F.R. (Rund), & Van der Meer, A.L.H. (2024). Handwriting but not typewriting leads to widespread brain connectivity: A high-density EEG study with implications for the classroom. *Frontiers in Psychology, 14*, 1219945. https://doi.org/10.3389/fpsyg.2023.1219945

Waldinger, R. & Schulz, M. (2023). *The good life: Lessons from the world's longest scientific study of happiness.* Simon & Schuster.

Wanigatunga, A.A., Dong, Y., Xue, Q.L., Lindquist, M.A., & Crainiceanu, C.M. (2025). Moderate-to-vigorous physical activity at any dose reduces all-cause dementia risk Regardless of frailty status. *Journal of the American Medical Association, 26(3).* https://doi.org/10.1016/j.jamda.2024.105456

Webber, J.M., & Mascari, J.B. (2018). *Disaster mental health counseling: A guide to preparing and responding.* American Counseling Association Foundation.

Weller, F. (2015). *The wide edge of sorrow: Rituals of renewal and the sacred work of grief.* North Atlantic.

White, A., & Ernst, E. (2004). A brief history of acupuncture. *Rheumatology, 43(5)*, 662–663.

White, M. (2007). *Maps of narrative practice.* Norton.

Wolpe, J. (1969). Subjective units of distress scale (SUDS). *APA Psyc Tests.* https://psycnet.apa.org/doi/10.1037/t05183-000

Index

active listening: conversation 119–120; healthy limits 121; interruption 170; open-ended questions and clarifying questions 169; paraphrase and summarize 169; in relationship 120–121; to understand 169; use encouraging language 170; use minimal encouragers 170; use silence 170
acute stress disorder (ASD) 4, 7, 73; alterations in arousal and reactivity 11; avoidance 10; criteria on exposure 11; duration 11; exclusion 11; functional significance 11; intrusion symptoms 10; negative alterations in cognitions and mood 10–11; specifications 11; stressor 10; symptoms 12–14
adverse childhood experiences (ACEs) 7
anger: effects of holding 92; expressing 109–110; in healthy, appropriate manner 111; wound 110
anxiety: management 1, 108–109, 123–124; narrative trauma management exercise 61; negative thoughts 108–109
Aurelius, M. 184; *The Meditations of Marcus Aurelius* 184

beliefs: about power and control 100–101; about power of choice 21, 101; negative 88, 89; regarding trauma 88–89; shame 114
body: body-oriented interventions 42; communicating with 200; flashbacks 45–46; focus to another area 200; healing light 200; liberation 206; posture language 169; preparing mind and 199; scan 28–29; self-compassion 96; and vagus nerves 202
The Body Keeps the Score: Brain, Mind, and Body in the Healing of Trauma (Van der Kolk) 6
box breathing 4, 5, 44, 46, 47, 49, 56, 58, 60, 75, 79, 80, 82, 84, 107, 108, 111, 120, 128, 129, 131, 148–149, 174, 179, 199
Boyle, G. 19, 20
breath: flashbacks 46; healing 116–117; self-guided healing meditation 199
breathwork 148; vagus nerve 149–150
Brooks, A. C. 50
Brown, B. 2, 196
burnout (BO) 72, 88, 163, 165, 168

Cappachione, L. 105
chair yoga 155–156
charting, healing from trauma: award ceremony (optional) 197; daily or weekly healing chart 195–196; daily visual encouragers 197; healing journey 192–194; journaling for continued growth 196; personal resilience award 197; self-exploration in trauma recovery journal 196; trauma narrative 195; trauma timeline 195
chest center (CC) 47
chronic stress 148, 155
cognitive behavior therapy (CBT) 88
cognitive processing therapy 4, 175
commitment 91–92
compassion: bracket judgment 170; conversation 170; delay and reschedule 170; referrals 170; setting healthy boundaries 170; time limit 170; validating speaker's perspective 170
compassion fatigue 72, 163, 168
courage 63–65

daily gratitude practice 96–97
depression 111–112
deShazer, Steve 67, 87
Diagnostic and Statistical Manual of Mental Disorders (DSM-5-TR) 5
dialectical behavior therapy (DBT) 20, 34, 36, 41, 52
disappointments: daily gratitude acknowledgment 205; drawing or collage 204; empty chair conversation 204; failure, requirement for future success 203; focus on new challenges 203; increased self-reflection and awareness 203; journaling 204; lessons learned 203; meditation 205; Meridian tapping 205; mindfulness routine 205; movement 205; resilience development 203; seeking support 204–205; self-acknowledgment 205; self-compassion development 203; success, developmental process 203
dissociation 40–41; dissociative disorders 41; film analogy 72; future rehearsal 72; learned about 77; normal dissociation 41; problem with 71; replaying 72; rewinding 72; safe space visualization 72; trauma-related dissociation 41–42
distractions: body posture language 169; calm facial expression 169; eye contact 169; mind wandering 169; removing distractions 169; still mind 169
drawing (or collage) journal, reflective questions 189
drawing therapy: emotion drawing 188; free drawing 189; gratitude drawing 188; healing process 188; life journey 188; meaning in life drawing 189; meditation 188; miracle drawing 188; sample exercises 188–189; self-compassion drawing 188; suggestions 188

early life recollections (ER) 185
Ellis, A.E. 21, 24, 67, 88, 115, 123, 131
empty chair exercise: example 85–86; forgiveness 95, 99; practice 86–87, 167–168
Epstein, M. 169
exposure, types of: imaginal exposure 80–82; in vivo exposure 81–83

fear, dysregulation 105–108
first responders: addressing survivor guilt 172–173; asking for help 164–165; developing presence to help others 169–170; good listening friend or colleague 165–168; narratives 175–178; past trauma, narrative responses 170–171; re-entry questions for exploration 171–172; survivor guilt signs 173–175; trauma recovery journal 178–180; writing and PTSD 175
flashbacks: body 45–46; and management 42–43; mind 45; replay and review technique 44–45; spirit 46
forgiveness: defined 92; empty-chair forgiveness 95, 99; miracle questions 95
4C's (clarity, communication, consistency, and consequences) of boundary setting 139
4-Square Breathing 107
Frankl, V.E. 26, 37, 53, 100, 101, 112, 131, 181, 182, 189

Gestalt Empty Chair Exercise 85
grounding: body scan 28–29; 5 senses exercise 28; gratitude acknowledgment 29; journaling 29; meditation 29; movement 29; safe place 29; solid ground 28; special or sacred object 28; talking with friend 29
guilt 111–112; self-compassion intervention 113; terrible twins 113; unpacking feelings of 113

Hanh, Thich Nhat 120, 121, 131
healing: action 96, 115; breath 116–117; charting healing from trauma 195–197; contemplation 115; disappointments 203–205; healing meditations 198–200; journaling 24–25, 201; life lessons 205–210; maintenance 115; mind 115–116; movements 151–152; physical activity 117; postscript 210–211; precontemplation 115; preparation 115; relapse 115; shame beliefs 114; significant reflections 191–192; spirit 117; vagus nerve guided meditation 201–202
healthy communication 117–118; flexibility 118–119; identifying needs

118; knowing options 119; listening to partner 118; needs 118
Herman, J.L. 22
hurting 85–86, 91–93, 95, 97–98, 131, 136

The Joy of Movement: How Exercise Helps Us Find Happiness, Hope, Connection, and Courage (McGonigal) 151

Kabat-Zinn, John 34, 36, 121; *Wherever you go, there you are—30th anniversary issue* 36
Kornfield, J. 33; *Kornfield's Meditation for Beginners* 35–36

Levine, P. 22, 24, 27, 48; *Waking the Tiger: Healing Trauma* 48
life lessons: accepting human fallibility 207; body liberation 206; cognitive reframing 207; emotional regulation (ER) 208; emotional well-being 206; healthy boundaries 206; peer support 206; reclaiming selfhood 208; *why* (meaning) 207
light stream technique 42
Linden, Marsha 20
Linehan, M.M. 34, 41, 43, 44, 52, 69
logotherapy 101, 112

Mascari, J.B. 27
master or mistress of the ceremony (MC) 197
Matsakis, A. 110
McGonigal, K. 117, 151, 156; *The Joy of Movement: How Exercise Helps Us Find Happiness, Hope, Connection, and Courage* 151
meaning in life journal 50, 53, 181, 182, 186; discomfort as teacher 185; early life recollections 185; focus questions 185; grief 186; as if meaningful 185–186; journaling 185; love's impact 186; MIL specifics 183; questions regarding 183–184; routines 186; self-defined 185; simple conversations 186; suggestions for writing 186–187
Meaning in Life Questionnaire (MLQ) 182
meditation 148; new to meditation, tips to remember 198; self-guided healing meditation 199–200; tips for practicing 33–34
The Meditations of Marcus Aurelius (Aurelius) 184
Meridian tapping 150–151, 205
mind: and body, preparing 199; distractions 169; flashbacks 45; healing 115–116; wandering 169
mindful meditation 46, 149
mindfulness: defined 34–36; disappointments 205; narrative trauma management exercise 61; safety and security 34–36
Moreno, J.L. 85, 204, 209

narratives 175–178; reflections on storytelling 176, 177; responses for past trauma 170–171
narrative trauma healing exercise: facts entry 62; thoughts and feelings 62–63
narrative trauma management exercise: coping strategies 61; emotional processing 60; identifying triggers 60; just facts 60; mindfulness 61; physical activity 61; practice self-compassion 61; professional help 61; reauthoring 61; self-monitoring anxiety 61
nightmares 50–51; revising 52; suggestions for facing 51–52

O'Hanlon, B. 31

Pennebaker, J.D. 24, 175
Perls, Fritz 85
persistent negative emotions 104–105
post-event factors 8–9
postscript 210–211
post-traumatic growth (PTG) 7, 190, 191, 195, 196, 205
post-traumatic stress disorder (PTSD): alterations in arousal and reactivity 11; avoidance 10; criteria on exposure 11; duration 11; exclusion 11; functional significance 11; intrusion symptoms 10; negative alterations in cognitions and mood 10–11; specifications 11; stressor 10; symptoms 12–14; Type II PTSD 14; Type I PTSD 14; and writing 175
post-traumatic stress disorder checklist (PCL-5) 16; instructions 16–19
procrastination 66–67
prolonged exposure caution: imaginal exposure 83–84; practice: prolonged exposure therapy 83; in vivo exposure 84
prolonged exposure therapy (PET) 80

Qigong 157
"Qi" or life energy 156

Rational Emotive Behavioral Therapy (REBT) 21, 67, 88
relaxation 32–33
remembrance for healing 21–24; phase III: reconnection and integration 23–24; phase II: remembrance and mourning 23; phase I: safety and stabilization 23
rescripting and revising dominant narrative 70–71
resilience record 53–54
Rogers, C.R. 120, 121, 185

safe place visualization 31, 128, 129
safety and security: establishing 27–28, 30–31; feeling grounding 28–29; lessons learned 38; in life 30–31; mindfulness 34–36; recess from workbook 36–38; reflective exercises 29; relaxation 32–33; safe place visualization 31; safety checklist 32; tips for practicing meditation 33–34; visualizing safe place 31–32
secondary traumatic stress (STS) 168, 180
self-affirmations 101–102
self-compassion 10, 25, 95–96; acknowledging present moment emotions 96; behavioral examples 96; comforting body 96; gentle and reassuring self-talk 96; nurturing 96
self-forgiveness 97–99; *see also* forgiveness
self-guided healing meditation: communicating with body 200; connecting to ground/earth/floor/seat 199; focus to another area of body 200; gratitudes 200; healing light, areas of body 200; inhale healing light 199–200; pay attention to breath 199; preparing mind and body 199; reflect on experience 200; visualize healing light 199; *see also* meditation
self-injurious behaviors (SIBs) 79–80; symptoms of 77; treatment for 78–79; and ways to reduce and stop them 77
self-injury, forms of 78
self-soothing interventions: concluding paragraph 63; courage 63–65; final draft 63; managing triggers 59–60; narrative exercise 60–61; narrative trauma healing exercise 61–63; soothing triggers 57–59
self-talk 88
setting healthy boundaries, with others: clear communication 93; consequences 94; consistency 94; respect others' boundaries 94; self-reflection 93
shame: beliefs 114; healing 114; symptomology 113
Sheehan, G. 151, 156
SMART (specific, measurable, attainable, relevant, timely) 158–159
Steger, M.F. 182
stress management 123–124; box breathing 148–149; breathwork 148; chair yoga 155–156; chronic stress 148; getting started 158–160; healing movements 151–152; Meridian tapping points 150–151; mindful meditation 149; Qigong 157; Tai Chi 156–157; tapping 151; therapeutic massage 154–155; trauma release exercises 152–154; vagus nerve breathwork 149–150; voo exhale (voo breath) 150; walking meditation 149, 157–158
Subjective Units of Distress Scale (SUDS) 39, 40, 42, 44, 45, 60, 61, 63, 68, 75, 78, 81–84, 159
suicide intervention plan 112–113
survivor guilt signs: addressing 172–173; coping techniques 173–174; feeling 173; pay-it-forward behavior 174; reflective questions 174–175
survivors, trauma's impact on 5–6; event factors 8; pre-event factors for Trauma 7–8
symptomology, trauma: active listening 119–121; anger, expression of 109–110, 111; depression and subsequent guilt 111–112; fear 105–108; guilt and shame 113; healing shame beliefs 114; healthy communication 117–118; manage anxiety or stress 123–124; mind, body, breath, and spirit 115–117; negative thoughts 108–109; persistent negative emotions 104–105; responsibility to heal 121–123; self-compassion intervention 113; suicide intervention plan 112–113; wound 110

Tai Chi 156–157
tapping: additional information on 151; Meridian 150–151, 205
Tedeschi, R.G. 190
therapeutic massage: acupuncture for trauma reduction and healing 155; benefits of 155; somatic concerns 154
3Cs practice 89–91
trauma, addressing: ability to 9–10; body-oriented interventions 42; detailed EFT/Meridian tapping points 46–50; dissociation 40–41; flashbacks 45–46; lessons learned 56; light stream technique 42; and managing flashbacks 43–44; nightmares 50–51; replay and review flashback technique 44–45; resilience record 53–54; SUDS scale 39–40; three-part question in healing journal 54; vagus nerve voo exhale 42
trauma healing 54–55
trauma management: ability to address 9–10; arms of love exercise 24; ASD criteria *see* acute stress disorder (ASD); defined 5–6; examples 5; healing journal 24–25; impact on survivors 5–8; lessons learned 25; memory and reframing 19–20; PCL-5, 16–19; post-event factors 8–9; power of belief 21; promises made and kept 20–21; PTSD *see* post-traumatic stress disorder (PTSD); remembrance for healing 21–24; self-compassion 10; storytelling 2–3
trauma memory and reframing 19–20
trauma recovery journal: establish writing routine 178–179; facilitating journal writing 179; honest 179; ongoing self-care 179; safe and comfortable space for writing 178; self-fulfilling prophecy 179–180
trauma-related dissociation 74–75
trauma release exercises (TRE) 152; cat-cow pose 153; child's pose 153; neck rolls 153; reclined knee to chest pose 153; reclined pigeon/ figure four pose 153; seated side bending 152–153; standing forward bend 153
traumatic memory: purpose of 69–70; self-talk 70; into smaller sections 68–69
trauma timeline 54, 195
trauma treatment: common triggers 75–77; empty chair exercise 84–87; forms of self-injury 78; learned about dissociation 77; managing dissociation 71–72; miracle question 67; PET *see* prolonged exposure therapy (PET); potential trauma 73–74; problem with dissociation 71; procrastination 66–67; prolonged exposure caution 83–84; rescripting and revising dominant narrative 70–71; self-injurious behaviors 79–80; self-injurious behaviors 77; self-talk 70; trauma-related dissociation, addressing 74–75; traumatic memory 68–70; types of exposure 80–84; untreated dissociation, behaviors resulting 72–73
triggers: EFT/Meridian tapping 58; facing common 75–77; grounding techniques 58; healthy friendships 58; journaling or empty chair 59; management 59–60; momentary delay 58; peer support 58; practice 58–59; professional help 58; reframe self-talk 58; self-compassion 58; taking break 58; warning signs 57
trust: anger, effects of holding 92; beliefs about power of choice 101; beliefs regarding trauma 88–89; challenging beliefs about power and control 100–101; cognitive revision example (3 Cs) 90–91; commitment 91–92; 3Cs practice 89, 91; daily gratitude practice 96–97; defined 99; empty-chair forgiveness 95, 99; hurting 97; miracle question applied to forgiveness 95; negative beliefs and self-talk 88; practicing self-compassion 95–96; reflections on previous trust exercise 100; Scott (case) 89–90; self-affirmations 101–102; self-forgiveness practice 97–99; setting healthy boundaries practice 94–95; setting healthy boundaries with others 93–94

vagus nerve breathwork 149–150
vagus nerve guided meditation: breathing and focusing on sensation 202; getting comfortable 201; position hands strategically 201;

pre-check, noticing areas of tension 201; present moment return 202; senses and gratitude acknowledgment 202; vagus nerve and calming body 202; voo exhale 201–202
Van der Kolk, B. 6, 71, 104, 105, 195; *The Body Keeps the Score: Brain, Mind, and Body in the Healing of Trauma* 6, 104–105
visualizing, safe place 31–32
vivo exposure 81, 82, 84
voo exhale (voo breath) 32, 150

Waking the Tiger: Healing Trauma (Levine) 48
walking meditation 149, 157–158
Webber, J.M. 27
What's the Story You Are Telling Yourself? (Brown) 2
Wherever you go, there you are—30th anniversary issue (Kabat-Zinn) 36
writing: journal 179; meaning in life journal 186–187; and PTSD 175; trauma recovery journal 178–179
writing exposure therapy (WET) 4, 175

For Product Safety Concerns and Information please contact our EU representative GPSR@taylorandfrancis.com Taylor & Francis Verlag GmbH, Kaufingerstraße 24, 80331 München, Germany